For Mike

I hope you find
a few useful nuggets
in here,

Phil Jones.

Strategy Mapping for Learning Organizations

Dedicated to my wife, Deborah, who put up with me during the writing of this book, and our two big lads, Adam and Matthew.

Strategy Mapping for Learning Organizations

Building Agility into Your Balanced Scorecard

PHIL JONES

GOWER

Published by
Gower Publishing Limited
Wey Court East
Union Road
Farnham
Surrey
GU9 7PT
England

Gower Publishing Company
Suite 420
101 Cherry Street
Burlington
VT 05401-4405
USA

www.gowerpublishing.com

Phil Jones has asserted his moral right under the Copyright, Designs and Patents Act, 1988, to be identified as the author of this work.

British Library Cataloguing in Publication Data
Jones, Phil, 1958 Aug. 21-
   Strategy mapping for learning organizations : building
   agility into your balanced scorecard.
   1. Organizational effectiveness. 2. Organizational change--
   Management. 3. Strategic planning. 4. Organizational
   behavior.
   I. Title
   658.4'012-dc22

ISBN: 978-0-566-08811-7 (hbk)
ISBN: 978-1-4094-3701-7 (ebk)

Library of Congress Cataloging-in-Publication Data
Jones, Phil, 1958 Aug. 21-
   Strategy mapping for learning organizations : building agility into your
   balanced scorecard / Phil Jones.
     p. cm.
   Includes bibliographical references and index.
   ISBN 978-0-566-08811-7 (hardback) -- ISBN 978-1-4094-3701-7
   (ebook) 1. Strategic planning. 2. Communication in management. I. Title.

HD30.28.J664 2011
658.4'012--dc23

2011021029

Printed and bound in Great Britain by the
MPG Books Group, UK

Contents

List of Figures

List of Tables

Foreword

BY DAVID P. NORTON
Author: *The Balanced Scorecard*
Founder and Director: Palladium Group, Inc.

It has been almost 20 years since Bob Kaplan and I published the initial article about the Balanced Scorecard. Since that time, we have published five books that have sold over one million copies in 22 languages. Research shows that companies using the Balanced Scorecard (BSC) achieve 30 percent greater growth in shareholder value than companies using some other approach to performance management. Many organizations are now creating their "Office of Strategy Management" in an attempt to replicate these results.

How does the BSC approach to performance management help leaders achieve such results? I believe there are two essential ingredients:

1. *Focus* – Organizations are made up of thousands of people, each with their own unique set of skills and their own unique view of organization objectives. To succeed, these people must adopt one common view of the organization. That common view of purpose is the organization strategy. The BSC is effective because it helps to clarify and translate the organization strategy into a critical few objectives that can be measured and acted upon.
2. *Alignment* – With the critical few strategic measures as the target, all parts of the organization can become aligned. It begins with the alignment of executive teams and the Board, cascades to business units, support units, external partners and ultimately to every employee of the organization. To be successfully executed, strategy must be everyone's job.

How does the Balanced Scorecard achieve focus and alignment? Many people know the BSC as a set of methodologies and tools for managers. The approach is known for methodologies such as Strategy Maps, Strategic Themes, Balanced Scorecards, Cascades, Stratex (Strategic Expenditures), Strategic Readiness, Strategic Change Agenda, etc. These tools, and others like them, present a degree of structure that allows organizations to cut through the complexities inherent in their size and structure. The toolkit of the Balanced Scorecard appeals to the engineers among us that look for structure to deal with complexity. The BSC appeals to our "left brain."

Our experience, however, indicates that effective leaders need more than a toolkit. Successful leaders are *intuitive*; they have a sense of what needs to be done. Successful leaders are *change agents*; they need to create a sense of urgency. Successful leaders are *communicators*; they need to simplify and target complex messages. Successful leaders are *motivators*; they need to show "what's in it for me." Successful leaders have a strong "right brain."

The reality of a performance management system is that it must support both the left brain (structure) and right brain (intuitive) of a user. In fact, the left and right brain activities should be integrated. An executive senses a need to improve the teamwork of his/her management team (a "right brain" need). Jointly building a strategy map (a "left brain" approach) helps create the teamwork. An executive senses a need to break down traditional siloes (a "right brain" need). Cascading the strategy map (a "left brain" solution) helps to cut across siloes and create a holistic view of the organization.

We tend to think of a performance management system as a collection of structured methodologies and tools. By its very nature, it is easier to describe that which is structured than that which is unstructured. I believe the Balanced Scorecard approach has been effective, in part, because the left-brain structured approaches complement the right brain needs of a leader.

But what are these leadership needs that help mobilize, focus and align the organization? This is where the work of Phil Jones makes a unique contribution to the field of performance management. Using the BSC/Strategy Map methodologies as his point of departure, Phil describes their use in practice from the perspective of a facilitator. He asks the simple question, "What happened here?" Why did an executive team come to the conclusion that they did not agree upon the strategy? Why did it happen in this meeting instead of the hundreds of other meetings where these people worked together? They used a Strategy Map. How did this influence the "quality of conversation"?

This book is a "drivers manual" for anyone who is implementing a Balanced Scorecard performance management system. Whether you drive on the left or the right, it is required reading.

David P. Norton
Boston, MA, USA
October 2011

Preface

At first glance this book may seem to be about strategy, strategy mapping and balanced scorecards. It is. It is also about raising the quality of thinking, quality of conversation and quality of action amongst all involved in developing and implementing an organization's strategy. It is about how organizations learn and develop and grow and change, through their strategy. It is about how decisions are made. It is about being more agile and responsive in complex environments. It is about engaging and empowering people. It is about managing, implementing and executing, strategy better. Ultimately, it is about delivering results.

At the beginning of Chapter 1 I recount an experience, back in 1999, of working with a FTSE 100 retailer's executive team on the introduction of their 'Strategy Focused Balanced Scorecard'. At the time I was a senior consultant working for Renaissance, the organization Kaplan and Norton had set up to deliver balanced scorecard consultancy. The chief executive wanted help to get the strategy out through the organization because, as he put it, 'They didn't get it'. It turned out that it wasn't just that the people in the company didn't get the strategy; neither did several of the executive team.

As you will read, we helped that team agree on their strategy, communicate it and go on to execute it well. Seeing the effect we had on this team, and many other teams, promoted questions for me. 'What behaviours, beliefs and ways of working, are we changing?' 'How are we changing them?' 'What thinking underlies this?' This curiosity has led me on a journey of exploration that has resulted in this book.

Three Important Messages

I choose to write about strategy maps because they are the central spine around which all the other balanced scorecard techniques hang. I also think they are mis-understood. In doing so I wanted to emphasise three important messages. First, the importance of the basic principles and thinking we used in those early days, and continue to be important: principles that seem ignored by many balanced scorecard practitioners. Second, there is often too much focus on measures and too little on the thinking and conversations that they should create during design, implementation and during use. Third, I wanted to explain the developments and improvements, since that time, that extend how strategy is captured, communicated and managed. Developments that help organizations to capture their strategy better. Developments that help organizations become more flexible, agile and learn, as they implement their strategy. Strategy mapping is central to all of this. This book is my attempt to communicate these messages.

UNDERLYING PRINCIPLES AND THINKING

Omit the underlying principles and thinking and you destroy the approach. Many organizations still seem to think of the balanced scorecard as a measurement system and implement it as such. They fail to think of it as an overall approach to managing and implementing strategy and so fail to communicate, execute and learn from their strategy. This is particularly true of the role of strategy maps and strategy mapping, the central theme of this book. I often say, if you do not have a strategy map, you do not have a proper strategic balanced scorecard: merely a collection of operational measures. Strategy maps must capture and communicate your strategy, business model and the drivers of change. Omit these and you will fail. That is why understanding strategy mapping is so important.

Strategy maps were a fundamental part of the work of Norton and Kaplan. Their principles are described early in their first book, *The Balanced Scorecard*, and they are used extensively in their second, *The Strategy Focused Organization*. They provide the basic from which the scorecard should be developed. I think of Kaplan and Norton's third book, *Strategy Maps*, as a plea to practitioners to realize the importance of strategy maps, before their most recent books moved on to emphasize the value of organizational alignment and the premium gained from successful execution of the strategy. I intend this book to build upon their work to provide further insights and more details for the reader. Those familiar with Norton and Kaplan's thinking will find much in here that builds upon principles that are familiar. Those unfamiliar with their thinking will find much that illuminates the approach, strategy mapping being central to that.

QUALITY OF CONVERSATION

Over the years I have come to the conclusion that 'quality of conversation' is central and essential, to strategy formulation, implementation and execution. This is true, inside the boardroom, between managers and staff, and amongst the people executing strategy. Unfortunately that quality is sometimes lost. A major emphasis within this book is the facilitation of conversations about the strategy and about its implementation. Facilitation of conversations that invites managers to ask questions of the strategy, performance and each other, to look deeper into their organization and to encourage their people to do the same.

Napoleon is reputed to say that it was planning, not plans, that were important. Similarly I believe that strategy mapping and the conversations they generate, rather than the map itself, are important. Strategy mapping is an approach to stimulate thinking and facilitate conversation and understanding about the strategy. The resulting strategy maps are an elegant, succinct picture of your strategy and how the organization will change. Strategy mapping provides a vital tool to support the management of strategy and organizational learning. Understand the principles, thinking and conversations and you are on the way to a more responsive, agile, learning organization.

Over fifteen years of using this approach I have seen many examples of how effective strategy maps are at engaging people. I once placed in front of a senior manager the single page strategy map for cancer care in his hospital. It instantly engaged him: he didn't stop talking for nearly 15 minutes elaborating the hospital's ambition and strategy to be a leading cancer research and care centre. A technology company still had the latest version of their strategy map on the wall five years after I had initially worked with them. It had changed slightly, but still represented their strategy and was still used to ensure the team concentrated on what mattered. The IT department of a bank in the Far East were still using their strategy map, and its detailed balanced scorecard, when I talked to them six years later. Clearly there is something about these diagrams and the approach that both engages and has persistent value.

Nowadays when facilitating a strategic balanced scorecard I pay attention to whether the individuals in the team understand the techniques and principles. I track the quality of conversation amongst the team, and later the quality of conversation with the organization. I obviously track the development of the content of the strategy, though that will often be refined and developed as it gets used. I track the ownership that all of this creates. It is these characteristics that create persistency.

This quality of conversation continues during the implementation of the strategy and monitoring its progress. Strategy maps help you to raise the conversation from operations to strategy, change and improvement. As you will see they support a more flexible responsive approach to managing strategy and refining it as it develops.

DEVELOPMENTS AND IMPROVEMENTS

There are various extensions and improvements to the strategic balanced scorecard approach in this book. Some are relatively simple extensions of the perspectives model. The values perspective will help you make links from the organization's values to its strategy. The environmental and social impact perspective will help you capture your strategy for Corporate Social Responsibility.

Some are more subtle, for instance how you capture your organization's strategy and business model. I once heard Charles Handy speak, and one phrase of his stuck in my mind, 'If you really want to understand a subject, try writing a book about it'. Writing this book has helped me recognise the subtlety of the layers of strategy mapping. At the bottom the fundamental model of how organizations work, captured in the perspectives, where learning and growth drives processes which affect the outcomes for customers and finances. In the middle, capturing the organization's business model or service delivery model, adapting the customer perspective to represent perhaps franchises, distributors or the layers of customers. On this we overlay the strategy which gets captured in the selection of themes and objectives. This book has also allowed me to gather together my experience of strategy in many different types of organization. The techniques for capturing strategy and particularly, developing the subtleties of the customer perspective, have been with me for a long while and writing this book has given me a chance to present them for you.

Perhaps the most important part of this book, for me, is how the strategic learning model provides a framework for management to think more systematically about how they manage their strategy. This is increasingly important with the recent financial crisis and the continuously changing environments that we all work in. As well as treating strategy as a learning process, it provides a route for executive teams to be more responsive to changing circumstances, learning from the strategy, using the external perspective to monitor assumptions, uncertainties and risks. Strategy is no longer an annual process, but one of continuous learning and refinement, which the strategy map supports. For me, the most important developments in the whole strategic balanced scorecard approach are about supporting a more agile, responsive way of managing organizations. This is about helping organizations and management teams to learn from their strategy as they execute it.

Commercial and Not for Profit Organizations

The underlying principles and messages in this book apply to any organization, be it commercial, not for profit or some hybrid arrangement. After all, management is management, and strategy is still about choice, focus and positioning your organization to serve your market (or community). This is true whether your customers pay you directly or not, whether you distribute funds to shareholders or retain the surplus for reinvestment. This book includes both commercial and not for profit examples. I originally wanted more not for profit examples, and particular sections on not for profit and public sector organizations, but the book was simply getting much too large. If you are in the public sector or a not for profit organization, there are still a large number of examples and all the underlying principles still apply. If you are impatient for further insights into the public sector or not for profit sector, or are after more commercial examples, you can contact me directly via my company website at Excitant Ltd www.excitant.co.uk.

Acknowledgements

I am grateful to all my many clients over the years who have been a part of this journey. They have set tough challenges for their own improvement. They have often challenged me to think hard about what is needed to help them in a sustainable and persistent way. They have been a delight and an inspiration when they have adopted, and often adapted, my approaches to bring about change and improvement in the way they manage and deliver their strategies. There are too many to mention, but I am grateful to them all. I am also grateful to my many fellow consultants who, when having a quiet coffee, have shared and discussed these topics.

Particular thanks go to my patient editor at Gower, Jonathan Norman, who guided me through various manifestations of this book. Thanks also to Mike Brooks who went through an early draft of the book providing useful guidance, direction and improvements.

Finally, I would like to thank David P. Norton for providing the foreword. As one of the originators of the Balanced Scorecard approach, I am extremely grateful for his contribution and kind words.

If you have comments, or wish further insights, you can contact me directly via my company website Excitant Ltd, www.excitant.co.uk or via this book's dedicated website www.mappingstrategy.co.uk.

Phil Jones
August 2011

I

Strategy and Strategy Management

Part I sets the context for strategy maps: strategy formulation, governance and strategic management.

Chapter 1 explains the potential benefits, useful for anyone making the case for well implemented strategy maps, strategy mapping and strategic balanced scorecards.

No strategy map or balanced scorecard works in isolation. They operate in an overall organisational context. Chapter 2 raises the discussion to overall organizational governance and the overall strategy management process. Understanding the governance model helps you avoid problems with existing governance systems. The strategic learning model considers how managers learn when they execute strategy and manage performance. Putting strategy maps and scorecards in this context brings the approach up to date, supporting emergent strategy and rolling plans and budgets. It allows executives flexibility over their approach to managing and executing strategy, especially in complex, changing environments.

Chapter 3 explains how strategy maps can capture the many different aspects of organizational strategy. It looks at strategy from a variety of perspectives and explains how the multiple aspects of strategy maps capture them. Once you have captured your strategy fully and richly, you will make it much easier to communicate your strategy and engage your people in it.

1

The Benefits and Principles of Strategy Mapping

As I looked around the management team, I was both puzzled and curious. We had only been working with this management team for three weeks and this was the first facilitated workshop. This was a team who had worked together for a long time. They had much well developed market analysis, detailed strategy documents and various plans they were implementing. They knew their business well, many having worked in it for a long while. It was a FTSE 100 company, so we were not dealing with anything small. Ostensibly all we were doing was playing back to them the strategy that they had written about and told us about. Yet, in this workshop, we had hit a critical moment.

The workshop had only been going for a short while and yet we were uncovering contrary views and beliefs amongst the team. Admittedly there was a clue to potential difficulties in the first meeting with the chief executive, when he said, 'They don't get the strategy'. The most critical issue was that some of the team believed their objective for total shareholder return (TSR)[1] was sacrosanct: they had to achieve it. However, two of the team were questioning it and did not believe that the total shareholder return target was achievable. As the topic was discussed, the tension in the room seemed to rise. Eventually we asked, 'So, who believes in this target?'

The seven executives on the left, including the chief executive, put their hands up. The two on the right did not. 'So, who does not believe in this financial target?' The remaining two members of the team raised their hands. One was the relatively new human resources director, who had been promoted to his position nine months before. The other was the finance director.

It felt as if a curtain had fallen across the room dividing those who believed in the target from the two who did not. The tension rose further. The facilitator turned to the chief executive and said, 'Tell us what you believe'. He replied simply and clearly, 'It is not in question. It is what we have to achieve. It is what our bonuses are based on'. The facilitator turned to the finance director and asked him the same question. He replied, 'It is completely unrealistic, unachievable and outside our control'.

---

1   TSR: The total return on a shareholder's investment in shares, from an increase (or decrease) in value of the shares plus any dividends distributed to that shareholder.

At this point some of you might ask what we were doing there. I was tempted to ask it myself at the time. We had been invited to help them to develop a balanced scorecard to support their strategy. We read through their strategy documents and interviewed them. We were presenting them with their collective view of the strategy in the form of a view of the future five years hence and a draft of a strategy map. All we had were the story that had been told to us and the figures they gave us. The future view showed how they thought the future would develop for them, how their offering would evolve, how it would lead to achieving the shareholder value target. The strategy showed the same story, but from the view of what they had to do to be successful. Yet, somehow, we had helped them uncover a massive issue. An issue that lay undiscussed in the management team. An issue that seemed to say the chief executive had a financial target, TSR, that the finance director believed was unrealistic.[2] That was the big first of several issues that we uncovered during our meetings.

This team did resolve this issue, and several other similar issues, to become better at discussing their strategy amongst themselves and with their staff. After some discussion they refined the strategy map and developed a scorecard that reflected their strategy, both of which were rolled out through the organization. Over the next two to three years their share price performance was around ten per cent better than the average for their sector. Whether this balanced scorecard work was a significant contributing factor to that improvement in their relative share price is hard to tell, especially as the circumstances are not repeatable. Some might claim it was responsible, but I am too realistic to make such a claim, taking into consideration the many other factors that might affect an organization's overall performance and its share price. What I am more confident about is the effect the approach had on the team we were working with, and the subsequent teams to whom the strategy map and balanced scorecard were later rolled out. Their success was more likely given the clarity of their strategy and the improvements in the quality of conversation that they held.

I was curious as I left that workshop. What were we doing with these tools that brought about the richer discussion and realization? What principles were we applying? Bear in mind that we had not even started to look at the measures, targets or the detail of the scorecard. We were only mapping their strategy and creating a simple view of the future at this stage. The simple strategy map we used is shown in Figure 1.1. Yet there was something about how we had captured and presented this strategy that changed the way they thought and worked. What were we doing that improved the quality of conversation amongst that team?

---

2   The finance director was naturally concerned that absolute shareholder return should be more dictated by the overall stock market's performance than by the effects of one player in that market.

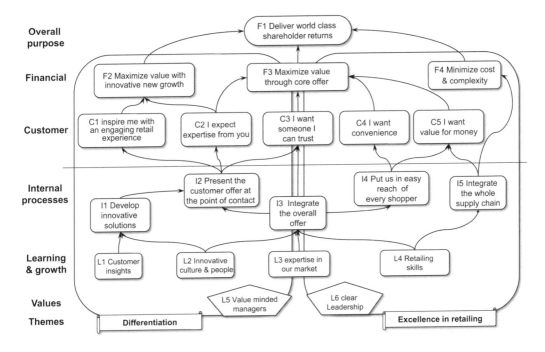

Figure 1.1   A retailer's corporate strategy map

The Superficial Tools

That meeting was back in 1999 and the strategy map shown reflects the approach from that time. Since then these techniques have been tested, developed and enhanced. This book presents fifteen years' experience of using such techniques and adapting them in a variety of organizations, teams and strategies.

This organization wanted a balanced scorecard that would support them over the next five years, a balanced scorecard they could cascade to all their retail outlets and departments that would help them to track and manage their strategy better. Superficially we were only using two basic tools to model the strategy: a picture of the future and a strategy map. The picture of the future described how they saw the organization in five years' time. The relatively simple technique used then has since evolved into a far richer tool which is now called a 'tangible future'. This describes the landscape through which the organization is heading with its strategy, uncertainties, risks and decisions, and how the organization is expected to change over the same timeframe. How the organization will change is described with the strategy map.

In turn, the strategy map frames its balanced scorecard to support the strategy. This avoids an operational scorecard. Careful design of the strategy map makes sure that the scorecard you develop from it will actually address the strategy. The process of strategy map design, the ways in which strategy maps capture strategies and the principles embedded within the approach are the subject of this book. This book also explains how you can use them to manage your strategy better, learn from your strategy and become a more agile and responsive organization.

The Underlying Thinking, Principles and Techniques

Even though this meeting was a long time ago, it has remained with me ever since. I realized that the deeper things that we were doing were having a much more fundamental effect on how this team met, discussed the strategy and would operate: deeper than the mere superficial techniques would suggest. This realization started me on a journey, a journey that has included understanding the various forms of strategy and the ways strategy is discussed, described and expressed; understanding how models of change and models of learning are embedded in the approach; how to create a high quality of conversation amongst the team; how performance management influences behaviour and brings about change in an organization; and, ultimately, how strategy is implemented and managed. I have continued to work with management teams in many different organizations on their strategy, its communication, implementation and subsequent management. I have continued to explore and pursue the underlying thinking, capabilities, skills, language and patterns of behaviour that make some balanced scorecards strategic and successful, whilst others fail. Much of this is deeply embedded in the principles, thinking and deeper processes of the strategy mapping and the balanced scorecard approach, and often not explicit.

This thinking can easily get lost or ignored. When the thinking is lost, so too are the benefits. The underlying thinking raises questions that are essentially simple, yet extremely powerful. For example, one question is about focus in your strategy. If the question is omitted you can easily end up with a hundred measures on your scorecard. Ask the question correctly and you will have a manageable number that work as a set and focus attention on what matters most. Questions like this require managers to think hard about the answers and the consequences, to discuss the answers in a way that leads to clarity and consensus within the team. If these questions are avoided, not thought through or not answered carefully, you will not capture your strategy. The resulting balanced scorecard will omit the strategy and degenerate into an operational view. The strategy map will not represent your strategy. Implementation of your balanced scorecard may even have a deleterious and ultimately costly effect on how you manage your strategy's implementation.

This book is about the underlying thinking, behaviour, assumptions and values that make a balanced scorecard a useful strategic performance management approach, and the role of strategy mapping in that process. They are the 'difference that makes the difference' between a 'strategy-focused' balanced scorecard and an operational one. They make the difference between a culture of performance that encourages the right behaviours and a culture of measurement and target setting that can create dysfunctional behaviour. They make the difference between an organization that learns about and from its strategy, and one that formulates its strategy and then concentrates mainly on the operational implementation. They are the capabilities that both management and the organization as a whole need to learn, grow and develop to move towards strategic performance management. Strategy mapping is central to this. Understanding and applying the principles of strategy mapping in this book will help you to avoid potential problems, so that you have an effective tool of strategy implementation, execution and management.

The Executive Perspective on Strategy Mapping

How might strategy mapping help you and your organization? Let me assume that you are an executive in a management team working on your strategy.[3] You may well have carried out some market research, looked at the state of the organization at the moment, considered various options and, together with your team, chosen your strategy from amongst the options available. You have prepared some outline planning, thought through some of the resource allocation implications and have a good idea where change is required and the extent of that change. The organization has anticipated that a new strategy is coming. Like most clients I meet, you are an experienced management team who know your market and your organization. You have a good idea of your strategy and what you want to achieve.

You want to make sure that the strategy is successful. You need your staff to understand where you are, the pressures for change and where you are going. You want to ensure they understand the imperative for change, the rate of change and how that change will happen. You want them to take on the strategy and be a part of shaping it and implementing it.

You want to make sure that, as you implement your strategy, you can tell whether it is having an effect, can see progress and can show people progress. You know that what you have created is good, but is probably not perfect. You know that the strategy will need refinement as you progress and learn more about the environment, the market, customers' reactions and the responses of competitors. This is where your strategy map will help.

You may already have a balanced scorecard that you use. You certainly have some form of performance management that you use. It will be an early generation of balanced scorecard that does not use strategy maps and is therefore more operationally focused. It probably provides good information on financial performance and operational performance. It may serve you well, but it is time for improvement. The balanced scorecard approach has moved forward since the early versions and a more modern approach might help you deliver your strategy better.

Why might a strategy map help you? Many performance management approaches concentrate on measuring and monitoring operational performance. In contrast, a strategy map-based balanced scorecard concentrates on how the strategy will improve the organization's performance. The emphasis is on how strategy drives change and improvement. It captures operational detail as a part of the approach, but focuses the attention of the organization on the management and implementation of the strategy. Some of the potential benefits for strategy formulation and planning, operational performance management and strategic learning are shown in Figure 1.2 as a strategy map. When these benefits are being delivered you are moving towards a strategy focused organization. How do strategy maps help you with specific aspects of managing strategy performance and learning as an organization?

---

3   If you are in the role of supporting your management team, this perspective will help you as well. You will find it especially useful to think through the design from the executive team's perspective.

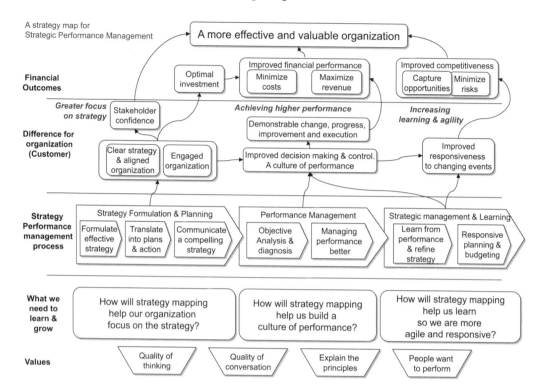

A strategy map for
Strategic Performance Management

A more effective and valuable organization

Financial Outcomes

Optimal investment

Improved financial performance
| Minimize costs | Maximize revenue |

Improved competitiveness
| Capture opportunities | Minimize risks |

Greater focus on strategy — Stakeholder confidence

Achieving higher performance — Demonstrable change, progress, improvement and execution

Increasing learning & agility

Difference for organization (Customer)

Clear strategy & aligned organization

Engaged organization

Improved decision making & control. A culture of performance

Improved responsiveness to changing events

Strategy Performance management process

Strategy Formulation & Planning
| Formulate effective strategy | Translate into plans & action | Communicate a compelling strategy |

Performance Management
| Objective Analysis & diagnosis | Managing performance better |

Strategic management & Learning
| Learn from performance & refine strategy | Responsive planning & budgeting |

What we need to learn & grow

How will strategy mapping help our organization focus on the strategy?

How will strategy mapping help us build a culture of performance?

How will strategy mapping help us learn so we are more agile and responsive?

Values

Quality of thinking

Quality of conversation

Explain the principles

People want to perform

Figure 1.2   The benefits of strategy mapping expressed as a strategy map

STRATEGY MAPS CAPTURE YOUR STRATEGY AND SET THE AGENDA

Strategy maps do not map the whole operation of an organization, otherwise they would be called operational maps. As their name suggests, strategy maps are about the strategy. They are explicitly designed to capture a management team's strategic thinking and intent. They therefore ask questions about the strategy to capture the management team's thinking, choices and intentions. A well designed strategy map explains, on a single page, what these choices are, how the strategy will bring about change and how you will deliver your strategy. Strategy maps focus on the few things that will make the biggest difference to the organization.

Strategy maps describe the organization's strategy from the perspective of the management team for which they were designed. Your team's strategy map should describe your strategy. If you are the top executive team in an organization then you describe the organization's strategy from your perspective. The teams that support you will have their own strategy maps for their own part of the strategy. Each strategy map sets the strategic agenda for each team and how they implement their part of the strategy.

STRATEGY MAPS DESCRIBE HOW CHANGE WILL HAPPEN

Strategy is about change. Your strategy needs to describe what will bring about that change and what the changes will be. Strategy maps help by describing the changes you wish to bring about and, just as importantly, the mechanisms that you will use to ensure those changes happen.

Strategy maps explain what will be different and how the organization will change from various perspectives. Most importantly they explain the underlying drivers of change. A failure to explain these drivers of change is what I call 'strategy by hope and magic'. The strategy map helps you to avoid strategy by hope and magic. It makes the underlying drivers explicit and helps you manage them explicitly.

Strategy maps contain a simple but powerful cause and effect model. The structure of the cause and effect model explains how performance is driven in an organization. It also provides a predictive model of business performance. Instead of merely tracking whether you *have achieved the eventual results*, the cause and effect model also tells you whether you *are making progress* towards the end result. The emphasis changes to 'how will we know we are succeeding?' The cause and effect model is fundamental to this description of organizational change, but it is only one of a variety of models and mechanisms of change that the overall approach captures. Strategic change happens through a variety of mechanisms: management communication; behaviours; management attention; projects; reorganizations; changing the measures, targets and incentives; and many more. Strategy maps and their scorecards capture these.

STRATEGY MAPS HELP THE COMMUNICATION OF YOUR STRATEGY

When a client used the phrase 'a piece of the strategy in everybody's pocket', I knew exactly what he meant. Strategy maps are a rich and succinct picture of an organization's strategy on a single page and a powerful tool of communication. I know many clients who have carried their strategy maps around to explain their strategy. Others have kept a large version on their wall, or the office wall, so that the whole organization can see what needs to be achieved. People can see where they contribute to the overall strategy and which particular objectives they and their team are responsible for. Marking improvements on these one page strategy maps helps people see where and how the strategy is working. With strategy maps everyone can have their piece of the strategy in their own pocket.

At a more detailed level, strategy maps help ensure your strategy is consistent with how you manage performance. You will want to avoid the situation where the message of your strategy is not the same as the message in your measures and targets. If your measures and targets do not reflect your strategy, it will confuse your staff and undermine your strategy's success. A strategy map-based balanced scorecard is central to ensuring you communicate the right message and a consistent message.

Strategy maps help with explanation of the strategy and engagement of your whole organization. The more people are engaged, the more they will understand how they can contribute to the development and implementation of the strategy. Embedded in the design of strategy maps are elements designed to help you engage as wide an audience as possible.

QUALITY OF CONVERSATION

At the end of an engagement, the chief executive will often say, 'You have helped us improve the quality of conversation amongst our team'. This is good to hear: it is how the management team think, work together and behave that affects the rest of the organization and the ultimate success of the strategy. Making a difference here makes a big difference elsewhere.

Strategy maps are a tool of thinking and conversation as well as communication. Napoleon is reputed to have said, 'I give not a jot for plans; it is planning that is important'.[4] The questions and techniques in strategy mapping are designed to help a management team explore and discuss the strategy in more detail than they perhaps would normally. They ensure that quality thinking has gone into the strategy. They ensure your management team share their views and beliefs about why this particular strategy has been chosen and how it will be implemented. The approach develops a shared understanding of the strategy amongst the management team and consensus over how to implement it. I call this 'the quality of conversation'.

On occasions a chief executive has expressed a concern to me that their team, or perhaps some individuals, do not work well together. Perhaps someone does not seem to understand the strategy or appears not to want to understand the strategy. At the start of this chapter was an example of this. The issue of TSR had become undiscussable[5] and the team had avoided the discussion. When this happens there is a tendency to dance around problems and never resolve them. Discussions become stilted. I have found that paying attention to the quality of conversation during the development of strategy maps has led to such situations being brought to the surface and, most importantly, resolved.

This quality of conversation should extend to how your strategy is communicated and rolled out. If the quality of conversation is good within the management team, it is likely to ripple through the organization and engage staff at each level as the strategy is cascaded and implemented. Engaged staff are one of the consequences of a culture of performance, rather than one of target setting and measurement.

IMPROVING HOW PERFORMANCE IS MANAGED

Strategy maps are fundamental to improving how performance is managed. A significant part of the approach can be characterized as, 'don't start with measures'. This surprises those who still believe that balanced scorecards are about measures and targets. They may have experienced the early balanced scorecards or simplistic measurement systems masquerading as 'balanced scorecards'. These people have often been subjected to measure mania, the tyranny of targets and feeding the beast. Measure mania is the obsessive creation of measures for everything, usually resulting in such a confusing picture that you cannot see the wood for the trees. It is often driven by the mantra, 'what gets measured gets managed'. As a result everything gets measured. The tyranny of targets is an obsessive compulsive disorder that first thinks every measure must have a target. This creates an environment where management is only about achieving targets. Often these conflict and confuse or create dysfunctional behaviours to satisfy inappropriate targets. Feeding the beast occurs when the central body, or head office, demands measures and other information that have no relevance to those who need to provide them. They are often demanded with a frequency that would be impossible for the central body to actually respond to. The measures' only purpose appears to be feeding the beast of central

---

4   I have also heard this variously attributed to Paton, Eisenhower and many other military leaders. Also I assume Napoleon said it in French.

5   For a richer description of undiscussables and how they arise, see Argyris 1993.

bureaucracy. In each case, the measures, targets and incentives have been used as a blunt instrument of management and change. Using strategy maps will help you avoid this problem.

In this book, strategy mapping positions you to take the opportunity to focus on learning rather than merely control. You don't lose control: indeed you improve it. Your staff are also encouraged to learn and develop. Management team meetings can become more about how you as a team learn, develop and improve. Decision making also improves as better information is available and judgement is developed. When I explain the principles that are covered in this book, managers say they are obvious and wonder why others continue to apply such problematic approaches. Having a well designed strategy map that contains objectives in each perspective is at the centre of this approach. It is fundamental to making good decisions about what to measure and how best to learn and develop.

A MORE AGILE STRATEGY AND A LEARNING ORGANIZATION

This quality of conversation during design and communication leads to a quality of conversation about the strategy as it is being implemented. It helps you be better at learning from, refining and potentially re-communicating your strategy. Strategy maps sit in an overall process, called strategic learning, that links strategic thinking and planning with performance management and learning. Strategic learning is a way of assessing, adjusting and refining your strategy as it progresses. Events can also happen in the outside world that might cause you to adjust your strategy. The mechanisms and tools around strategy mapping help you to monitor these potential events and also to refine and adjust your strategy as they occur. Rather than being a thick plan, strategy maps are succinct, yet rich, models of your strategy in a far simpler format. This makes it far easier to refine your strategy and to communicate changes. Strategy maps support a more flexible responsive strategy and a management team who want to learn from their strategy as they implement.

In summary, strategy maps are fundamental to the balanced scorecard as a tool of strategic management. A strategy map is a pictorial representation of the strategy on a single page. It describes the strategy and tells the story of the strategy. It describes visually how value is to be created by the organization and what will drive change. Strategy maps are part of the overall balanced scorecard management approach. A strategy map sits in front of its balanced scorecard (the scorecard). Each scorecard has a strategy map. They make the difference between an operational view and a strategic perspective. They raise the level of conversation from operational detail to strategy and change. They raise the focus of management from operational control to strategy execution, where strategy becomes a continuous process of learning and refinement.

A Roadmap to Navigate this Book

This book concentrates on strategy mapping: how you design and use strategy maps. When you design your strategy map correctly, it makes it much easier to design the subsequent scorecard and manage the strategy. The book is therefore about strategy mapping rather than strategy maps. You will find that much value comes from thinking through the questions strategy maps ask, the process of design and the discussions that take place as they are developed and also used.

With these benefits in mind, this book is made up of seven parts which pull together the 21 chapters into logical groups that explain the various aspects of strategy mapping principles, design, implementation and use. Figure 1.3 provides a map through these parts and chapters.

Part I (Chapters 2 and 3) concentrates on the strategic management process and how your strategy can be captured and represented in your strategy maps. Chapter 2 explains how strategy maps support management's need for governance and their strategic management process. This chapter treats strategy conception, design and implementation as a learning process where the strategy is refined as management learns and the environment changes. This is the strategic learning model. Chapter 3 explains how you can capture various aspects of your strategy within your strategy map. It also shows how extensions to the basic balanced scorecard perspectives support aspects of strategy and strategic management that a simpler balanced scorecard would otherwise omit.

Part II provides tools to capture the wider view of your strategy: how your strategy interacts with your environment, context and market; how you expect your strategy to develop over time. This is achieved through three techniques: the context diagram, value chain model (Chapter 4) and the tangible future (Chapter 5). Together these tools create the context for your strategy map and its scorecard.

Before we describe more detailed design, Part III helps you to think through how you will structure your corporate strategy map and your set of strategy maps. This involves strategic themes (Chapter 6) and the cascade (Chapter 7). Strategic themes help you explain the story of your strategy, the tensions within the strategy and the threads that run through your strategic thinking. They help you to avoid common problems that affect strategy map design. Your strategy will have to be communicated through your existing organizational structure, so Chapter 7 helps you think through how you might

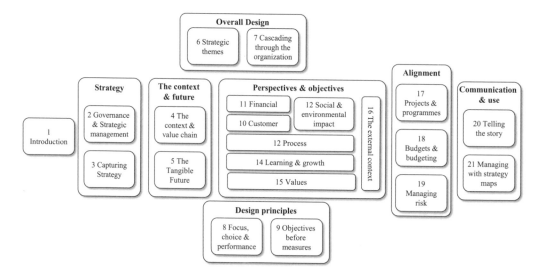

Figure 1.3   A roadmap through the chapters of this book

best cascade the strategy maps and balanced scorecards to ensure your strategy has the desired effects. Thinking through your themes and cascade before you start the design of your overall strategy map will ensure you capture the essence of your strategy, first time.

Part IV addresses the design principles within strategy maps that ripple through to your scorecards. Chapter 8 explains how the principles of strategy as focus and strategy as choice are used during design and manifest themselves in the structure of strategy maps. It provides a set of questions to ask during design that will expose the performance gaps you have. Your choices about how to close these performance gaps determine the content of the strategy map and the subsequent scorecard. The idea is introduced of managers using both judgement and evidence, which is applied during the design of the strategy map and the subsequent management of the strategy. Management teams use a variety of techniques to develop their strategy and make choices about how they will address the resulting changes. Understanding the various ways management teams make such decisions will help you capture the underlying thinking behind their strategic choices. Chapter 9 explains a fundamental principle of strategy maps and scorecards: objectives before measures. It explains how the temptation to leap straight to measures causes a narrow view of how to manage and what to manage. It also causes your staff to have to mind-read what is really required. Developing your objectives first dramatically improves the design of the scorecard that sits behind the strategy map. It makes it easier to communicate the intention of the strategy and to manage the implementation. It makes it easier to refine measures and targets as the strategy develops.

Part V explains how to detail your strategy in the objectives within each perspective of your strategy map and balanced scorecard. Each chapter provides you with both the underlying thinking and the techniques to capture your strategy within each perspective of the strategy map. Chapter 10 explains how the customer perspective captures your market position and customers' needs. Chapter 11 explains that the financial perspective contains your planned financial outcomes. Financial activity, capability and financial inputs are captured in the lower perspectives. Chapter 12 adds a social and environmental perspective that captures the environmental impact and social impact of your organization's activities. Chapter 13 explains how to use the process perspective to capture what you want your organization to focus on and deliver. Chapter 14 explains the vital role of the learning and growth perspective in defining the persistent, sustainable skills, knowledge, capabilities and technology that will drive the organization's strategy long term. Chapters 15 and 16 provide extensions to the traditional balanced scorecard perspectives so that aspects of strategy that are often missed can be included. Chapter 15 explains how adding an organizational values perspective at the bottom of the strategy map provides a foundation for the strategy and the persistent values and behaviours of the organization. Chapter 16 adds the organizational context or external perspective, to include information that is not normally monitored in balanced scorecards: namely the changing context in which the strategy is being implemented and the assumptions, risks and uncertainties that you will have captured in previous chapters. This part of the book will help you think through each perspective of your strategy map to ensure you capture its richness properly.

Part VI will help you align the organization once your strategy map is built. Chapter 17 explains how to align programmes of change and projects with your strategy map, adding detail that will drive change and improvement through your organization. Chapter 18 will help you link your strategy map to your budgets and assess the implications for budgeting. Strategy includes risk, and so Chapter 19 explains where strategy maps capture risk and where they omit it, for good reason. It also explains how aspects of risk can be included and managed in the strategy map and scorecard.

Finally, Part VII is about communicating your strategy and managing meetings using strategy maps. Chapter 20 explains how the finer points of strategy maps can help you communicate your strategy more effectively through the organization. It explains how the more subtle communication elements within a strategy map can be brought out and exploited to get your message across and engage your staff. Finally, Chapter 21 brings together the aspects of managing with your strategy map, tangible future and scorecard. It provides a management team agenda for meetings and explains how you can refine your strategy as you learn from it, using the strategy map as the basis for that refinement.

Extending Balanced Scorecard Thinking

Those of you already familiar with some aspects of balanced scorecard design will already have noticed a number of extensions to the normal way it is described. These extensions include: positioning the balanced scorecard in a model of strategic learning; using judgement and evidence; extra perspectives that cover values, the external context, and environmental and social impact; having a tangible future; and addressing the discipline and culture of performance. Together these extensions form what I consider natural developments that make up fourth generation balanced scorecards.[6] Whilst the features described in this book correspond to fourth generation balanced scorecards, no knowledge of previous generations is required as all the aspects needed to understand this state of development will be explained as we go along. Rather than describing different types and applications of balanced scorecard and their different generations here, those interested, can find more information on my website www.excitant.co.uk.

Learning from the Case Studies

To help any reader to appreciate what strategy maps are and what they can do, there are a number of examples and case studies used throughout the book. The examples have been chosen to illustrate particular parts of the strategy map design process, rather than to be complete case studies. They have been chosen to reveal the thinking behind each part of the design of strategy maps and the variety of situations that you might encounter and need to consider. This approach is designed to help you understand how to think about strategy mapping, rather than illustrate finished strategy maps. Unusually for case studies, they do not concentrate on the end result, but on the process used to achieve it. For this reason sometimes only parts of strategy maps are used, and often short cameos from different projects have been chosen to illustrate particular aspects or to contrast different approaches.

I often say that there is no rocket science in strategy mapping, but as with rocket science you do need to understand the principles and how to apply them. You do need

---

6   For further information on the development of fourth generation strategic balanced scorecards, go to my website: www.excitant.co.uk

common sense, precise questions and clear thinking. Strategy maps are intuitive and powerful. When I explain the structure and thinking behind strategy maps, the usual reaction is, 'Well of course that is true'. However, people sometimes find it difficult to answer the questions prompted by the strategy map. This is because the questions are quite penetrating and address the depth, clarity and integrity of the thinking behind the strategy. Strategy mapping helps you think through these issues and have a clearer strategy, and the structure of the chapters in this book is designed to help you do this.

2 *Managing Strategy: A Context of Governance, Strategy and Learning*

When you consider the wider process of organizational governance and the process of devising and implementing the strategy, then it is easier to understand how strategy maps fit into these processes and contribute to them. It is also easier to see when not to use them, and how to use them effectively as a tool for managing strategy.

Strategy maps sit within the context of the governance, strategic management and performance management processes of an organization. This chapter explains that context through two complementary models that throw light on the governance and strategic management process.

The first model, the learning board model, describes a frame of governance around the strategy map and balanced scorecard. It explains what an organization's board need to pay attention to and the distinct ways in which they need to govern, influence and control the organization. The model of governance raises the level of the discussion away from merely reporting and managing performance. I have known this model to create nearly an hour's discussion amongst a management team, when I hoped to spend only five minutes raising the agenda.

The second model, the strategic learning model, positions strategy maps and balanced scorecards in an overall model of planning, implementation and learning about the strategy. It changes the discussion from managing performance to strategy and how organizations learn.

These two models will help you to understand how your strategy maps and balanced scorecards, with different emphases, can contribute and address problems within your processes of governance, strategic planning and implementation. They will help you sell the benefits and value of strategy maps. They will help you to identify where more fundamental problems of governance or strategy lie and need to be addressed, before strategy maps are introduced. They will help you to think through and improve how you plan, manage and review strategy as a team and as an organization.

The Roles of Governance and Management

The first thing we need to be sure of is whether a strategic balanced scorecard is appropriate at all. Are there other problems that need fixing first? Or might the attempt to be strategic be overtaken by the need to solve more fundamental governance problems?

How do we identify this potential pitfall? The way an organization is managed is a consequence of the way it needs to be governed from the very top: the board. What and how managers need to manage is a reflection of the needs of the board of the organization. To understand the demands on managers, we need to start at the top of the organization, the board, and see how that might ripple through the organization. We need to understand what the board need to pay attention to and the potential implications.

Garratt (2010) provides a framework for a board's governance activities. This framework, which he calls the 'learning board model' (Figure 2.1), suggests that the board need to pay attention to the short- and long-term performance of the organization as well as the organization's internal activities and the external environment. The combination of these two dimensions leads to the board having responsibility for four roles of governance.

ROLES OF GOVERNANCE

The first role of governance is driven by short-term, internal attention. It is characterized by supervisory management; oversees management performance and budgetary controls; and reviews key business results. The second role of governance addresses short-term, external activities and needs to demonstrate accountability to owners, shareholders, legislators and other stakeholders, and ensure that appropriate audits are carried out.

The third role concerns long-term, external attention and addresses policy formulation. This includes establishing the purpose of the organization, its vision and values; developing the corporate culture and climate; and monitoring the external

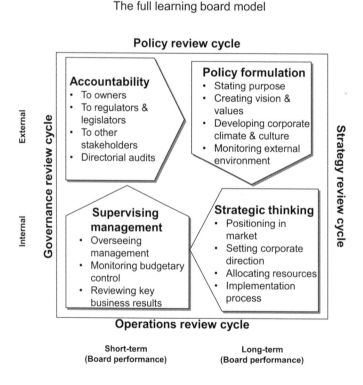

Figure 2.1   The learning board model of governance

environment. The final role addresses long-term, internal attention. It concentrates on strategic thinking, setting corporate direction, positioning in the market, selecting the strategy, reviewing and allocating resources, and deciding how to implement strategy.

GOVERNANCE CYCLES

Garratt explains that the board need to cover all these roles, systematically reviewing each aspect in turn. He suggests that moving through these four roles creates a natural rhythm for a board and the transition from one role to another creates review cycles. This starts with a review of policy that reflects upon the changing world in relation to the espoused purpose, vision and values. In turn this leads to a review of the strategy and strategic thinking, where the external factors link to the long-term positioning of the organization.

Progress against the strategy is reviewed through the monthly review of supervision of management, using key performance indicators, budgets, cash flow and detailed project management information. The board should not do this in detail, but they should be looking for broad changes in patterns and trends. As Garratt puts it, 'We all think we know better than the present managers how to do their jobs and so will get bogged down in detail if the chairman gives us a chance'. He continues, 'The annual cycle of the board ends with the careful checking of their accountability at least three months before the end of their financial year. This process ensures that the board is legally and emotionally in synchronization with the needs of the company itself, the shareholders, legislators and regulators, customers, staff, suppliers, the physical environment and local communities'.

These roles, cycles and demands do not just apply to the corporate board. They ripple through to create demands on every level of management. The natural rhythm at the top drives lower management to also ensure they formulate policy, set strategy, are accountable and carry out their supervisory management duties. More importantly this rhythm influences the agenda of the board and the choices they make.

EXERCISE:

For each of these responsibilities of a board, choose a score (out of 10) for how well your organization performs these roles:

- Accountability
- Policy setting
- Strategic thinking
- Supervisory management.

How informed are you on each aspect? How long do you spend on each aspect of governance? How confident are you on each aspect, as a management team and when briefing the board? Make a note of *why* you scored as you did.

Reviewing how well you conduct each of these roles and governance cycles will help you to identify where improvements may be needed. An organization that scores low on accountability will need to fix its basic statutory, regulatory or financial reports before it can put too much emphasis on strategic intent. An organization with little operational control or detail will find it difficult to make informed decisions about the strategy, where the organization should be improved and where to allocate resources to best effect. Emphasis will need to be on the basic capability of the organization to gather, use and understand operational information before more fundamental, strategic decisions can be made. A poor score on policy formulation might suggest a need to be clearer on purpose, vision, culture or organizational values. Insufficient attention paid to strategic thinking might suggest a lack of direction or clarity on the strategy. More likely where an organization is changing its direction or developing a new strategy, it might suggest uncertainty as to how the new strategy will be managed and how the board may become confident that the new strategy is moving in the right direction and going to deliver results.

A deficiency in any area at board level will have implications for management all the way through the organization. As the organization pays attention to fixing any deficiency it will alter the emphasis of any performance management approach being adopted at the time. This will alter the emphasis you will need when designing your strategy map and balanced scorecard.

IMPLICATIONS FOR BALANCED SCORECARDS AND HOW PERFORMANCE IS MANAGED

This model of governance helps to explain why are there so many different views of a balanced scorecard and its purpose. Why do some help with strategy and others remain operational? The answer is simple. The designers of these various scorecards were responding to differing performance management needs and using different approaches to understand, influence and change their organizations. Each of the resulting scorecards put emphasis on a particular aspect, and that will have remained until the scorecard was fundamentally revised. It will also have influenced how the scorecard is used. If the current emphasis is on compliance and regulatory reporting, then it will be no surprise that that is where the emphasis of the resulting scorecard will lie. If there is a deficiency in operational information then operational detail will be where attention is focused. Once such deficiencies are embedded in management practice, it can be hard to redress the balance.

If you understand where recent attention has been paid, where emphasis needs changing or improving, it will help you to understand where governance problems reside. This will help you identify which aspects of governance your strategy map will need to emphasize and support, and so judge how to focus the attention of your strategy maps and balanced scorecards to best effect. It will even tell you if you should not try to implement a strategic balanced scorecard approach just yet. If there are fundamental accountability or regulatory issues, or where there is a fundamental deficit of operational information, these will need addressing first. At best they need addressing in parallel to provide the basic information against which decisions are being made and progress can be judged.

Putting discussions about the strategy map and balanced scorecard in the context of the board's governance raises the profile of these issues at board level. It will also help the board to appreciate its role in using the approach, and help you, as an executive, manage their expectations about what it will and will not deliver. Placing the balanced scorecard in a role of strategy management will mean that the board will still want reassurance of the operations, governance and policy cycles. As chief executive you will need to manage these expectations. As a manager in the organization, you will need to be conscious of how these implications ripple through to your level.

My experience is that an imbalance of governance is often not the presenting issue, though it might be the deeper issue. Rather, the board want reassurance that success will continue. I often encounter boards that say, 'We have been successful in the past, but now we want to be sure our current strategy will succeed. How will you (the executive) demonstrate that to us?' Strategy maps and balanced scorecards help the executive to provide that assurance to their board.

The strategy map's power lies in its ability to help an organization articulate, communicate and then ensure the implementation of strategy. As this governance model shows, this is where strategic thinking and strategy formulation link to the implementation of the strategy and operational supervision. Understanding these governance roles, and how the strategy map will help them, will help you ensure that you design and use a strategy map that contributes appropriately to the current and future needs of your organization.

Strategic Planning, Management and Learning

Having checked that a strategic balanced scorecard is appropriate, given the state of governance of the organization, you now need to ensure that it supports your processes for managing strategy and managing performance. The strategic learning model is used to describe this fully. It includes the activities of strategic thinking, planning and implementation. It explicitly gathers feedback on the strategy and its implementation, so you learn about it as it is implemented. The model also links strategic planning closely to the management of performance in the organization. It takes a much wider view than the more traditional approaches to strategic planning and performance management.

TRADITIONAL STRATEGIC MANAGEMENT

There are many models of strategic planning and many philosophies about how strategy can be developed. Ten variations or schools of strategic management are well described and categorized by Mintzberg, Ahlstrand and Lampel (1998). Most organizations choose a particular time to do their strategic thinking and prepare their plans from which they implement their strategy. The processes are usually conducted annually, at the same time each year. Depending upon the organization they can take up considerable resources and time (Hope and Fraser 2003: 3–15).

This approach of developing your strategy followed by a period of implementation is represented in Figure 2.2. This diagram corresponds with two parts of the learning board model. The top half of the diagram represents the strategy review cycle as policy formulation links to strategic thinking and the strategy is articulated as direction, position, resources, budgets and the implementation process. The operational management loop maps across to the operations review cycle where supervisory management ensures that budgets and responsibilities are met, staff and resources are managed, and the results are

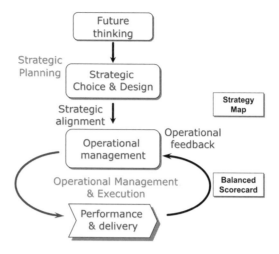

Figure 2.2   Traditional strategic planning and performance management

delivered. The strategic alignment stage is where the planning and budgeting processes take place.

Many strategic planning models start off by establishing a view of a desired future. This might involve reviewing the organization's purpose or mission, how it expects the future to evolve and how it will influence that future. Often a vision statement will be used or developed to describe the organization's position at some time in the future. Typically the strategy team establishes what the organization's customers will want and how the environment might change. They consider the gap between where it is now and its desired future, as well as the effect of the environment and external factors. There may be several routes that the organization could take towards the desired goal and, from this choice of routes, a particular strategy is chosen. This determines the broad choices that the organization has to make given the resources it has available.

The details of the strategy are then developed and expressed as detailed plans. Strategic alignment typically includes resource demands, budgets, targets, responsibilities, programmes of change and implementation projects. Resources and responsibilities are allocated. The strategy is then communicated to the organization through briefings and the various mechanisms of programmes, projects, resource allocations, budgets and responsibilities. The functions, departments, teams, processes and people within the organization then have the role of executing the strategy as represented on the diagram by performance and delivery.

Finally, operational performance management is used to track progress with the strategy. Performance management ensures that the choices in the strategy are implemented. It checks that the operational parts of the organization, interacting with the customers, are performing effectively and that any improvements are bringing results. It also ensures that the programmes and projects designed to bring about change are being implemented effectively.

This performance management loop is usually drawn as a simple feedback loop because it is concentrating on the implementation of the strategy. In this way of thinking, the choices made during the strategic design are rarely revisited or changed. Attention is on their correct implementation, given the resources available, rather than whether they are correct or working.

If a strategy map is developed during the strategic design phase it will typically remain static during the implementation phase, the work of managing the delivery of the strategy resting with the scorecard. If any form of detailed future vision statement exists it will be used in the future thinking stage. The performance management loop is where the scorecard is used. The scorecard is often designed in the strategic alignment stage by selecting measures and targets, projects and responsibilities that represent the strategy in each part of the organization. Management attention then concentrates on the delivery of these targets and projects as a part of the delivery of the strategy and the operation of the organization, using the balanced scorecard as a direction setting, control and reporting tool.

EXERCISE:

1. How often do you review your strategy?
2. How often do you discuss the strategy as a team?
3. How often do you check that your strategy is being implemented as per the plan?
4. How often do you check whether the strategy needs to be refined, changed or revisited?

However, this is not the only approach adopted by organizations. Many organizations have a more iterative approach. Often this manifests itself as a rolling planning and budgeting process where the senior management team review and revise their plans perhaps every quarter, using an 18 month to two year planning horizon that has greater detail in the first few quarters. This approach has become more popular, with organizations trying to move away from annual budgeting and performance to a more responsive, rolling forecasting and budgeting approach (Hope and Fraser 2003). This, of course, has implications for how the strategy and planning processes meet the budgeting and performance management processes. The origins of this thinking go back to those management thinkers such as Quinn (1982), who thought of strategy as an incremental process, and further back to Lindblom (1959), who described policy making as a messy process that he referred to as the science of muddling through, rather than a neat, ordered strategy planning process, which many pretend the process should be. More recently Mintzberg et al. (1998: 189–195) contrasted emergent strategy with the more deliberate strategy of the systematically planned approach. To accommodate both these emergent, incremental learning approaches as well as the more systematic, structured schools of thought, I use a much richer strategic learning model.

The Strategic Learning Model

The strategic learning approach treats strategy and performance as a more complete, continuous, iterative process. The model is shown complete in Figure 2.3. It brings strategic thinking, planning and performance management closer together and keeps strategic progress and review much higher on the management agenda. A simpler, early version of this model is described in Kaplan and Norton (2001: 275, Figure iv-2) as the way to make strategy a continuous process.

Once the strategy has been chosen, the traditional model puts emphasis on whether the strategy is being implemented. The strategic learning model adds a further important question: given what we have learnt from implementation so far, is our strategy working, or does it need refinement? If so, what should we do about it?

The strategic learning model helps you ask systematic questions about the progress of your strategy (and not just its implementation) and to learn from the answers you get, so you can refine the strategy as your implementation progresses. This model accepts that the strategy may not be perfect at the start, rather than leaving it a year before it is revised. The organization can (and should) learn from the implementation of the strategy and need not wait until the next cycle of strategic planning: it can refine the strategy as the implementation provides feedback. This approach invites the organization to learn from and refine the strategy as it is implemented.

The idea of organizations learning is not new. The question has always been how to learn. Arie de Geus (1997) asked whether an organization was like an organism and could learn and develop. His conclusion was that it could, but that most organizations did not develop this capability and so died early.

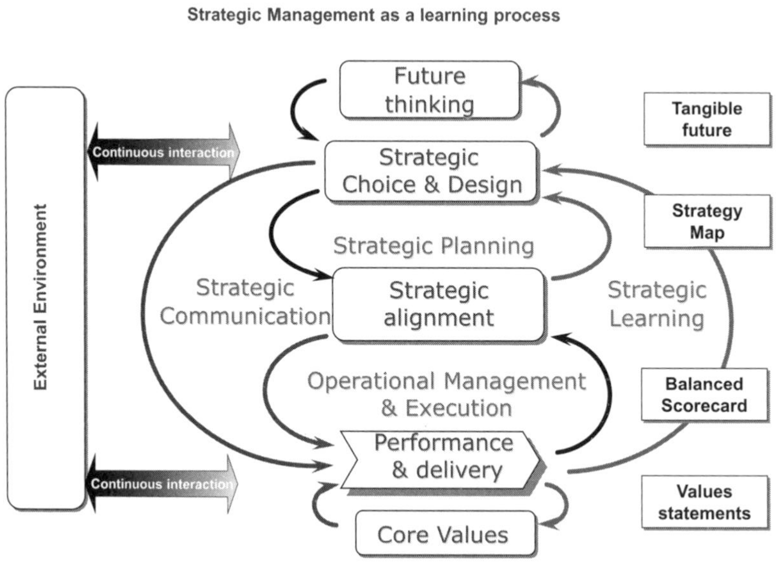

Strategic Management as a learning process

Figure 2.3   The strategic learning model, showing where the tangible future, strategy map and scorecard support it

---

EXERCISE:

1. Do you learn from your strategy as you implement it?
2. How would you describe your organization's ability (or inability) to learn?
3. Why would you describe it this way?

The emphasis in the strategic learning model is not the boxes but the arrows that describe the relationships and interactions between the boxes. In many pictures the arrows merely suggest some sort of coherence or relationship between the boxes. When confronted with such diagrams it is useful to ask, 'what does this arrow specifically mean?' In this model each of the arrows between the boxes has a specific meaning and asks a specific question. The arrows are as important as the boxes. They show how the elements of the model interact, illuminate the relationship between elements of the model and provide questions about how the strategy is managed and communicated. The questions they ask are vital to understanding the approach.

LEARNING MODELS AND BALANCED SCORECARD THINKING

Around the time of the publication of the first balanced scorecard book (Kaplan and Norton 1996), Norton formed an organization (Renaissance Worldwide) to deliver balanced scorecard services.[1] The strapline for the company was, 'Implementing Strategy: measurable, rapidly, knowledgably'. The balanced scorecard provided the measurable. 'Rapidly' was provided by emerging internet technology. 'Knowledgably' was provided by the knowledge management practice, led by Harry Lasker, who had a background in cognitive learning, had worked on the television programme *Sesame Street* and was applying these theories to the practice of organizational learning (Lasker 2006). Renaissance was as well known for its knowledge management practice as it was for its balanced scorecard work, and the two teams worked closely together. The cognitive and organizational learning work was strongly influenced by Chris Argyris and his model of double loop learning (Argyris and Schön 1978, 1996). The origins of the strategic learning model were sown with this work. This thinking was so fundamental to the approach that it is referred to in the first chapter of the first balanced scorecard book (Kaplan and Norton 1996: 17–18). It also appears as a simple diagram in *The Strategy Focused Organization* (Kaplan and Norton 2001: 274–75), but with an emphasis on budgeting. Yet, despite this, the model is rarely mentioned when describing balanced scorecards today. However, this thinking was deeply embedded in the work from the start. The fuller strategic learning model I use has evolved from this original thinking, having been developed from subsequent experience with many clients.

The fourth perspective of balanced scorecard and a strategy map is properly called 'learning and growth' for this very reason. It is about organizational *learning* and asks the question, 'how do we *learn and grow as an organization*?' Those balanced scorecard practitioners who rename this perspective 'people', 'culture' or anything else are discarding this fundamental piece of the jigsaw and removing the emphasis on learning and growth. These other names describe a narrower perspective and ask a narrower question, such

---

[1]   Prof Bob Kaplan was a non-executive director.

as, 'how shall we measure people/quality/culture?' This is a much less progressive or developmental question and produces a far narrower answer than, 'how shall we learn and grow as an organization?'

EXERCISE:

If you have an existing balanced scorecard that uses perspectives (and I hope you do), look at the names of the perspectives. Are you using 'learning and growth' or has someone renamed it 'people', 'culture' or something similar?

If it has been renamed, do you know why they did that?

BUILDING UP THE STRATEGIC LEARNING MODEL

The move from the more traditional way of thinking about strategy development and implementation to the overall strategic learning model requires adding some extra pieces to the original picture. You can build this up in stages.

First we add two arrows on the right hand side that represent explicitly looking for feedback on the strategy, rather than just the operations. These arrows represent processes that gather and assess feedback on the strategy associated with 'strategic learning'. These arrows ask two separate groups of questions about the progress of the strategy. The arrow feeding into the strategic alignment box asks:

1. Are we making progress with our strategy?
2. Is the alignment of our strategy working as we intended?

Feeding the information back into the strategic choice and design box asks:

1. Is our strategy working as we intended it?
2. Should we refine, revise or re-communicate the strategy?

These questions explicitly invite management to think about the progress of their strategy: to continue to question the assumptions; to check whether the strategy is working; to ask whether the strategy needs to be refined, changed or re-communicated. They invite management to regularly review the strategy as well as operational progress. As the strategy map is developed, we put in place the essential components to promote this management discussion.

These two sets of questions appear similar, but are quite different. 'Are we making progress with our strategy?' asks about the stages of implementation of the strategy and whether they are being achieved. 'Is the alignment of our strategy working as we intended?' asks a very different question. It asks whether the choices you made in the alignment of the strategy, such as the allocation of resources, choice of measures and targets, allocations of responsibilities, project design, programme design and its communication, are having the intended effect. The emphasis is on whether management have made the right decisions, rather than whether the staff are implementing them correctly.

DIRECTLY COMMUNICATE THE STRATEGY

We have also introduced a new arrow on the left hand side from strategic choice to operational performance and delivery. This arrow represents direct communication of the strategy. It explicitly asks, 'how should we communicate our strategy?' and 'are we communicating our strategy effectively?'

These questions ensure that the strategy is communicated as it was initially conceived and not simply as it was translated into operational details. At its most simple, this includes communicating objectives as well as measures so people can work out why particular measures have been chosen. At a richer level it is sharing management's understanding of the environment, context, assumptions and beliefs so that staff can appreciate why management believe what they do, can engage in the strategy and contribute to it. Of course, part of the monitoring of feedback will include, 'is our communication of the strategy successful and is it being understood?' Jones (2008) provides a more detailed view of the communication of your strategy.

MONITORING THE EXTERNAL ENVIRONMENT

This strategic learning model also includes a continuous monitoring of the external environment for changes to the assumptions on which the strategic choices were based. This connection to the changing environment is fundamental to strategic thinking, planning and successful implementation, especially where strategy is seen as a process that is reactive to its environment and where the organization adapts to its environment (Mintzberg et al, 1998: 286–300). This is represented by the arrows that connect the external environment to both the strategy and operational management loops.

Back in 2009, the UK was in the middle of the credit crisis – a crisis that few anticipated. The lack of availability of credit and its consequential effect on trade, markets, and consumer and bank behaviour was probably not considered by many organizations. The assumed availability of credit is just one example of many assumptions that were made when most organizations' strategies were being conceived, only a year or so before. An important part of the learning model is the identification of these assumptions.

The connections to the external environment help you to avoid similar mistakes in the future. The strategic learning model includes two links to the external environment designed to act as reminders of two important interactions. First, the strategy and future vision were based on assumptions and beliefs about how the external environment would evolve, adapt and change. These need to be monitored. We do this by looking at the assumptions behind the strategy and the assumptions and uncertainties in the future vision. The external monitoring is looking for changes in the environment that might affect the assumptions behind the strategy. The second link to the environment is where the operational processes are interacting with the outside world and therefore providing the opportunity to gather information and learn. In effect they are a day-to-day sensor of the strategy's effectiveness.

The external environment has a large affect on what an organization can achieve. In good times it is much easier to achieve growth and profitability than in difficult times.

The external environment sets the context in which performance should be considered. Failing to consider this context means that you may have targets that are either unrealistic or too easy. This is why fourth generation balanced scorecards add an external perspective to the standard Kaplan and Norton strategy map.

EXERCISE:

Pause for a moment and consider these questions:

1.   What assumptions did you make during your strategy formulation?
2.   Did you assess the external environment correctly? Is it changing?
3.   Would you notice if the external environment changed?
4.   Are you monitoring the external environment and these assumptions to see if they are still true?
5.   Is feedback from the interaction between operations and the outside world being used to inform the strategy and its progress?
6.   Do you have any way of refining, or more radically adjusting, your strategy if a significant change were to manifest itself?

FUTURE VISION

In the same way we introduced feedback on the strategy, you also have to monitor whether the desired or expected future has changed and consider any implications. To accommodate this thinking there is an arrow from strategic choice back to the future vision. This represents two questions about the future vision that were the basis of the strategy. First,

1.   We based our strategy on assumptions about the future. Are these assumptions still valid? Does our strategy need to change given what we have learnt?

The strategy is a choice about how to travel towards a desired future, so you also have to ask:

2.   Is our strategy moving us towards our intended future?

ADDING ORGANIZATIONAL VALUES

Finally, the addition of organizational values, together with their links to performance and delivery, invites questions about how your organization's values influence behaviour, contribute to the strategy and are effective. The arrows here raise two questions:

1.   Are we demonstrating and communicating the organizational values that underpin our strategy and our way of working?
2.   Are we seeing the effects of that communication and do our people exhibit these core values?

The arrows from the values box reflect how the values are intended to influence the activities and behaviours of the people operating the processes, and the feedback from those processes of the consequences of the values.

PLACING STRATEGY MAPS AND SCORECARDS IN THE MODEL

As you work through the strategic learning model, you will also see in Figure 2.3 that the strategy map, balanced scorecard and a tangible view of the future provide central components that support the model. Placing the balanced scorecard components within this strategic learning framework gives them explicit roles that contribute to the parts of the strategic learning process.

The tangible future forms a central part of the approach. The tangible future makes explicit the management team's expectations of the future and provides clear statements of what is expected to happen by when. This makes establishing the organization's objectives and level of ambition much easier when you reach that point. Consequently, target setting is also easier. Of course, there will be uncertainties and ambiguities. Recognizing them and doing something about them is all part of the strategy process.

The strategy map articulates how the strategy will move the organization towards its future, the choices that are within the strategy, where the value lies and how the organization will get there. The arrows from the strategic choice activity indicate its role in setting the context for operational planning and in communicating the strategy to the organization. The arrow into the strategic choice box indicates the need for the strategy map to be flexible enough to gather feedback on the strategy and be refined.

The balanced scorecard provides the mechanism to capture the operational aspects of the strategy: the measures, projects, budgets and responsibility. It also has an important role in communicating the operational detail to those who are implementing the strategy and gathering feedback on that detail. Those who are implementing the strategy can learn from the operational execution. Management can refine the approach and the messages. The components of the balanced scorecard also provide input into progress with the strategy, and tell you whether your choices about your strategy, embodied in the strategy map, were correct.

The strategic learning approach asks two further questions: 'is our strategy actually working?' and 'should we refine it in the light of what we now know?' Again strategy maps provide the mechanisms to do this because they provide a very simple, but effective, view of the strategy and its progress. They are also far easier to refine, develop and re-communicate than highly detailed plans. When changes are necessary the change is seen less as a 'change in direction' and is more easily seen as a refinement and improvement in the strategy in the light of experience.

The strategy map plays an important part in assisting with strategic planning, communication and learning, as we shall see as this model is developed further, both in this chapter and in subsequent ones. We shall also see how balanced scorecards derived from strategy maps provide better support for the management and implementation of the strategy than a balanced scorecard on its own.

Moving from traditional strategic planning and implementation to a strategic learning model is substantially eased by using strategy maps, though, as we will see, it is substantially enabled by the attitude of management. You can use strategy maps and *not* move to a strategic learning process. However, this would be a missed opportunity. Once you start to use strategy maps the movement to this model is made easier.

The questions in this chapter are designed to invite you to think about how well you are implementing the various parts of this model and where you might improve. The questions provide a basis for your agenda for action.

A Model of Leadership and Management

One subtle aspect of this model is the way it embodies both leadership and management. There are many definitions of leadership. Mintzberg (2007: 17) suggests strategy formulation 'can fruitfully be viewed as the interplay between a dynamic environment and bureaucratic momentum, with leadership mediating between the two'. I also like the useful definition of leadership as 'creating the space for people to perform'.

In contrast, management is about making sure it happens: being specific about what is required, setting and communicating direction, ensuring people have the resources, skills and knowledge to deliver what is intended. It is monitoring behaviours, activities and results, and pulling the levers within management's control to influence those results. When you cover up the future, values and external environment, then the centre of the model represents management, where management is ensuring that performance happens (see Figure 2.4). This leads to management being 'ensuring that people are performing', as represented by the strategic performance management loop and the operational performance management loops.

If you cover up the centre of the strategic learning model, leaving just the future thinking, values and external environment, the model represents aspects of leadership (see Figure 2.5). In other words, if you communicate what you want to achieve and how you want people to behave, and help them understand (and interact with) the external environment, you have created the space for them to perform.

This model neatly encapsulates the important role of leadership and management in the strategy implementation process. It also exposes the difference between strategy maps and their scorecards. Strategy maps set the stage whilst scorecards make sure the detailed script is followed.

Figure 2.4   Management includes strategic and operational performance management

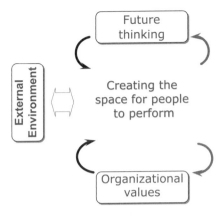

Figure 2.5   Leadership is about creating the space for people to perform

What does this Mean for the Management Agenda?

The first question this chapter asked was, 'is your overall approach to governance in a fit state to discuss strategy and managing the implementation of your strategy?' 'What needs to be fixed before you start, or alongside, the development of your strategic balanced scorecard?' This will stop your project starting in an inappropriate context.

If you are one of the many organizations which do their strategic thinking and planning once a year, followed by a period of strategy implementation and operational focus, you will recognize that things change. If an organization's ability to learn determines its success, how can we build that into the overall strategic management process? The answer is to think of the traditional strategic management process as merely part of a richer strategic learning model which asks additional questions that support strategy review and refinement as the strategy is implemented. The model of strategic learning integrates strategic planning and performance management to create a much more continuous process of learning, refinement and delivery. You can consider which arrows on the diagram you pay least attention to, and how you might improve in these areas.

If you have already embraced a more incremental, emergent approach and perhaps also adopted rolling plans and budgets, then you are simply moving around this strategic learning model more quickly. The full strategic learning model allows you to review the effectiveness of each stage of this process and where strategy maps can help you.

The strategic learning model helps us ask questions about the strategy, its implementation and how the management team are monitoring the strategy to learn from its implementation. If these questions are asked through the year, the organization is less likely to be implementing a strategy that is not being as effective as was originally intended. It is also less likely to be taken by surprise by changes in the external environment or assumptions that were made when the strategy was conceived. These provide an agenda for a management team to continuously review their strategy as it is being implemented. The questions are:

1. Has the outside world changed in a way that will influence our strategy?
2. Are we making progress with our strategy?
3. Is our alignment of the strategy working as we intended?
4. Is our strategy moving us towards our intended future?
5. Are we communicating our strategy effectively?
6. Do our values support our strategy?

And finally

7. Given what we have learnt, does our strategy need refinement or revision?

3 *Capturing Strategy and Change in Strategy Maps*

Strategy maps capture various aspects of strategy in different ways. The key to describing your strategy well is to understand these different mechanisms for capturing your strategy and business model, and to design strategy maps that represent them for your particular organization. Your strategy map describes how your organization will change, what will bring these changes about and the effects of these changes on the environment in which you operate. If you understand how the various aspects of strategy and change are captured, then constructing an appropriate strategy map for yourself becomes far easier and the result will be more effective.

The process of developing a strategy map involves asking precise questions about the thinking behind the strategy, the strategy itself and its expected consequences. Different questions tease out different aspects of your strategy at each stage in the design process. That you have asked and answered some of these questions is immediately obvious from a strategy map, whilst others are more subtle. At each stage the answers to the questions will capture, explain and communicate your strategy. Unfortunately, there are no shortcuts. These questions require thought and insight into the strategy. Because of this, there is often the temptation to either avoid a question or not to answer it fully. Sometimes practitioners do not realize these questions need to be asked and fail to ask them. Sometimes managers feel they need not answer them, or answer them without sufficient thought. Failing to ask these questions is a severe and fundamental mistake in the strategy mapping process. Not to obtain answers to these questions is as bad. In either case, your strategy map (and probably your strategy) will drop back to a view of today's operational detail, rather than a view of the future, strategy and change. In contrast, if you ask the questions, promote conversation and get thoughtful answers, you will focus your strategy map, your scorecard and your organization on strategy and the drivers of change and improvement. Remember, it is as much about the process of strategy mapping and the conversation and thinking it produces, as it is about the result.

This chapter provides an overview of how your strategy and business model can be captured and represented in your strategy map. Further chapters will provide the detail. Different aspects of your strategy will be captured in different parts of the strategy map and its supporting elements. You will capture aspects of your strategy in the pieces that surround your strategy maps, the tangible future and the scorecards. You will capture parts of your strategy in the perspectives that describe how your strategy will ripple through the organization and the effects you expect. You will capture detail of your strategy in the way you use objectives in each perspective and the relation between objectives in different perspectives. Being clear about what you are using and how you are using them will help your design, communication and implementation. First we will describe the generic cause that strategy maps use to describe how all organisations operate. On top of this you can capture specific business models and strategies.

Strategic Themes and Perspectives

There are two mechanisms used to capture and frame your strategy in a strategy map. The most obvious one is the perspectives, which provide both the balance of the balanced scorecard and a cause and effect model between the perspectives. We shall look at how the perspectives work in a moment. An equally important part of a strategy map, but one little understood, is the strategic theme. This is such an important concept that Chapter 6 is entirely devoted to strategic themes and the variations that you might need.

Strategic themes work across a number of perspectives to divide your strategy into its major parts that work together. Figure 1.1 provided an example of a strategy map that used two strategic themes: one for costs and the other for growth. This is a good example of using strategic themes to explain the tension within a strategy: in this case the desire for growth whilst controlling costs. There are many other variations on the use of themes, which you can use for your strategy as you understand their role.

Strategic themes remove the need to add any extra perspectives to account for ideas such as innovation, quality or the environment. Such ideas are best represented in themes that cross the cause and effect relationship of the perspectives. This technique works because there are usually aspects of the ideas that are relevant to each perspective of the strategy map. One important distinction between themes and perspectives is that the strategic themes are chosen by you. You will label the themes with names that reflect parts of your strategy. In contrast, the perspectives remain labelled with the standard balanced scorecard labels, yet each will describe a specific perspective on your strategy, or your strategic theme. Between themes and perspectives you should be able to describe any strategy and all aspects of your strategy. When you understand how perspectives and themes work, strategy map design becomes a far simpler process.

The Cause and Effect Model between Perspectives

The cause and effect relationship builds upon the principle of having objectives in each perspective. The strategy map's cause and effect model provides a clear description of what drives performance and creates change. This cause and effect model is fundamental to capturing your strategy (see Figure 3.1).

The basic cause and effect model is represented in the four main perspectives of the strategy map. They are called perspectives because they look at your strategy from different perspectives. The cause and effect model is very simple and straightforward, deceptively simple in fact. Money (represented in the financial perspective) comes from your customers, so you have to satisfy their needs (represented in the customer perspective) to get revenue. To make the biggest difference to your customers you have to ensure you focus on doing things that will make the biggest difference (the process perspective). The learning and growth perspective describes what you have to learn and how you have to grow as an organization. It is far wider than just the people in your organization. It can contain your critical capabilities, skills, knowledge, culture, behaviours, intellectual property and technology that will make a difference to your strategy. If you deliver these learning and growth objectives, it will improve how you perform your processes and activities, so you can deliver what is most important for your customers, so that their objectives are satisfied and they will provide your revenue, as long as you deliver at an economic cost. That, in essence, is the basic cause and effect model.

This cause and effect model is deceptively simple. However, as we shall see, it asks powerful questions about how you will deliver your strategy, the drivers of change and improvement, the timing of that improvement and how the organization will influence its market and deliver its financial rewards.

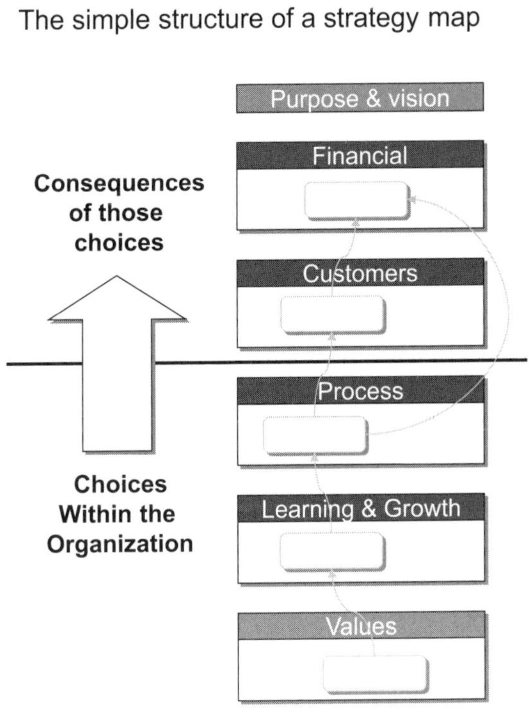

The simple structure of a strategy map

Figure 3.1   The basic strategy map structure is framed by the organization's purpose and values

AVOIDING THE SIMPLISTIC VIEW OF PERSPECTIVES

This cause and effect model also renders the original cruciform picture of the balanced scorecard both outdated and misleading (see Figure 3.2). This picture was used by Kaplan and Norton (1996: 9), and consists of a box labelled 'vision and strategy' surrounded by four other boxes labelled 'financial', 'customer', 'internal business process' and 'learning and growth'. The original picture included a question that linked each perspective to the strategy. It also included a simplified scorecard consisting of objectives, measures, targets and initiatives. As the adjacent text explains, this picture was merely intended to associate each perspective with the strategy and vision. There is no cause and effect model in it. The cause and effect model is initially described three pages on, and then made explicit in the next chapter (Kaplan and Norton 1996: 30–31). The cause and effect model is fundamental to balanced scorecard design, yet you can still find many articles on the balanced scorecard that refer to this cruciform model. They seem not to have read further than page 9 and so ignore a fundamental part of balanced scorecard thinking, the cause and effect model that this picture hides.

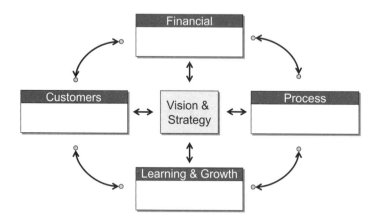

Figure 3.2   The misleading cruciform model of a balanced scorecard that merely shows that perspectives relate to the strategy (adapted from Kaplan and Norton 1996, Figure 1.1, p. 9)

SEPARATING PERFORMANCE AND RESULTS

It is helpful to think of the cause and effect model amongst the main perspectives in two halves as Figure 3.1 shows. The top two perspectives of the strategy map represent the value that is created by the organization, the consequences of the implementation of the strategy, for customers and for the organization's finances. The lower two perspectives of the strategy map (process, and learning and growth) describe how the organization will create that value. It is helpful to think about this lower half as the operational part of the strategy. The two halves of the strategy map are clearly distinct; do not be tempted to merge the perspectives in the two halves. It is the questions within and between perspectives that illuminate your strategy and will help you explain it. This approach clearly shows the distinctions between results and performance. The top half of the picture represents the results of the organization's efforts. The lower half is where the performance of the organization takes place. This is the distinction made by Parmenter (2007), where he uses Result Areas (RA) and Performance Areas (PA) to establish a distinction between Key Result Indicators (KRIs) and Key Performance Indicators (KPIs). This distinction is helpful in understanding where the strategy takes place and where the strategy affects the customers and delivers the financial results.

THE CAUSE AND EFFECT MODEL IS FUNDAMENTAL

The cause and effect relationship between the perspectives is richer and deeper than merely result areas and performance areas. If there is a most common cause of failure in strategy map design it is the failure to think through and apply the cause and effect relationship correctly. Designers that ignore the relationship and simply ask for objectives, or worst still measures, in each perspective cause the whole strategy map and scorecard design to collapse. Get this right and you will capture, communicate and be able to manage the changes your strategy describes. A test of any strategy map is whether the link between any two objectives is capable of being described with an explicit effect. For instance, to ensure we create an integrated design to manufacturing process (process objective) we need to develop our design integration skills and ensure that designers understand the effect they have on the factory (skills and capabilities in the learning and growth perspective). It is this clarity of the questions between objectives that describes the strategy and its cause and effect relationship. As you work through this book you will be describing your strategy by answering some questions that develop objectives within a perspective, and other questions to develop the relationship between objectives in different perspectives.

If a management team cannot describe the explicit relationship between specific objectives, except through vague statements and hand waving, they do not have a strategy that is thought through. The people who have to implement it will not know what to do. Even if they achieve what the strategy says at the lower levels, it might not have the desired effect. That is why the cause and effect relationship exists. I have seen many strategy maps with objectives in each perspective but no explicit links *between* the objectives in different perspectives. This would perhaps *imply* a cause and effect relationship between objectives but you would not have made an explicit relationship.

This simple cause and effect model seems obvious. It is deceptively obvious. As soon as it is explained, people understand it. Yet you only have to look at the internet to find many examples of balanced scorecards and strategy maps where this cause and effect model has been ignored, lost, or destroyed by changing perspectives, rearranging the perspectives or ignoring the cause and effect relationships between them.

Framing your Strategy with Mission and Values

Strategy is about your orientation towards the future and the direction you will take. Strategy is not about monitoring where you are now, as that is the remit of the operational governance. Strategy is about leaving where you are now and heading off in a chosen direction. Strategy maps capture this in a variety of ways, through the mission statement, using forward-looking objectives statements and through the tangible future.

STRATEGY POINTING TOWARDS MISSION OR PURPOSE

Many organizations have a purpose or mission statement which represents why they exist or a vision statement that represents where they want to be in the future. These statements all describe the aspiration of the organization and can usefully be placed at the top of the strategy map to remind the organization of its overall mission or purpose and ensure that the strategy is directed towards that purpose, mission or vision. This same purpose or mission statement is used at every level. This makes your aspiration an integral part of the telling of the story of your strategy through your strategy maps, at every level of the organization to which they are cascaded.

STRATEGY UNDERPINNED BY THE ORGANIZATION'S VALUES

The story of the organization's strategy becomes more complete when you add the organization's values as the lowest perspective of your strategy map. This perspective sits below the learning and growth perspective. I have been using an organizational values perspective since I first realized its significance when working on a project with a major retailer back in 1998. Almost every organization refers to their core values underpinning their capability and directing how they should behave. Collins and Porras (1998: 220–21) treat an organization's core values, alongside its core purpose, as a part of its core ideology. The organization's values are often fundamental to its strategy. It seems incongruous that almost every balanced scorecard ignores them.

Placing the organization's values in a separate values perspective has two major benefits. First, it separates the more persistent organizational values from the slightly more transitory objectives in the learning and growth perspective. The organization's values are usually more persistent and remain in place when the objectives in other perspectives are updated and refined. Second, having the values explicitly identified positions and communicates the values as a core part of the strategy along with the vision. Having a consistent set of values on the strategy map means that the values will be applied as the strategy map is cascaded to each department or function, regardless of its specific learning and growth objectives.

Using Objectives to Orientate you Towards the Future

Strategy maps contain objectives, not measures. The measures will be in your scorecard that supports your strategy map. It is the objectives, and how they are chosen, described and communicated, that orientate the strategy map towards the future. You must always develop your objectives in each perspective before you start choosing ways to measure them.

Your objectives need to be statements about where you want to be, rather than where you are. The process of mapping strategy is about developing these forward-looking objectives, which you can later choose how to measure. The principle of objectives before measures is central to capturing the richness of your strategy and to the design of effective strategy maps and balanced scorecards. The approach is to develop objectives in each perspective and ensure that these objectives have a description of their characteristics and qualities. These characteristics and qualities describe how the objective will be achieved and what will be the result of achieving it. Only when these are completely defined do you start the measure selection and design process. This does not mean you ignore measures during the strategy map development process. You still need to gather facts, evidence and numbers that indicate the level of activity and ambition, and the gaps to be closed. The emphasis is first on developing and articulating your strategy as a set of linked objectives, across the perspectives, objectives that look forward to describe where you want to be, how you will get there and what you have to achieve on the way.

A MORE COMPLETE STRATEGY MAP MODEL

As we develop the cause and effect model in this book we will add some perspectives that will help you capture some further subtleties of strategy and business models. These include a perspective for environmental and social impact, a perspective that reflects regulatory demands and a perspective that captures the external context and assumptions. This full cause and effect model is shown in Figure 3.3 and will be explained further in subsequent chapters.

If you are working in a not for profit or public sector organization there will be some variations on this model. Figure 3.4 shows that you may have beneficiaries rather than customers and that your sources of funds come from bodies that may themselves create demands on your services. The essence of the top half of the public sector and not for profit strategy map model is a three ball juggle: satisfying the needs of their community, customers or beneficiaries; whilst also managing their finances and budgets; yet also satisfying the needs of politicians and/or those people who provide their funds.

You can read the cause and effect model from the top to the bottom and from the bottom to the top. If we develop these capabilities, our organization will learn and grow so that our processes will improve. As our processes get better at delivering for our customers, our customers will be more satisfied and they will give us more money. As long as we can do this economically, we should achieve our financial goals. The basic cause and effect model is a set of objectives, in the four perspectives, framed by the organization's purpose and the organization's values, with questions linking the objectives in each perspective.

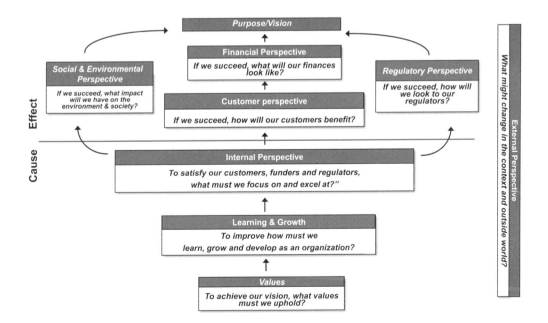

Figure 3.3   The full strategy map framework for commercial organizations

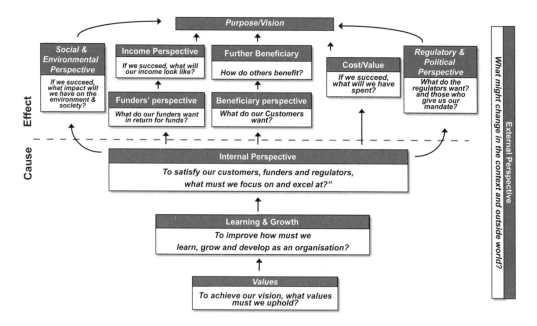

Figure 3.4   The full strategy map framework for not for profit and public sector organizations

THE SCORECARD SITS BEHIND ITS STRATEGY MAP

It is behind this strategy map framework of perspectives that the actual scorecard sits. Whilst the scorecard contains such detail as measures, targets, initiatives, actions and responsibilities, the scorecard layout does not show the relationships between objectives. It does not show how improvements in the lower objectives and measures should drive performance and ripple through the organization. That is why, as a management team, you need both the strategy map and the scorecard. Figure 3.5 shows a simplified example of how these fit together.

Using objectives and the cause and effect model is vital to capturing your strategy, but they also hide a deeper question that is used to fully represent your strategy. If you ask simplistic questions about which objectives you should have in each perspective you often get so many answers that you do not know what to deal with. There is no prioritization, and limited selection within the answer. To achieve this prioritization you have to ask specific questions about the strategy in specific ways so you limit the range of responses and you get to those that are most critical. This gives you an essential quality of strategy maps: choice and focus.

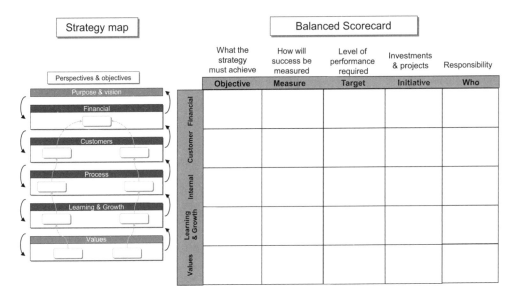

Figure 3.5   The balanced scorecard sits behind the strategy map to detail the objectives in each perspective

Strategy as Choice of Position and Differentiation in a Market

The most crucial part of any strategy, and therefore any strategy map, is how you represent the value your customers want, how you engage with your customers and how you will serve their needs through your value proposition. This is described in the objectives you choose for your customer perspective, as they need to spell out clearly which customers you will serve, how they (the customers) expect your products or services to serve their needs and where that fits into their value chain. It is described in the relationship between these objectives and the objectives you choose for your process perspective. This is the area where you identify and segment your customers, define what they want and need, that is distinct for you, and it is where you describe how you will directly satisfy those needs.

TRADITIONAL CHOICE AND FOCUS

Porter (1996) suggests that strategy is about what we choose to do, and what we choose not to do. We make choices about the market we serve, our position in that market, what makes us distinct in that market and how we will serve it. We also make choices about which markets and customers we will not serve. This choice helps us position the organization in a market, and helps to differentiate ourselves from our competition.

This idea of position and differentiation in a market is fundamental to strategic thinking. Marketing talks about focus in the form of a Unique Sales Proposition (USP) that differentiates one organization's products and services from those of their competitors. In competitive theory, Michael Porter (1985) talks about sources of sustainable competitive advantage leading to long-term economic value. That advantage comes from a choice of market focus and how to differentiate a product or service (either through cost or features).

Your market position and customer proposition are vital to your strategy. This is why so much emphasis in strategy mapping is put on understanding the business model and market and clearly identifying the customers through the context diagram, the value chain model, the tangible future and then the objectives in the customer perspective. The customer objectives need to make clear which customers or segments of the market you are serving, and represent those customers' needs. You also need to show how you will serve those customers' needs as you add value for them. You have to be clear that your value proposition distinguishes your offering from those of your competitors.

Much strategic thinking is about choosing, establishing and protecting a part of the market that provides long-term value and can be protected from competition. Mintzberg et al. (1998: 81–122) refer to this as the 'positioning' school. Porter calls this 'sustainable competitive advantage' and treats strategy as fundamentally about choice and differentiation. However, there are other ways to think about this. Recently the idea of blue ocean strategy has been popular (Kim and Mauborgne 2005). Whilst Porter's competitive analysis is seen as fighting against competitors and shedding blood that creates the red ocean, blue ocean strategy thinking encourages you to step beyond the market boundaries, to look at other industries, to identify and create aspects that are not being addressed by competitors and are therefore in a blue, rather than red, ocean. These two approaches may use different tools of analysis and ways of thinking about strategy, but they have more similarities in their models than differences. Both look at the competitive space. Both seek value from the market. Both seek to differentiate themselves from their competitors, either by positioning in the competitive space for sustainable competitive advantage from cost, differentiation and focus (Porter), or by positioning in the blue ocean, seeking partners and cost innovations (Kim and Mauborgne 2005). It does not matter which approach you take, or whether you use a completely different approach, they should all provide you with a value proposition that you can represent in your strategy map.

This value proposition will extend from your customer perspective to your process perspective. Michael Porter (1996) says, 'Competitive strategy is about being different. It means deliberately choosing a different set of activities to deliver a unique mix of value'. He continues by distinguishing strategy from merely being operationally efficient or effective, 'Strategy is the creation of a unique and valuable position involving a different set of activities'. Kim and Mauborgne (2005: 132–4) suggest there are three levers that will help you find the cost target to serve your chosen market: streamlining operations and introducing cost innovations; using partnering to secure capabilities, leverage of another company's capabilities or secure economies of scale; and changing the price model of an industry.

In 'Are you sure you have a strategy?', Hambrick and Fredrickson (2005) go further and say that a strategy is only complete when you are clear: where you are active; how you will win; how you will get there; what speed and sequence of moves you need; and how you will obtain your economic returns. Furthermore, these aspects all have to align and work together.

POST INTERNET THINKING: RETURN ON ENGAGEMENT

More recently some writers have argued that the internet has changed the situation for customers where previously there was scarcity of choice and now there is an abundance of choice. This has undermined uniqueness of propositions because there are so many alternatives available (Leboff 2011). Marketing texts now talk about return on engagement, citing how organizations communicate with their customers through various social media. Other writers have described how the historical broadcasting of marketing has been replaced by conversations amongst customers which marketing departments can no longer control (Levine et al 2000). Godin suggests that brand marketing has changed from 'top down internally focused, political and money based' to tribe management, where brand is about the permission or 'privilege of delivering anticipated, personal and relevant messages to people who want to get them', and that people want to connect with people, not companies (Godin 2008). These changes emphasize the importance of understanding the relationship with the people who interact with your company, and not just assuming standard models of marketing.

UNDERSTANDING YOUR CUSTOMERS' NEEDS

Whichever of these schools of thought you are in, the objectives you choose in the customer and process perspectives need to describe your customers, their needs and your proposition. The objectives in the process perspectives will describe how you will deliver them. As we shall see when we develop the customer perspective, the earlier ideas, particularly Porter's positioning, have led Kaplan and Norton to provide standard templates for the value propositions in the customer perspective and influenced how they recommend choosing objectives in the customer perspective (Kaplan and Norton 2001: 86–89). From these standard templates you can choose customer objectives that suit your particular choice of positioning. Whilst these templates are useful as a checklist, I believe they are limited in value and restrictive in choice. There is more value in establishing where and how you specifically add value to your particular customers by mapping their value chain and the problems they may have or the points where you wish to influence. This more flexible approach is described in Chapter 10 and enables you to understand your customers' needs, their value chain and how you can specifically engage with them and serve them.

What remains persistent is how your choice of customer objectives will need to show how you serve your specific customers and also position yourself against your competition to deliver your strategy. This representation of choice, position and differentiation is fundamental to strategy maps. It is what distinguishes them from other models or descriptions of an organization's operations and its strategy. Develop the objectives in the customer perspective correctly and all the rest of the strategy map will fall into place.

Strategy as Focus, Leverage and Improvement

Whilst differentiation, position and choice are about markets, strategy contains the ideas of focus, leverage and change to deliver the strategy. Focus, leverage and change are deeply embedded in strategic theory and therefore strategy map design (Porter 1996: 11–18; Kim and Mauborgne 2005: 39). Focus is about where to put most attention amongst the many things that are going on. Leverage is about getting the most from the assets you have. Change is about improvement, about what will make the difference. The same concepts are built into questions that are used to develop the strategy maps and objectives.

To drive out these aspects of strategy, we ask a simple question about the objectives that have been identified: to achieve this objective, what are the few things that we will have to focus on to make the biggest difference? This appears to be a simple question, but its construction is deliberately designed to tease out choice, leverage, change and focus.

FOCUS: PAYING MOST ATTENTION

Focus is about where management and organizational attention is to be put. An organization looking for improvements should not try to change too much, otherwise it will get overwhelmed. You may only have limited resources for investment and change. If you have a list of a hundred things that might all contribute to closing the performance gap, management attention will end up dissipated and internally focused, rather than looking at the outside world. We want to concentrate management's attention to focus on the few things that will make the biggest difference, and they want the organization's attention focused in the same way.

What to focus on is embedded in the way the cause and effect model is elicited. That is why you ask the question, 'to achieve this objective, *what are the few things that we will have to focus on* to make the biggest difference?'

Focus will require that you manage other aspects by exception. This means you have suitable exception reporting processes in place and other teams are clear what they have to escalate. Whilst it is a strategy map for a management team, this does not prevent a management team looking at the strategy maps of the teams that report to them, for exceptions and issues that need escalating.

LEVERAGE: THE BIGGEST DIFFERENCE

Strategy is also about leverage. It is about finding less resource-intensive ways of achieving your ambitious goals. This is where leverage complements the strategic allocation of resources (Hamel and Prahalad 1993). Warren Buffet says this is about allocation of financial capital (Cunningham 2002). It might be about the people, capability or human capital of the organization.

The critical part of the question associated with leverage is the phrase, 'what will make the biggest difference?' This is about the lever and the effect of the lever. It is not simply what needs to change, but what will bring about the biggest change. The problem with the simpler question 'what shall we focus on?' is that there is no criterion for choosing the answer. You might potentially get thirty answers. By adding '… to make the biggest difference' you are making it clear that you are looking for the few things that will make the biggest difference from amongst the many that might make some difference. As you ask the question it is important to put the emphasis on the critical words: the *few things* that will make the *biggest* difference. This will help you identify where the greatest leverage is. It is this attention on the few things that will make the biggest difference that creates the focus of attention in the strategy map for any given level of management team.

STRATEGY IS ABOUT CHANGE

The question is also about change and improvement. The question asks, 'what will make the biggest *difference?*' It is not about what will keep things the same, but rather what will improve things. In subsequent chapters we will introduce further questions that are designed to establish the performance gap and the size of that gap, so that subsequent questions can be used to identify improvements or changes that will close the performance gap.

STRATEGY MAPS MUST NOT CONTAIN ALL THE OPERATIONAL DETAIL

It is vital that you are selective and that you ensure your strategy map avoids trying to capture too much operational detail. The question of focus, choice and leverage is designed to shift attention from the operational detail, where everything potentially has an effect, to the few things that will make the biggest difference. It moves the thinking from operations to strategy and change. Strategy is about choice, focus and change. This is fundamental. You are not trying to create a complete model of the detail of the organization. You are creating a model of the strategy and how that will change critical aspects of the organization's operations and behaviours, and so impact on the results. Whilst a single strategy map does not contain all the operational detail, the total cascade of maps will eventually become more operational and specific.

Strategy as a Persistent Behaviour

There is another aspect of strategy that you can capture in your strategy maps if you are thoughtful about their design: that of strategy as a persistent behaviour. Strategy as a persistent behaviour manifests itself as a persistent behaviour in a market. It manifests itself as the persistent behaviour of the organization and through the development of core competences and capabilities that position the organization to establish and sustain its competitive position.

You will represent your persistency through the choice of objectives in each perspective and the wording of those objectives. The more you craft your objectives to represent persistent actions, positions or behaviours, the more long lasting your strategy map design will be.

If you can correctly select and design the objectives, even though the characteristics and emphasis of those objectives might vary over time, you will have a more persistent strategy map that communicates the long-term strategic intent. I have found this with several clients where they have been using their strategy map for over five years. Over that time there have been some amendments, changes to wording, some new objectives added and refinement of the learning and growth objectives, as some have been achieved and other imperatives have replaced them. Despite the refinements, five years later their strategy maps were clearly derived from the ones they started with. Their strategies, and their strategy maps, had been persistent and successful.

This persistency will of course depend upon the time horizon of your strategy. I have worked with organizations whose strategic thinking horizon varied from one year to 60 years, though more normally we work around five to ten years forward. The organization with a one year horizon was facing a crisis in its market and wanted to focus the organization's attention on overcoming that crisis and positioning itself to survive for the future. The organization with a 60 year horizon was looking at its legacy and the people it would affect long-term. The timescale of your strategic thinking will affect how you construct your tangible future, the thinking about the strategy map and the choice and working of the objectives.

The planning horizon you choose, and the persistency of your strategy, particularly affects the planning horizon for your learning and growth perspective. This represents how you will grow as an organization to develop capability that positions or differentiates you. As Porter says (Porter 1996), 'Competitive advantage grows out of the entire system of activities... the competitive value of individual activities – the associated skills, competencies or resources – cannot be decoupled from the system or the strategy'. Likewise, Mintzberg (2007: 11) is quite clear that strategy is a persistent pattern of behaviour over time and managing strategy is about detecting emerging patterns (Mintzberg 2007: 379). This helps us to make a clear distinction between strategy and tactics. Strategy is the persistent pattern of behaviour, whereas tactics are a set of the shorter-term solutions used to solve local problems at that point in time. Tactics are in the armoury of choices and tools, but are used only intermittently, when appropriate, rather than persistently used. On the other hand the behaviours that represent the strategy are persistent.

> I was talking to an organization whose managing director had banned the use of the word 'strategy'. He told his staff he did not want it used. So I got a blank response when I asked such questions as, 'What is your strategy?'
>
> However, when I changed tack and asked, 'What has been the persistent pattern of behaviour as an organization over the past five to six years?', immediately I got the response, 'To get close to insurance companies'. That, in essence, was their strategy.

This has implications for how you capture your strategy, design your strategy map and choose objectives on your strategy map. How does your persistency manifest itself? Framing the strategy map with the organization's purpose and its values provides a persistent frame of reference. Asking yourself whether the objectives you are choosing are going to be persistent, and for how long, helps you check that you are not including more tactical considerations. Using objectives as your point of reference, instead of using measures and targets, means that you have the space to create a more persistent statement for which measures might develop and the targets might change. This adds to the persistency.

Validating your Strategy

The great advantage of the strategy map's cause and effect model is that it allows you to trace the sequence of improvements in objectives, through the objectives' measures and targets, over time. The timing of the improvements has logic behind it that the strategy map, scorecard and associated documentation easily capture and make available for others to understand.

VALIDATING THE LOGIC AND TIMING

The changes and effects in the lower perspectives are expected to work through to the customers and financial consequences, as shown in Figure 3.6. This example is from an engineering company and how it delivers projects for customers. Both the theme of the strategy map and the diagram show how the increased application of project management disciplines is designed to improve the organization's project management processes. This means that projects will be more likely to be on time and deliver to time, cost and quality. In turn, this will mean that the customer has more confidence in the solution as it emerges, as well as getting more benefits from the solution. Financially the organization wastes less time on re-work, delivers more economically, gets paid earlier because there are less client problems, and therefore improves revenues, costs and cash flow.

However, the improvements will not happen overnight: they are expected to work through slowly. Perhaps a third of projects will already be on schedule and so the improvements will make little direct difference to them. Perhaps another third of the projects will get immediate benefits from the improvements and so will deliver to a higher quality over the following six months as they move towards completion. Whilst the improvements in perhaps another third of the projects will either take longer to bring into line or the new practice will expose problems that were previously hidden. So, the financial benefits will take some time to filter through, even though the improvements in project management quality and confidence in the projects will rise much earlier.

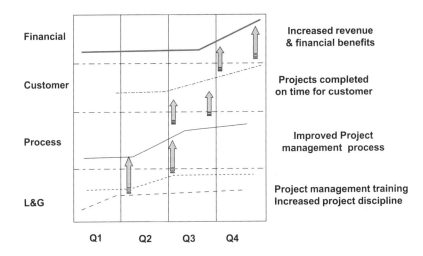

Figure 3.6   Performance is expected to ripple through the perspectives over time

IS OUR STRATEGY PROGRESSING, OR GOING WRONG?

A valuable use of the strategy map is to tell you whether your strategy is succeeding or whether it is delayed or going wrong. To show how each objective is performing you can place scores on each objective of the strategy map. These might be a simple RAG status (red, amber, green), marks out of 10 or actual measures. Showing the status of objectives in this manner is useful to provide an overview of how your strategy is progressing and whether it is bringing about the changes you required in the timescale required. You would expect the lower objectives to move from red or amber to green as you succeed in implementing the objectives in the learning and growth perspective. If you have your cause and effect model correct, then you would also expect to see higher level objectives progressively turn green as time progresses. However, if the new capabilities were developed but the operations did not improve on time, then you would need to investigate what was slowing down the changes that you envisaged.

The strategy map, together with the timing diagram, allows you to test the logic of the strategy and ensure it is viable in the timescales envisaged. This gets carried forward to the rate of change of targets in the balanced scorecard. Often the improvements lower down are designed to bring about changes higher up the cause and effect chain. However, in a different example, what looked satisfactory at the time turned out to have the potential to go wrong in the near future.

> An organization's innovation pipeline appeared to be performing well. It had been delivering the flow of new products that were starting to get to market and generate revenue. On this basis we would have expected the business to continue to bring a flow of innovative products to market.
>
> However, while examining the pipeline's drivers of performance, we discovered two deeper problems. The underlying investment to develop new products had been cut. Also, there was little movement of staff into the innovation team to provide fresh ideas in the wider areas of the business. As a result, it was likely that the innovation pipeline would soon dry up. Objectives that were 'green' at the time would be turning 'orange' or red in the future as the effects trickled through. As this was a two year pipeline, it would have taken a long time to rectify the problem if it had not been noticed until the financial consequences were eventually noticed.

You want to be tracing both the logic of the strategy and the timing of the improvements so you can see how the chain of impact is working through your organization. The strategy map and the scorecard together enable you to capture the logic and timing of the changes and diagnose where problems might be occurring.

Strategy Exists at Different Levels

What is strategic and what is operational depends on your position in the organization. You will be aware that strategy exists at various levels in an organization, such that a more detailed functional strategy can be embedded within a wider organizational strategy. For instance, any department's local strategy, whilst important to that department, could be said to be merely operational detail from the perspective of the overall organizational strategy.[1] From that department's management perspective, the organization's strategy defines their agenda, constraints and ambition, and sets the level of resources available. The same would be true for marketing, sales, IT, operations or finance. Any operational strategy should be supporting detail within an overall organizational strategy.

You can represent these embedded strategies with your cascade of strategy maps. At any level of management team you need to be clear about the scope of their strategy and whose responsibility it is. This way you create a strategy map for a management team with the scope of their strategy defining the scope of the strategy map. As a consequence, you will have a set of strategy maps cascading through the organization, defining how the strategies are embedded within one another. They also define how higher level strategies govern and constrain the lower ones. This has implications for the design of the cascade, as the strategies need not follow existing functional boundaries, and you may choose to have strategy maps that cross existing silos with the aim of joining up thinking and working. This is a theme we will return to in later chapters, as the cascade is designed, and again as each perspective of the strategy map is developed.

Strategy, as Distinct from Planning

In any discussion of strategy it is useful to recognize the distinction between strategy and planning. I find that the most simple and useful distinction between strategic thinking and planning involves thinking of the organization as a box. Strategy is thinking about the box, working on the box, choosing its position in the landscape, how big the box should be and whether it should really be a box or not. Planning is about what you do once you have chosen the configuration of the box. Planning is working inside the box with the resources that you have and the actions you wish to take. So strategy and planning are relative to the system you are dealing with.

The strategy map provides the framework to capture the strategy, against which the planning is captured within the scorecard through the measures, targets, projects, initiatives, and allocation of resources and responsibilities. So, strategy maps help you bridge the space between strategy and planning: from working on the organization, the box, to working in the organization, inside the box. They then help you with implementation and delivery.

Strategy is about Understanding your Landscape

The tension in the need to think about the sustainability and persistency of the organization's strategy in a changing landscape is neatly summed up by Mintzberg (2007: 17 and 24). He wrote, 'Strategy formulation can fruitfully be viewed as the interplay between a dynamic environment and bureaucratic momentum, with leadership mediating between the two'. This clearly explains the tension between the often volatile

---

1   Of course, this underplays the potential of a specific department to be the source of strategic differentiation.

environment and the need to have a more consistent set of operations, processes, practices and policies within the organization.

I take this further and say that strategy *implementation* can fruitfully be viewed as a persistent pattern of behaviour to create and maintain that bureaucratic momentum, with leadership responsible for monitoring the environment and learning from the strategy as it is executed.

Both these expressions capture the need to connect to the landscape and respond to its changes. The strategy map alone does not capture or describe this landscape. That is why we use the tangible future, the external perspective and the strategic learning model to establish these connections. They help by creating a context within which the strategy is to be executed and by providing points of reference against which any changes can be monitored and their consequences managed.

Two Warnings

Now you have a better understanding of how strategy maps represent strategy, I have some warnings for you about how you approach mapping your strategy. If you are familiar with the early balanced scorecard model and thinking you will, by now, have realized that we are a long way from the simplistic cruciform model of a balanced scorecard as merely a collection of measures in different perspectives. It is common in such simpler operational measurement approaches to simply copy measures and KPIs from other sources. However, such an approach has severe dangers when one is dealing with one's strategy. You need to think about where you obtain the content of your strategy map from and you need to be careful that the process you use does not bypass thinking, conversation and ownership.

WARNING ONE: MAP YOUR OWN STRATEGY: DON'T COPY SOMEONE ELSE'S

This warning is about the content of your strategy map and where it comes from. Your strategy map should represent *your* strategy, not some other organization's strategy. Do not be tempted to copy another organization's strategy map as your own. You will also be copying their strategy, not yours. There are examples of strategy maps in this book and other balanced scorecard books. They may be elegant and you might think they contain good ideas. You might be tempted to copy these strategy maps and apply them in your organization. You must not copy them. They are someone else's strategy.

An organization that copies the strategy of a competitor completely devalues the choices, conversation, analysis and decisions that should underpin their strategic thinking. Organizations competing in the same industry are likely to have some similarities in the top half of their strategy maps (the financial and customer perspectives) and face the same industry economics and perhaps serve similar customers with similar overall needs. If two organizations adopt the same strategy (and have identical strategy maps) they are either competing head on or one has adopted a copycat strategy from the other. In reality you would expect differences of operational emphasis depending upon the products or services of each organization, and where they are coming from in terms of existing capabilities and the capabilities they wish to develop to compete in the future. For this reason you should expect differences to reflect the different propositions, ambitions and business models. An identical operational strategy would also suggest that you are in the same place as your competitor, with the same strengths and weaknesses, creating value in the same market. Of course this is highly unlikely. You will not be starting in the same place as they are. You will have your culture, with different competences and capabilities that you want, or need, to develop. The bottom half of your strategy map should be unique for your organization and your strategy. It may have some structural similarities to other competitors, but your choice of strategy, structures, themes, objectives, capabilities and competences should set you apart from others in your industry.

> *The client showed me 'their' strategy map. A consultant working for the company had said he would construct a strategy map for the organization. He worked in isolation and produced what was obviously a copy from an example in one of Kaplan and Norton's books. The consultant had not involved any of the management team in the process. They did not even know it existed. It did not reflect their words, nor the words in their business plan. It broke almost every rule of strategy map construction.*

Of course, were you to get hold of a competitor's strategy, or their strategy map, it would allow you to understand their intentions, weaknesses and how they wish to position themselves to address the market. This does not mean you should copy the content. Rather, you would use it to understand what they believe and then position yourself differently, to your advantage.

For these reasons, you should not be prescriptive about the content of a strategy map in the sense of the objectives it should contain and the wording of those objectives. As this book explains, there are rules about the structure and the questions you should ask to tease out the strategy and how objectives are worded, but not about what the objectives are. Obviously a commercial organization will have some form of objectives centred around costs, revenues and profits, but we do not say what they are. A strategy map is not prescriptive about what you should manage or what you should measure. There are guidelines for what it is likely to contain. The 'rules' are there to help you choose a logical, complete and well structured framework for measuring and managing what is most important to address your strategy.

Generic strategy maps are useful guidance by way of example. Specific maps illustrate and expose a particular team's thinking. They may suggest ideas and prompt your thinking. However, it is your process of thinking about the strategy and the strategy map that is significant. From your thinking come your insights, ownership and the ability to own and tell the story with commitment and congruence. After all, it is your strategy. For this reason we concentrate on the techniques and thinking, and use examples to illustrate the result of the techniques and thinking rather than as examples to be copied. In summary, apply the principles, and test with typical models, but do not dictate the content.

WARNING TWO: DO NOT BYPASS DISCUSSION DURING DESIGN

This warning is about the process of development of your strategy map. Your strategy (and your strategy map) is a reflection of the quality of your thinking and your conversation. Do not be tempted to bypass the questions and conversations designed into the strategy map production process. They are there to improve the quality of conversation, depth of thinking and collective understanding of the strategy and the strategy map. The result of this understanding is a strategy that the whole of the management team agree with and that they can all communicate effectively. It is the quality of your conversation as a team that determines the success.

The process of discussion and questioning is designed to ensure the words used by the management team are represented in the strategy map: to ensure that their detailed thoughts are captured in the characteristics and detail behind the objectives. If the strategy map does not reflect your words and thinking it will not be owned by you and your team, and they will be unlikely to have confidence and congruity when they present it. If you bypass this part you will undermine its value in the communication of your strategy, and use in tracking and refining it.

The process is designed to create ownership so the whole of the management team walk out agreeing on the strategy and comfortable with the way the strategy map represents their strategy. If you present the rest of your team with 'one you prepared earlier' it is likely to remain 'his' or 'hers', rather than 'ours'. The strategy mapping process is designed to build understanding, and create ownership, so that it is your story. It is the collective ownership that matters. How you design and present your strategy map should reflect the thinking of you and your team. Your strategy maps should reflect the thinking and personality of your organization.

> I chaired a balanced scorecard conference where there were over 120 organizations represented. There seemed to be 120 different ways of doing balanced scorecards in the room. Over dinner the person on my right said, 'This balanced scorecard thing is a heap of junk'. Intrigued, I asked him why he thought that (and separately wondered why he was at a balanced scorecard conference at all).

> He explained that he worked for a large telecoms organization. Their scorecard had over 60 measures on it. He complained, 'With so many it was impossible to work out what was important. There seemed no logic to it. It just created confusion'.

> I asked, 'So, if your organization's scorecard is a reflection of the quality of the thinking and clarity of the strategy in your organization, what does your scorecard tell you?'

> He was rather pensive for a while and then replied, 'It's a mess'.

Either the strategic thinking was muddled here, or the understanding of the principles of strategy maps and balanced scorecards was flawed. Whichever it was, the confusing design communicated a confused message to the organization. Assuming you have a good consultant or practitioner facilitating the process, you can think of the approach as holding a mirror up to the management team's thinking.

EXERCISE:

- What does your current 'scorecard' tell you about your strategy and your organization?
- Can you read and deduce your strategy from your scorecard?

Conclusions

You need to ensure you capture your strategy in your strategy map. Strategy maps are rich enough to capture many variations of strategy as well as ways of thinking about strategy. Using the perspectives, objectives, cause and effect model, and strategic themes you should be able to represent any strategy.

Overall your strategy map should describe how your organization's values will affect how it learns and grows to improve its processes, satisfy its customers and deliver its financial results, so that the overall purpose and ambition of your organization is achieved.

When you have this correct for your strategy, then your management team will be able to communicate the story of your strategy. The subsequent chapters will help you apply the design principles so that your strategy map helps you implement your strategy better.

The Organization's Context

Part II is about ensuring we understand the organization's context so we can design an appropriate strategy map.

Chapter 4 provides techniques for exploring and understanding how the organizations context and value chain affect its strategy. These techniques not only raise the level of conversation about the strategy, and where it adds value, but provide important clues for correct the design of the strategy map's most important perspective, the customer perspective.

Chapter 5 looks forward across the time horizon of the strategy. The tangible future creates conversation about how you expect the context and organization to develop and captures your teams thinking and beliefs. Being a rich picture it also captures uncertainties, risks and assumptions. This information sets the rate of ambition for your strategic objectives. More importantly it provides the agenda for monitoring those aspects which might re-rail your strategy or cause it to need refinement. An agenda that informs management team discussions as the strategy is implemented, helping you to avoid costly mistakes.

4 *Exploring the Organization's Context and Value Chain*

It is vital to understand the context, the landscape and the industry in which your organization operates, because effective decisions about your strategy rely on understanding your environment. It is also important to recognize when changes in this landscape or context might influence your strategy or alter the assumptions upon which it is based.

The techniques in this chapter will help you describe your context and your organization's value chain and business model. You and your team can validate the picture you have developed and then use it as a framework from which you can put in place monitoring systems for when the external environment changes. The techniques will help you identify groups of customers and how the organization adds value for them, so that you include the appropriate customers and stakeholders in your strategy map. This work will also ensure you cover all the various players that have a part in the future of the organization, when you later develop the tangible future.

Two techniques are used. The context diagram is used to identify the various players associated with the organization, their roles and any pressures or issues they create. The scope of this is quite wide and can include customers, regulators, suppliers, competitors, political influences, funding roles and ownership. The second technique, the value chain, is used in two ways. The first is to analyse specifically how a customer is served and how you add value to them as an individual or to their organization. Secondly, industry value chain analysis is used to look at the structure, profitability and power across the industry structure.

The two techniques in this chapter work together. The context diagram is used to identify the various players with which the organization interacts. In some cases this may be sufficient. The value chain analysis helps you unpick the more complex structures that often exist in an industry, so that you understand the rich relationships that can occur between various players. Both help you to understand how various customers' needs are served and where financial value comes from. Both help you with the external perspective. Both help the management team reach a common understanding of their environment.

FOCUS ON THE QUALITY OF CONVERSATION

Whilst it is helpful to have a context diagram and value chain, they are not ends in themselves. Much value lies in their construction and the discussion and debate that their construction generates. A management team that are well plugged in to the external environment may find only small additional value from this exercise. It may serve to confirm what they already know, and know they jointly agree on. However, even amongst management teams that do talk often, I find that this exercise creates debate and discussion, and often identifies information that is known only to a few, or beliefs that only a couple hold. Wider sharing of the information, assumptions and beliefs can only do good. So, as you use these techniques, treat them not as an exercise in producing a context diagram and value chain. Rather treat them as a tool to create discussion, clarity and ideally consensus. Even where there is no consensus, at least knowing that people disagree is useful, so that the situation can be monitored to see which one does transpire to be correct. These are tools of conversation that should be revisited regularly as the strategy is implemented.

IDENTIFYING ISSUES TO MONITOR

The context diagram and value chain are the first places you might identify assumptions, issues and risks that will need monitoring as your strategy is implemented. As issues are discussed, you will certainly identify assumptions, potential changes and even parts that you may be uncertain about. All of these are candidates for inclusion in the external perspective as items that need monitoring. That monitoring might be to wait for something to occur, or even to monitor for indications that a change is going to occur. The key is to have an open mind as you progress through the techniques, to ask what might change and what you need to monitor, building the agenda for the external perspective as you go.

HOW THE CONTEXT AND VALUE CHAIN HELP SHAPE YOUR CUSTOMER PERSPECTIVE

The organizational context and value chain will help you to develop the most appropriate customer perspective. They will also help to identify areas to be explored using the tangible future described in the next chapter. Do this analysis before you start putting any objectives in the customer perspective. When people first try to develop strategy maps they often have difficulty with the customer perspective. They dive straight in to the perspective and start trying to describe what their customers want, prematurely. However, the complexity of having many stakeholders and customers can create confusion that leads to questions about which to include and how to represent them. In extreme circumstances, some decide the approach is somehow inadequate or does not work, and criticize the approach for 'only having a customer perspective'.[1] Some even go to great lengths to include additional perspectives or create complicated pictures to accommodate what seems a complicated external environment. However, as you shall see through this chapter, all this additional complexity is unnecessary. With a little understanding, thought and analysis, you will find that the customer perspective is more than capable of handling the most complex commercial and not for profit organizational

---

1   Performance Prism (Neely, Adams and Kennerley 2002) is a excellent example of this. Whilst there are a lot of good ideas in the book, it presumes the customer perspective can only have customers and then suggests a three dimensional model of their performance in the shape of a prism.

context without destroying the cause and effect model or the simplicity of the story of the strategy.

Without this context and information, it is difficult to draw a strategy map that properly represents the strategy. They help you ask questions that cover all aspects of the tangible future and enable you to design an appropriate customer perspective for your strategy map. So, the understanding they provide makes designing your strategy map a lot easier. It can provide clues as to the appropriate shape and structure for your strategy map. The process of drawing and discussing these diagrams with the team helps to ensure that you have considered all the pieces *and* that everyone has a common understanding of how the organization relates to its environment. As with every technique in this book, the context diagram and value chain are as much about creating conversation and common understanding as they are about illuminating the design and use of the strategy map. These techniques make developing your tangible future and drawing the most appropriate customer perspective for your strategy map far easier. Everything else within the strategy map flows from this.

WHAT IS THE PROCESS?

The basic process outlined in this chapter is:

1. Identify the customers and players that relate to the organization (the context map of players)
2. Develop a value chain picture of the industry to identify the layers of players and their roles
3. From these identify the main customer groups and put these in the customer perspective
4. Then work on the objectives of each of these customer types

As you do this, use the knowledge you gather to inform discussion about the strategy and the organization's future.

In later chapters we will detail further the particular needs, demands and objectives of these separate groups of customers, and how they might evolve over time.

Building the Context Picture

The very first thing to do before drawing up a strategy map is to be clear about the various players involved. I find 'customer' is too narrow a phrase to describe the groups that an organization needs to influence to deliver its strategy. Unfortunately 'stakeholder' seems to extend to anyone who has a mere interest, rather than a stake, in the organization. This word seems more appropriate for corporate communications, yet has perhaps too wide a scope for strategy. However, neither customers nor stakeholders seem to suitably include the wider players such as regulators (who have an interest but not a stake); politicians, who may influence an organization's funding and direction; and advisory boards or controlling bodies, who may set agendas for an organization (especially in the public sector). I use the more neutral word, 'player', in the sense of one who *plays* a role in the strategy (which excludes mere observers and spectators). However, you set the scope, and whatever you call them, we create a simple diagram that lists the *main* players (customers, owners, regulators) and how they relate to the organization.

AN EXAMPLE CONTEXT DIAGRAM

You would think that most organizations have relatively simple groups of customers they serve. For instance, you might think a water company simply had water consumers. However, a little digging often exposes a much richer picture of the customer groups and their differing needs than you might first expect.

> *A water company had two main groups of customers, residential consumers and commercial companies. Within the consumers, some households were on water-meters and so paid depending upon the amount of water used. Other consumers' water charges were based on the value of the house, and so they paid a fixed amount each year, irrespective of the water used. The industrial consumers could be broken down into major users (e.g. power stations and large industrial processing units), as well as small businesses. The water company also allowed the public to use their reservoirs for various leisure activities.*

> *The company was regulated by the water regulator OFWAT, so how the company behaved, where and how effectively it invested in improvements in water infrastructure long-term, and the quality of its water and services were of vital interest to the regulator, who could regulate the prices it charged and the level of increases it made. The company also worked closely with the Environment Agency in relation to rivers and water quality. It was also accountable to shareholders and investors. At the corporate level the organization believed that they could ensure their share price reflected their capabilities better (and therefore lower the cost of borrowing) by improving investor relations.*

From this we note the main groups served by this organization: residential consumers (metered and un-metered), business customers, large industrial customers, leisure users, the regulator and the Environment Agency. We might draw a context diagram using this information, as shown in Figure 4.1. When you draw a context diagram, it is useful to label the arrows and describe the relationships between the organization and the different groups. I also ask clients to identify any particular relationships which are troublesome, have issues or create tensions. This is all useful information that provides insights as the strategy map is developed.

In this case the analysis suggests that the main groups of customers needed in the customer perspective would consist of those shown in Figure 4.2.

We do not have these customers' objectives yet. We have simply identified customers whose objectives we need to identify. From this you can ask questions about the specific objectives that these customer groups have. The objectives would then be placed within these holders, as shown in Figure 4.2. Do not place the names inside the boxes. This space is reserved for the objectives of the groups of customers. Place the names alongside so that they ask the question, 'what are the objectives of this group of customers?'

On further analysis, these groups of customers may have similar objectives and so you may consolidate the list further. For moment this is the high level framework we are looking for.

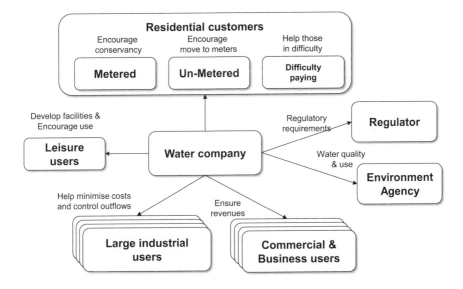

Figure 4.1   The simplified context diagram for a water utility

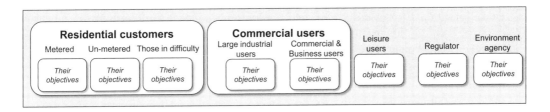

Figure 4.2   Framework for the customer perspective of a water utility

EXERCISE: DEVELOP YOUR CONTEXT DIAGRAM

Part A) From memory, and by systematically going through your business plan, make a list of all the main bodies your organization interacts with. This is likely to include groups of customers and the main groups within these customers. They might include:

- Types of customers in the same organization (e.g. procurement, end users, beneficiaries)
- Customers further up the value chain (e.g. distributors, retailers and end users)
- Distribution channels
- Natural groups with different characteristics such as national and overseas markets
- Any bodies made up of customer representatives (e.g. user groups or reference groups)
- Shareholders or owners (within which there might be groups such as investors, lenders and dominate shareholder groups)
- Regulatory bodies (for instance regulators in financial services or telecoms industries)
- Any bodies of political influence (for instance, a utility or telecoms provider may wish to lobby politicians about regulatory matters).

Part B) Draw a diagram that arranges these players around your organization at the centre. Draw it in a way that represents the relative importance of these groups of players to the organization, with those less influential further away.

1. Issues and tensions: On the diagram draw and annotate lines from the organization to the groups which describe the influences. Make notes about any issues, tensions or points of interest associated with any particular groups.

2. Monitoring assumptions and change: Identify any aspects of this diagram that should be monitored for changes and their impact. Identify any assumptions that should also be monitored. Make a note to monitor these issues and assumptions by including them in the external perspective.

The purpose of this exercise is to ensure the main players that influence the strategy, or that the strategy should influence, are included and considered. Just this simple exercise can reveal interesting facts about the organization and its strategy. Doing this on a context diagram, before the strategy map is drawn, allows you to explore the relationships and identify issues in any relationship, which can be addressed later when the customer objectives are developed. It also helps you plan the spacing and grouping of customers in the perspective.

In another case the approach revealed issues of governance and potential conflict.

Working with one supplier to a group of local government councils demonstrated the political complexity that can exist. The context diagram quickly exposed how the end users were local councils, but that the governing body, its board, which made decisions about the work the supplier should undertake, was made up of only a few elected senior managers from user departments in just some of the councils. Hence there was a sequence of political negotiation where the organization would agree direction with its board, but the board members would then have to sell the agreement to their individual councils, and latterly to other councils. The board members in effect wore two hats which they would swap: one being the representative of the sector as a whole, the other being the representative of their individual council. Quite often these would be in conflict, which caused problems for the organization. Managing the resulting tensions amongst their customers was a vital part of the management team's role, so understanding this dual role of the board members helped in the design of both the customer perspective and the themes of the strategy when the strategy map was developed.

In many circumstances, this level of analysis can be sufficient. However, some organizations serve more complex chains of customers and varieties of customers, or have particular parts that require a more detailed analysis. Adding additional detail to the context diagram to explore the value chain usually exposes these.

Value Chains, Strategy and Strategy Maps

A more sophisticated version of the stakeholder map is to use value chain analysis. I usually do a more sophisticated analysis using an industry value chain once I have developed an initial context with the client.

Value chain analysis of your organization helps you establish the scope and boundary of the organization. This makes it far easier to identify the critical activities of the organization and understand what you can control and influence. It also ensures you have covered the scope of the organization in the process and learning and growth perspectives of the strategy map.

Value chain analysis helps you to validate your understanding of the organization's relationship with its customers, and where value and money flow in the industry. Value chain analysis also helps you understand where financial value is being created for each player in the chain, how it is created and how much is created. For a commercial organization, you should be able to show where the margin lies and where profitability flows in the value chain. This helps you to make informed choices about how satisfying your customer objectives will create revenue, which you describe in the relationship between the customer and financial perspectives of the strategy map. This analysis ensures that the strategy addresses the critical issues which are then described in the structure and content of the strategy map.

Value chain analysis also helps you understand the different groups of customers and their perspective. One reason to link value chain analysis and strategy mapping together is to ensure that the strategy map's structure is correct, particularly how the customer perspective represents the business model. This is the stepping stone to understanding where financial value is to be created from the strategy. This chapter will explain how to describe on a strategy map how you add value to a single customer group, and to more complex layers of customers.

Developing your Value Chain

Value chain diagrams provide a view of the activities both in and outside the organization. They ask, 'which activities "add value" to the organization and to its customers?' There are two types: the value chain of an organization and the value chain across an industry.

Figure 4.3 shows the generic value chain model for an organization,[2] which is based on Porter's approach (Porter 1985: 33–36). In value chain analysis the main value-adding activities of an organization are called primary activities and run across the top of the diagram. These primary activities create the product or service, and typically include procurement, logistics to provide inputs, sales and marketing to bring the customers in, production, delivery to the customer and after sales support. The secondary activities, shown horizontally along the bottom, provide support to the primary ones. They do not deliver the product or service directly but support the primary activities to deliver to the customer. They typically include support functions such as HR, finance, purchasing, IT, legal and R&D. Whilst this is a manufacturing example, a service organization will have equivalent primary and secondary value-adding activities.

The value added by the organization is represented by the triangle on the right hand end of the diagram. This represents the excess value created over the costs of the rest of the organization embedded in the primary and secondary activities.

---

2   Porter draws the diagram with the primary activities along the bottom and the secondary at the top. I prefer to draw it the other way around. This way it is easier to draw a set of value chains in an industry and the relationship to strategy maps is clearer.

Whilst we have 'value added', we are missing any view of what that value is and how it is generated by serving the customer. This comes from looking at the overall market and how your organization's value chain adds value to other organization's value chains. It is this that helps us develop the top of the strategy map.

USING VALUE CHAINS TO UNDERSTAND YOUR CUSTOMERS

An organization's value chain does not live in isolation. The value chain will serve customers, be fed by suppliers and have competitors. Figure 4.4 is a generic diagram that

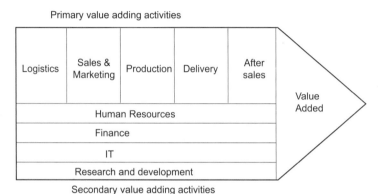

Figure 4.3   Generic value chain framework for an organization (adapted from Porter 1985: 60, Figure 2.2)

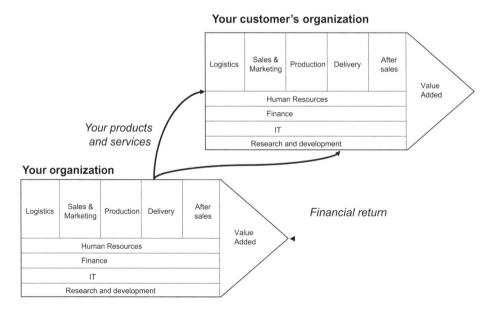

Figure 4.4   How two organizations' value chains interact

shows how an organization's value chain might connect to the value chain of one of its immediate customers. An organization might serve different parts of their customer's value chain: the arrows from an organization's value chain might connect with either their customer's primary or secondary activities. If you are a provider of financial software, you will probably support your customer's secondary value chain activities. If your customer outsources their whole call centre to you, you may be directly supporting their primary value chain activities. Of course, you may have many immediate customers, who might have similar or different value chains. If they are different, you will need to analyse each one separately. In all these cases, in return for your services, you should receive a financial reward from the customer.

COMPARING VALUE CHAIN ANALYSIS AND STRATEGY MAPS

There are similarities between the value chain model and the strategy map, but they are not the same. The primary activities of the value chain are equivalent to the process perspective of the organization's overall strategy map. The value chain describes activities, whilst the strategy map process perspective describes *the objectives* of those activities. An organization's value chain describes aspects of the bottom half of the strategy map. It omits the top half of the strategy map. This is a subtle, but important, difference.

The value chain of the customer is represented by the customer perspective of the strategy map. It tells us where the customer perceives our services add value to them.

Do not take the similarities too far. The secondary activities in the value chain diagram are not the same as the learning and growth perspective. The value chain asks what secondary *activities* support these primary *activities*. The learning and growth perspective asks what *skills, knowledge and capabilities* we need to *learn and grow* to support these primary activities. This is an important difference. In Porter's model the capabilities that support the primary activities of a value chain are *embedded within* each of the primary activity boxes. In strategy maps these secondary activities are treated as support functions in separate strategy maps.

The strategy map approach is to develop a strategy map for each support function and ask what capabilities are needed to support that secondary activity. Value chain diagrams deal with activities. Strategy map diagrams deal with objectives, which represent processes and, separately, skills, knowledge and capability.[3]

Despite these differences, understanding the organization's value chain provides a very useful starting point for your strategy map design. If you can identify the primary and secondary activities of an organization you will begin to understand how the organization fits together, and you will have a checklist of the areas which may add most value. These are areas that are likely to require or at least be covered by strategy maps.

EXERCISE:

Draw up your organization's value chain. Identify the primary activities and the secondary activities.

---

3   Both strategy maps and value chains came from Harvard Business School, so it is no surprise they are related. Value chain thinking does look at the capabilities, skills and knowledge within each activity. However, they are not represented in the value chain diagram.

DIFFERENT DEMANDS WITHIN A SINGLE CUSTOMER

Value chain analysis is most useful when there are different, and potentially conflicting, demands from within a single customer. For instance, an optical fibre manufacturer might supply high quality optical fibre to a cable manufacturing company. However, the supplier has to deal with three different parties in the cable company. Purchasing may want to ensure that the optical fibre is procured at the lowest cost, given the specification. The R&D department value the relationship with the supplier because they collaborate on improvements in transmission characteristics. The production department want on-time delivery and to minimize production hold-ups in the cable production process. In this case we have three different parties, with differing needs, in different parts of the organization. To represent these three contrasting demands from different parts of the same customer organization you might produce a structure for the customer perspective similar to that shown in Figure 4.5.

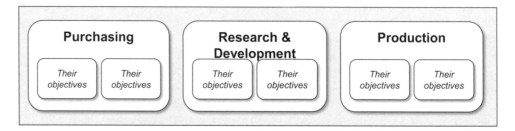

Figure 4.5   Contrasting demands from different parties within the same customer organization

Again, delving into their individual objectives will undoubtedly expose overlaps and common objectives. Nevertheless it is useful as a starting point to recognize the different perspectives of individual roles, even in the same company, as each will need to be satisfied.

EXERCISE:

Draw a diagram showing the value chains of your customers and how your value chain interacts with them. Identify where you add value for them. If you have customers with quite different value chains, repeat the exercise for the most important ones.

Value in the Chain of Customers

Value chain analysis comes into its own when you are looking at a chain of customers in a market. Most organizations don't just have a simple relationship with a single type of customer. The organization only 'adds value' in the context of an industry, customers, consumers, suppliers, competitors and any regulatory influences.

The reason we analyse chains of customers is to understand the structure of the industry and also to understand what the organization might seek to change in the future. How might the industry converge or break up? Will someone in the industry seek to integrate parts of the value chain or bypass parts of the supply chain? What is the timescale for change in the industry? How long do developments take to ripple through? Is a large amount of capital investment necessary (e.g. in oil exploration) or can new entrants start quickly?

Figure 4.6 shows an example of a more typical, extensive chain of organizations in a market. You will influence your direct customers' value chains and affect how your customers deliver value to their (second tier) customers. This chain will continue until it reaches end consumers. You will have chains of suppliers that are supporting you. You will have competitors that are trying to add value to your customers as well. Their objective is to divert that customer's revenue to themselves rather than to you. You may also have partners that are essential in helping you deliver the service or product your customers want.

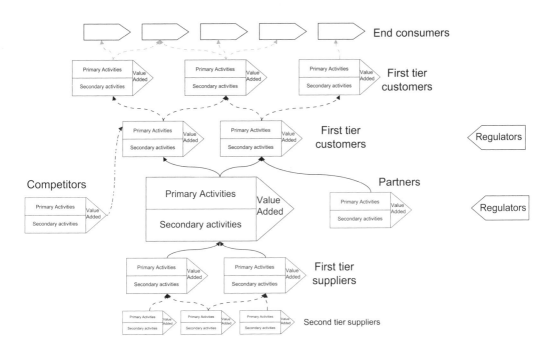

Figure 4.6   The wider value chain for a market

ANALYSIS OF COMPLEX CUSTOMER SITUATIONS

This sort of analysis can be used to unpick complex customer situations. This description was used to create an industry value chain for a provider of modular building components:

The organization makes fully furnished rooms in a factory. These fully furnished room modules are then transported to the prepared construction site to be stacked together, to construct the main part of a building. The mains services are then plugged in to the modular components, non-modular components completed and then the building is clad and the roof added to complete the build. This off-site modular manufacture means greater control over quality of build and finish, and a much faster construction once the site is available. The organization has to design the modular components, and the whole building, from the perspective of the whole value chain. The end user wants attractive accommodation otherwise they won't want to stay and pay an economic rent, but the end user is neither the buyer of the building, nor its eventual operator. The developer who has acquired the land is buying the building. They want assurance of build quality, predictable development costs and timescales, and assurance of the value of the building long-term. The developer commissions others to design, build and manage the build for them. The commissioned architect needs to be convinced that a modular approach allows them a design flexibility that fits in with building regulations and planning laws. The project manager wants to be sure that the building can be built and the modular components will fit with other components. The developer will also be employing a construction contractor to do the actual build. The contractor will want to be sure that they can deliver the building, despite not using a traditional way of building, that their people understand how to work in this new way, and that they understand the risks and potential liabilities that this approach means. They want to protect their margin on the job and their reputation, to win more work.

This situation was drawn up by the client as the chain of players shown in Figure 4.7. In actual fact, this turned out to be one of several alternative value chains that the modular building company described, each of which set out different ways to potentially design, fund and manage the build of a whole building.

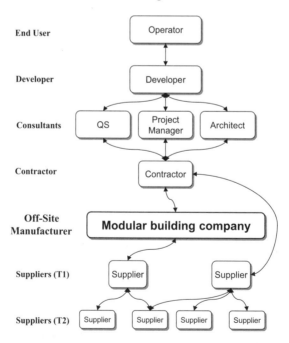

Figure 4.7   The value chain for an off-site modular construction company

REPRESENTING THE VALUE CHAIN IN THE CUSTOMER PERSPECTIVE

Clearly you do not want four or five layers in your customer perspective: one or two are sufficient and all that is needed. This value chain was simplified on the organization's strategy map, as shown in Figure 4.8, and then objectives were developed for the customers. As you can see, in the first stage the layers of the chain have been simplified into only two layers. One layer represents the objectives of the owner (who is both developer and eventual operator of the building) and the end users. These two are behind the layer of consultants and contractors who the modular building supplier interacts with to design, manage and build the building. The sequence of main players is actually laid out along the customer perspective in the order in which they are encountered.

In the strategy map we can see that we have two layers of customers. The primary ones are the architects, project managers and construction companies. This is because the company will have to interact and serve each of these directly. The secondary customers also have important needs. If the organization does not help the architect make the case for a modular building to the commissioning developer, then the architect will simply use a more traditional build approach. The project manager will need to be convinced of the approach and also convince the construction company that the approach lowers their risks and ensures they make their margin on the build. The challenge for this organization is to convince all these parties that their approach lowers risk and creates value for them, during both the build and the building's longer-term operation.

Stage 1: Identification of customers

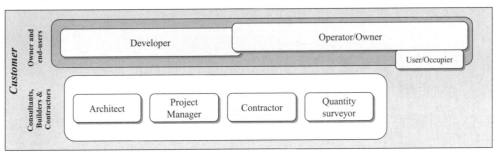

Stage 1: Objectives for those customers

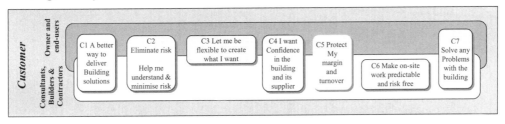

Figure 4.8   Two stages of development of the customer perspective for the modular construction company

This demonstrates two techniques you can use when developing the customer layer, especially in complex contexts. The first technique is to allow two levels of customers: immediate customers and those customers that are one step removed or ultimately served. This is an elegant solution to a very common situation.

You only ever need two layers because of the second technique. This is to arrange the customers from any value chain into a natural sequence of interaction. In this case you can see that the building goes from initial conception, when the developer acquires the land and gets permission to build, through to ownership and eventual use. The building itself goes through the natural stages of design by the architect, management by the project manager, building by the contractor and checking by the quantity surveyor before handover to the owner. There is an implied sequence along each of the perspectives. This sequence helps to explain the story of the building from the end customer's perspective and the various contractors' perspectives.

In the second stage of development of the objectives for each of these players, this eventually was simplified to the objectives shown in stage two of Figure 4.8. Now the common objectives amongst the consultants and builders have been combined and the common objectives between the contractors and owners have been shown by the overlap. This significantly simplifies this high level picture. However, those involved in its development also know the detail that lies behind it for each player and can use that in each of the customer perspectives of the cascade of strategy maps beneath this top level strategy map. The finished customer perspective was incorporated into the top level strategy map shown in Figure 4.9.

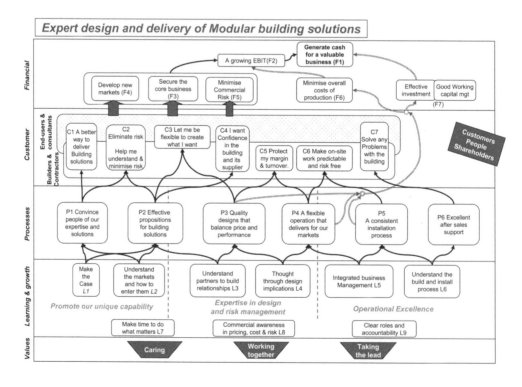

Figure 4.9   The eventual strategy map for the modular manufacturing company

HANDLING LAYERS OF CUSTOMERS

Multi-layered value chains are common. Car manufacturers, for instance, rarely deal with the end consumers (drivers) of their cars directly. The relationship is through their dealer franchisees, who are not a part of the manufacturing company but operate a franchise under the brand. The dealers have separate needs for new sales, used sales, and parts and servicing. The vehicle manufacturer will also have relations with financial institutions to provide finance, leasing and insurance deals that the dealer franchisee can offer. Some drivers may have cars provided through leasing companies that have their relationships with the manufacturer or the dealer franchisee. Again, here is a relatively complex value chain where, to the car manufacturer, the dealer franchisee, leasing companies and finance houses are the first level of customer. Individual owners and drivers sit beyond this layer. Similar, multi-layer value chain relationships exist in industries as diverse as mobile telephone service providers, consumer electronics, oil and many other markets.

Other Players in Value Chains and Strategy Maps

There are some players that need to be handled carefully when we later come to deal with them in the strategy map.

REGULATORS

Whilst an organization is attempting to satisfy its customers, in a way that creates profitable revenue, in a regulated industry the organization will also need to satisfy its regulators. However, its regulators do not provide revenue for the organization. Typically they are a party to be managed and satisfied. Therefore, if you are in a regulated industry, place the regulators and their demands alongside customers in the customer perspective. Typically there will be no link from them to the financial perspective (unless in exceptional circumstances you are incurring significant costs demanded by the regulator). The chapter on the customer perspective will provide more details of developing objectives for regulators within the customer perspective.

SUPPLIERS

Be very careful with suppliers in value chain analysis and strategy maps. The strategy map of an organization looks forward along the value chain. Suppliers are behind the organization and therefore you would not expect to see them in the top half of the strategy map. If they are to occur anywhere, they will appear in the bottom half of the strategy map, as they are adding value to your processes, represent a capability to deliver or are adding costs from which you create value. On a strategy map they are seen as contributory components in the process and learning and growth perspectives. Of course, changes in suppliers' costs would be reflected in the costs of the processes and ultimately in the financial perspective. However, they are not on the strategy map.

TRUE PARTNERS

The exception to this is true partner organizations. It is common for every supplier to be called a partner, even when the relationship is primarily transactional. However, you may have a few true partners who share risk and reward in the market with you. You might even be operating a joint venture. In such an integrated case the scope of the management team's responsibility would include the joint venture partner, and the partner's activities would therefore be contributing to the process objectives.

A deeper example of partnership would be where two organizations work together to deliver together and share revenue, such as Sony Ericsson or a group of companies jointly running a consortium. You would handle this by including these partners inside your organization's value chain and in the strategy map, bearing in mind how each contributes to delivering for your shared customers and how you share revenue.

COMPETITORS

Competitors are not represented on an organization's strategy map directly. However, there are ways in which competitor activity and thinking can be handled. You can always develop a value chain and strategy map from your competitor's perspective. This can be insightful simply because you are trying to describe their strategy from their perspective and therefore provide insights for your strategy.

Application in Not for Profit and Public Sector Organizations

These techniques are just as applicable in the public sector and for charities. For a local council it is vital to know where the cash flows from in terms of income from residents and grants from government, in order to balance the books. A local council also needs to understand how its actions will influence the prosperity of the people of the city it governs. The same is true for a central government body. A charity wants to know how its money is influencing those who receive its grants and both the direct and indirect beneficiaries. It will also want to know how its various targeted campaigns influence different donor groups to contribute to the charity or the overall cause they support. For instance, the charity may influence donors to give money directly to itself and may influence politicians to release money to fund changes in national policy.

Financial Flow along the Value Chain

Value chain analysis also helps you understand the flow of profits in the industry, which is valuable when you come to develop the financial perspective and its objectives. Once you have established the value chain you could progress to establish what value each element of the chain adds, where power resides, where revenues and profits flow. There will be a flow of money (or profits) in return for the products and services back down the chain. The 'value added' is the excess money that an organization can retain in such a chain. Adding greater value means that more cash will flow to that part of the chain.

Asking 'what value does this part of the supply chain add?' will expose the overall picture of how the whole value chain works and where profit flows so you understand the influential flows of money around the system. Who is the powerful player that determines the economics of the industry? Where is turnover? Where is the margin? Where are the costs? Where is the risk? What are the roles of the various players? What value do they add? Is there any conflict or ambiguity in the creation of value? Where do the products and services flow? Where does the money flow? What are the economic drivers?

Understanding the interactions with other bodies and the financial flows will help you construct the most appropriate customer and financial perspectives, no matter what the nature of the organization and its market.

Summary

Value chain analysis is a valuable tool of strategic analysis and thinking that relates closely to strategy maps. Understanding the value chain helps to you to structure and design the strategy map so that it represents the strategy, particularly in the financial and customer perspectives. Value chain analysis also helps you to check your understanding of the organization, so that you consider the whole of the value-adding activities. Value chain analysis ensures you understand:

- The scope of the organization you are dealing with;
- The value chain for the organization;
- The structure of the customer groups;
- Where value should be created.

Often there is not a simple answer for, 'who are your customers and what value do you add'. Most organizations will have different groups of customers with different needs. Interactions with customers may include both business-to-business and direct to consumers. Some organizations may have distributors or operate through a franchise. Look out for:

- Actual customers;
- Desired and potential customers;
- Eventual customers;
- Franchisees.

Make sure you understand how the money flows along the value chain. Who are the powerful players that determine the economics of the industry? Where are the costs, turnover and margin? Where is the risk? What are the roles of the various players and what value do they add? How will the structure of the industry change?

Value chain analysis helps us identify the groups of customers whose objectives we will develop more fully when we complete the customer perspective. It will also help us understand the financial consequences of serving these customers. Before we do the more detailed work, we need to use this knowledge to look at how the organization sees its future developing over the time horizon of its strategy. The knowledge gained from this will ensure we scope the future discussions to include the appropriate players. It will also ensure we ask appropriate questions about how the structure of the industry might develop and affect the organization's value chain. This analysis will also help you identify aspects to monitor, which we shall develop further with the tangible future that is developed in the next chapter.

5 *Future Thinking: Your Strategy and the Tangible Future*

This chapter provides a tool that helps you ensure that your strategy is leading you towards your ambition, and that that ambition and route is captured appropriately in your strategy map. This involves building a rich, tangible picture of the future across which you will navigate with your strategy. Reading through this chapter and working through the exercises, you will understand how the tangible future can contribute to the discussions of your management team. You will think through at least a part of your organization's tangible vision, and you will be clear on how the tangible future will contribute to capturing your strategy and developing your strategy map.

I call this rich, tangible picture of the environment, the organization and how they will evolve, the 'tangible future'. Vision statements are usually short, often intangible, lack detail and often omit timescales. In contrast, a tangible future describes the organization and its environment in an explicit, detailed, tangible way, at specific points in time. The strategy should be the driver of the organization, through its environment and through these points in time.

The tangible future has three benefits. First, the tangible future provides the basis for the level of ambition and rate of change of the objectives across all the perspectives of the strategy map. By providing specific statements about the development of the strategy at specific points in the future, the tangible future provides a picture of how the organization, the finances, the customers and market are expected to develop. It is a picture that can be checked for coherence of the story across its various parts. For instance, is revenue growth consistent with the market's needs and the competitive activity? Is our ability to grow capacity consistent with our expectations of market share? Are the changes we expect in technology and consumer demand consistent with our developments? Your degree of ambition and your speed of development, expressed in your 'tangible future', set the rate of change for the objectives in your strategy map and subsequent scorecard. As your strategy is implemented you should be able to mark off progress against the milestones you have placed in the tangible future.

Secondly, the tangible future exposes the thinking about the future amongst the management team and encourages discussion within the team of different views. The tangible future helps you, as a team, develop a common understanding of how you expect the future to develop. You will learn where you might disagree and, more importantly, why you disagree. Remembering that it is planning that is more important than plans, the primary aim of the discussion to develop the tangible future is to improve the quality of thinking, the richness of conversation and the shared understanding of the future. The value for the management lies in the process: the process of thinking through questions and having discussions (and arguments) with colleagues about what they believe and why. The physical product of this thinking is subsequently used to communicate the story of the future. However, it is the richness of the insights and understanding that are gained from the process that are important. Developing a tangible future requires you to really think through, discuss and describe where you will be at specific points in the future, what it will be like at that time, and to bring out any differences in perception, risks or direction. It helps your team develop a consistent view and be clear on where you disagree, and why, and what you are going to do about it.

The third benefit of a tangible future is to capture uncertainties, risks and assumptions about the future. Of course, the future is not certain and some disagreements about the future, the speed of development or how it might turn out, are inevitable. The strategy may be assuming that oil or steel prices stay within particular boundaries, or that bank credit will continue to be available. Recognizing that there are uncertainties, risks and assumptions means you can put in place monitoring mechanisms to identify whether the assumptions are still valid or whether the uncertainties and risks are manifesting themselves. Sensible monitoring of the strategy requires this connection to the outside world, but it is not captured within a strategy map unless an external perspective is added. The tangible future provides the basis for much of the external perspective, so that your management team can monitor uncertainties and assumptions to see how they develop as the strategy is being implemented.

If you omit development of a tangible vision you will not have agreed fixed points for setting targets. Nor will you have anything to check that progress towards those targets is feasible. Your management team may harbour uncertainties that remain undiscussed items of contention. Assumptions that underpin the strategy may become invalid and you may miss the emergence of signals that suggest your strategy needs refinement. Developing the tangible future, together, avoids these problems.

Creating a tangible future should not be an onerous task. Most management teams who are about to embark on their strategy implementation will have done much of the thinking, analysis and work that is needed to construct one. You may have already created something similar and discussed it amongst your team. Nevertheless, confirming the picture by creating and reviewing the tangible future provides your team with confirmation that you all agree on how you expect the future to develop, and you will know where you have uncertainties, disagreements and risks that you can continue to monitor.

The Tangible Vision and the Strategy Map

The overall relationship between the tangible vision and the strategy map was established in the strategic learning model: the tangible future describes how the future will evolve; the strategy map describes how it will be achieved. How do the tangible future and strategy map fit together in detail?

LINKING THE TANGIBLE FUTURE AND THE STRATEGY MAP

Although we talk about one tangible future, it is useful to build two separate tangible futures alongside each other. One represents the outside world. One represents how the organization will evolve in parallel and influence the outside world.

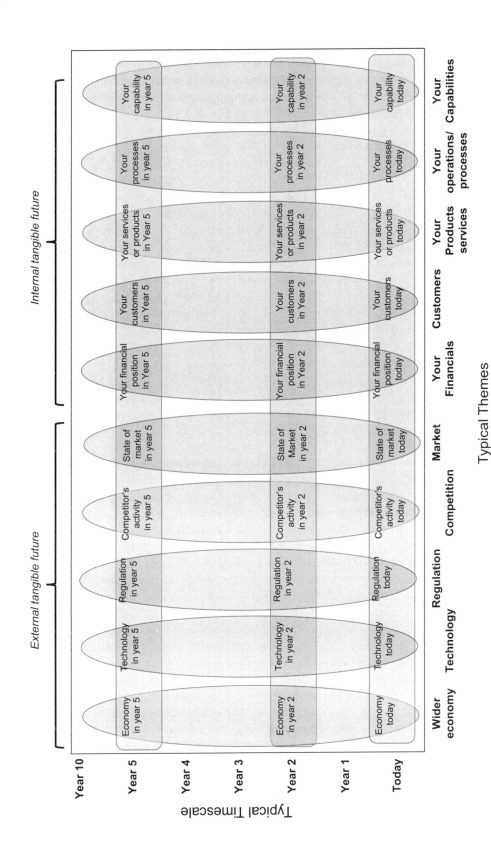

Figure 5.1   Simplified structure of the tangible future showing how themes develop over time

The most basic framework for a tangible future is shown in Figure 5.1. As you can see, at each point in time there are statements about the state of the external environment and the situation inside the organization. These statements set the pace of change and level of ambition for the objectives on the strategy map, so you can clearly see how each objective will improve over time, as shown in Figure 5.2.

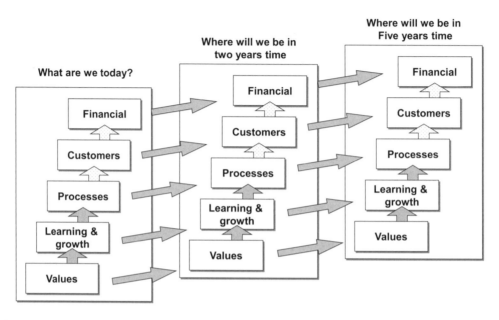

Figure 5.2   Individual objectives in each perspective should improve over time

The tangible future describes what the organization will be like in the future. It provides clear statements of the amount of progress that needs to be made between each step over a time period. Thus, if the revenue has to increase by 30 per cent by year four, then it is clear what makes this happen and where you would expect to be in years one, two and three, as well as year four. Likewise there should be corresponding statements for the customers, how their needs will develop, how the processes and activities of the organization will change and how its skills, knowledge and culture will develop.

Your strategy and strategy map describe your route through the tangible future. They describe the choices you are making and how the organization is changing, and the consequences for customers and finances. As a minimum then, the tangible future needs to include the changes over time affecting the four main perspectives of the strategy map and balanced scorecard: how the finances of the organization will change, how the customers' objectives and needs will change together with expected volumes and sales, how the processes of the organization will change, and how the skills, knowledge, behaviours and culture of the organization will grow. These are the minimum changes that need to be recorded to establish the rate of change for the objectives in the strategy map and subsequent balanced scorecard. By also including the wider strategic context, changes to the environment, and pressures and uncertainty in the market, you can provide a wider perspective that can be monitored within the external perspective.

WIDENING THE VIEW: FILLING A GAP IN STRATEGY MAPS

We need to be clear which aspects of the strategy the strategy map does not explicitly capture and what we should we should do to ensure they are not lost.

Strategy maps are about *how* the strategy works. They describe how the organization will change and serve the customers' needs to create revenue. Strategy maps do not capture *why* the strategy was chosen. There is no place on a strategy map to describe competitors' activities, economic changes such as oil price fluctuations or credit shortages, or to note changes in legislation that affect the strategy. Nor is there anywhere to capture the assumptions, beliefs and uncertainties that were embedded in the strategic thinking. We can enrich the basic tangible future to capture these and so make clear the assumptions behind the strategy (see Figure 5.3). Using symbols such as those in Figure 5.3, the tangible future can capture the assumptions, uncertainties and beliefs within the strategic thinking, which can be used when monitoring and managing the strategy. If any of these facts, beliefs, uncertainties or assumptions change, then the strategy may also need to change (with a resultant change to the strategy map). Without this background, the strategic assumptions may be lost and the strategy (and its strategy map) may continue to be implemented, despite it being no longer appropriate.

Recognizing that strategy maps do not capture these items is not to say that strategy maps are inadequate. On the contrary, they are extremely valuable. However, there are other pieces of information about the strategy that need to be captured and managed as well, items that sit around the strategy map and support it. We shall see how these are used later when we look at how strategy maps are used and maintained in management team meetings.

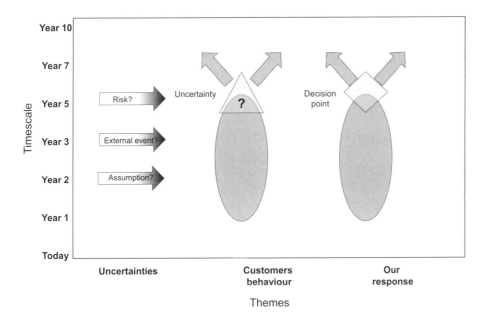

Figure 5.3   The tangible future can be used to capture uncertainties, decisions, risks and assumptions

Building the Tangible Future

Of the two views of the tangible future (the one that represents the outside world and the one that represents how the organization will evolve), I always ask clients to develop the external view first. This helps the management team think about the external environment before it thinks about the organization's response to it. You can establish a view of how quickly and in what way the market and competition will develop, before looking at how the organization will respond to it and seek to influence it. This section provides a step-by-step guide to developing a tangible future, with exercises and a simple example to guide you.

EXERCISE:

Take two large pieces of paper on which to develop your tangible future: one for external factors and one for the organization. (You might use a couple of pieces of A3 or a pair of flip chart pages.) Place them landscape on your wall and get a collection of different coloured sticky notes to write ideas on that you can later move around.

As you build your tangible future it may be helpful to refer to an example. Figure 5.4 is a simplified example of a tangible future from a manufacturing company, which shows many of the characteristics you would expect in any tangible future.

CONSTRUCTING THE FRAMEWORK

The first step is to construct the framework for the future thinking. This includes setting out a timeframe, identifying themes and understanding the factors that affect the economics of the market. You also need to be clear and realistic about where you are today. Include numbers that describe the future and how it is expected to evolve. You also need to accommodate an understanding of where there are uncertainties and critical decision points.

SETTING THE TIMESCALE

The structure of any tangible future has the timescale on the left hand side. The example in Figure 5.4 shows a five-year timescale. Typically I work with clients whose timescale goes from today, to three months, six months, one year, two or three years, five years and in some cases to ten and twenty years depending upon the organization and its strategic horizon. Some management teams need to, or are able to, think further ahead than others. In this example the team had market research that spanned five years and were setting out a five year programme for developing their products in the market. I have worked with a client who chose a timescale of sixty years. Sometimes imperatives might cause you to focus on a shorter timescale, as in this example.

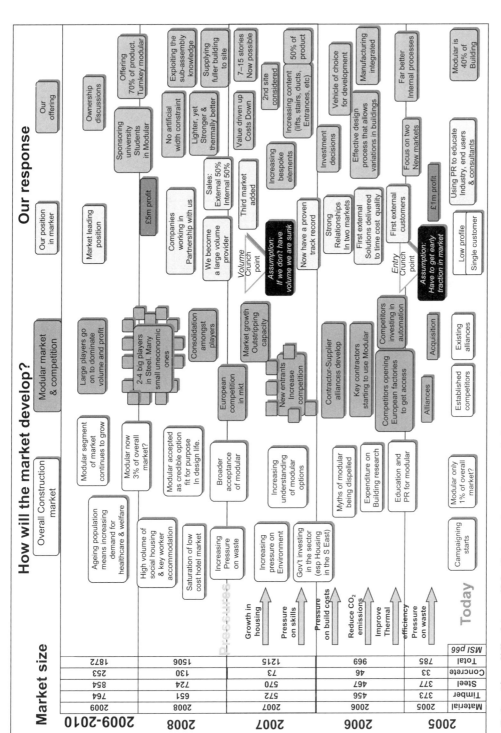

Figure 5.4 Simplified tangible future for the modular manufacturing company

In a service company serving public sector organizations, the costs pressures were so pressing that they needed to be radical this year. They needed to demonstrate that they were addressing costs and delivering what they had promised. Rolling the scenario forward, some of the team could see that if they failed to do this in the next nine to 12 months, their reputation would be ruined, and by year three they would face one of two scenarios. Either they would be closed down or the sector would revert to anarchy, choosing its services where it wanted (at a much higher overall cost) and their role would become redundant. However, if they succeeded this year then they had a chance to make a significant difference to the services, efficiency and overall costs of the sector. For this reason, a three-year focus was chosen with emphasis on the first year.

In other cases, where there are large capital investments (perhaps in oil exploration, building additional manufacturing capacity, or influencing social change over a generation), a longer timescale is appropriate. Choose a timescale that covers the reasonable life of your strategy.

EXERCISE:

Think about the timescale of your strategy. Put a scale on the side of your tangible future to represent your time horizon. Cover at least five years, if not ten. Include space for detail in the immediate future in the lower part of the page and space for long-term developments at the top of the page. Put an identical scale on both the external and internal tangible future. Include space for 'year nought'.

IDENTIFYING THE THEMES

Work on the external tangible future first. Start by thinking through the topics of the tangible future: aspects that you wish to track over the life of your strategy. Your external view may consist of your various markets, their size and development, the customers (in their various groups), the competition and how they will develop, economic factors, legislation, changes in technology, and any other external factors or events that might influence the market and the industry as a whole. Now revisit the value chain and context you produced earlier. The reason we analysed the context and value chain before starting the tangible future is that it helps to have an understanding of the value chain before you develop the tangible future. This is because it acts as a check on the scope of the tangible future and the elements to include or consider. It also helps when thinking about market extensions, competitors, customers and regulators.

Place these topics along the top of the external tangible future. (It is useful to use sticky notes for this. Use a colour specifically for the topic names to separate them from how the themes develop.)

EXERCISE:

Identify the topics or themes for your external environment. As a minimum include markets, technology, legislation, economic factors and competition. Check back to the value chain and context. Think about the other influences on your market. Do not worry if you have not identified them all initially. You can add extra ones as they come to mind.

ACKNOWLEDGE WHERE YOU ARE TODAY

It is important not to get carried away with grand ambitions but rather to recognize where you are today and where you have come from. That is why you need a 'year nought', which acts as a reality check. Use this to show the current numbers or describe the current state of products, services or the organization. The current strengths and weaknesses act as an anchor.

Recognizing where you are on the future vision acknowledges the strengths and weaknesses of the organization today and acts as a realistic anchor for the developments that you anticipate over the coming years.

When I do this sort of work there is usually a discussion amongst the team about how realistic the timing and pace of the change is. Within any collection of managers, you will find that they have different expectations of how long a situation will take to develop. Discuss the reasons for these differences, as they will be revealing. Often different managers will have different concerns, views on how easy things will be to change and thoughts about the pace of change. What seems reasonable in three years for one manager may, for another manager, seem more realistic in five years or one year. These discussions focus the attention of the team on what will make the biggest difference for their strategy and the potential pace of change. They provide a vital component for the choice of the strategy and the design of the strategy map.

EXERCISE:

Build a simple, but clear picture of where you are today. Place notes describing where you are against each theme or topic: for instance, current market penetration, state of competition, consumer awareness, current regulatory pressures.

DEVELOPING THE DETAIL

You now have a choice about how to start completing the detail. You can either work across the themes, completing the view at one point in time, or work on a theme and describe how the theme will develop over time. In fact, you could even fill in pieces as they come to mind. Whichever way you choose, make sure that eventually you check your story across for each given point in time, and follow each theme through time, to ensure you build a consistent and internally coherent story.

At each point in time, place a statement that describes the state of a particular aspect. In the example, the client has placed a statement about the state of the overall market and the state of their particular segment of the market at each point in time.

Some clients like to start at a point in the future, describe that and work backwards. This means they have to work back through the steps to get there. Also, to have achieved that point they have to have already overcome things that today are blocking them. This helps tremendously with the thinking.

You can also do this by going forward from today, asking where you want to be in, say, three months, then in six months, then a year, then two years. However, the problems of today often obstruct thinking about the future. You will may well receive a different quality of answer if you ask where you want to be in five to ten years, and then ask, 'so, what do we have to have achieved in five years, and therefore two years, and therefore in six months?'

When working across a single point in time, you are looking for the complete picture of the market at, say, five years out. Having completed the five years forward view, then look to fill in the same information for, say, three years, two years and one year out. What you are looking for is consistency of story across the development, working back from the ambition five years out. This provides a view across all the themes. Other clients prefer to describe how they will move forward from where they are now. They will start laying out one year out, across all aspects, and then develop that forward to three years and then, say, five. The choice will depend upon how they are thinking about their strategy.

Often a client will think through each aspect of the strategy separately. How quickly will this market develop? When do we expect environmental legislation to change? What is the timing of competitors entering the market? When will our new products be available?

Ensure you develop the tangible future at several points in time. Do not just rely on a tangible future for, say, three years out. Develop the detail of a number of points in the future, say six months, a year, two years, three years and five years out. This will help you develop a greater level of detail for the development and flow of the tangible futures. Tease out the timing and development story within each theme so that you explore each theme (vertically) through time. This allows you to establish understanding of the stages of development and change, and the pace that each manager anticipates is possible.

EXERCISE:

Start building your tangible future by placing sticky notes at particular points in time for particular themes. Make sure the notes describe the state at that point for each theme or topic: for instance, current market penetration, state of competition, consumer awareness, current regulatory pressures.

ANCHOR WITH KEY NUMBERS

Like the example organization in Figure 5.4, you probably have market research, financial predictions and existing analysis that can be put into the picture. This will provide numerical evidence to back up your view of how the environment and strategy are likely to evolve. You can see how the example organization's numbers have been summarized on the left hand side of the tangible future.

Always anchor your views of the future with explicit numbers. These add tangibility and create material realism. Choose those that describe the main characteristics of the future. Ensure that there is a logic and consistency between the organization and the environment in which it is operating.

With the manufacturing company, we used the overall market size, the size of the piece of the market they were targeting, their turnover and manufacturing capacity. This exposed when demand would exceed capacity and a new manufacturing facility would be needed. Given the lead time to create such a plant, it also revealed when the capital would be required and the business case should be presented to the main board. Whilst the factory was not needed for three years, the capital investment decision was only 12 to 18 months away.

With a city council, we used population growth alongside school performance results, employment statistics and the amount of investment income into the city. These provided a sense of how the city would be changing over the period being considered.

It is important to recognize that these numbers are often at best estimates and, at worse, informed guesses. They are markers that show how things are changing. They may be from economic analysis or market research, but they are only an indication of what the future may be like. Avoid the spurious precision you sometimes get in market research. Be willing to include ranges, such as plus or minus 10 per cent, to show the variability of the figures. These assumptions need to be understood and tested as with any other assumptions about the strategy.

EXERCISE:

Add key numbers and research to your tangible future. Use these to show how aspects of the external environment will develop and evolve. Make sure you make explicit any assumptions inherent in these figures and capture these for later.

ASSUMPTIONS

This process also exposes any critical assumptions in the strategy as it evolves. For instance, with a city council, it was vital to get a new school built and operational to improve the quality of education. With a credit union, it was about timing of income and being self-sufficient.

It was necessary to hold the operational costs of the new credit union at a level whereby the income from savings would exceed them. This relied on continued grant income over the next three to four years. It also relied on being able to recruit and retain volunteers cost-effectively and having low-cost premises as the main office and for other collection points. It also exposed the assumption that there were sufficient people, appropriately motivated, in the area of the credit union who would be willing to save with it. You can imagine the discussion about the quality of their market information that occurred at this point. How much was this based upon guesswork? How much was it based on hard facts? How much were these tested? Who actually had the figures and how credible were they?

These key assumptions become markers alongside the strategy map that are continually checked to ensure that they remain valid. If they change, the corresponding aspects of the strategy might need to be reviewed. These assumptions are items to be monitored in the external perspective.

EXERCISE:

Look through your tangible future and identify any assumptions that you are making. Note what they are, together with what information backs them up. These become items to monitor in the external perspective.

UNCERTAINTY AND RISK

Next identify your uncertainties and risks. You can mark a risk as simply a flag of some kind on the picture. An uncertainty might lead to one of two or three different things developing, and so I use a diamond shaped decision box when this occurs as shown in Figure 5.3. The box is labelled with the uncertainty and has the different outcomes emerging from each far side of the diamond.

Risks and uncertainties are similar, but with different characteristics. Risks are things that might happen. We may be uncertain about whether they will happen, but we are aware of the potential, the consequences and can take mitigating action. In contrast, uncertainties are things we do not know about and need more information on. For instance, there is the risk that oil prices will rise and alter commodity prices. In contrast, you may be uncertain whether a competitor is working on a rival product, but know that if they are there is the risk it will undermine your sales. The management team will recognize that there are aspects of the future that are uncertain and could go in one of several directions. Sometimes you can try to resolve these uncertainties through research, or explore the options using scenario planning, but this can take time. Sometimes it is necessary to simply recognize that the uncertainty exists and make decisions up to it or around it. Techniques such as scenario planning enable you to explore your strategy in the light of uncertain futures by putting detail on the alternative scenarios. This allows you to test your strategy in extreme conditions, just as an aircraft prototype is tested in a wind tunnel prior to being built and flying.

It is valuable simply to have the uncertainties and risks visible, so your team are aware of them and can resolve them later. A step further is to identify trigger points, and leading or advance indicators, that would suggest that things might be about to change, that risks are starting to manifest themselves or that assumptions are changing. I call these External Predictive Indicators (EPIs). Identifying external indicators that will predict whether risks or uncertainties are emerging means that you can monitor them as the strategy is implemented and ensures you are not caught out when they do emerge or become clear. Keep a note of assumptions, risks, uncertainties and triggers derived from the tangible future. Include these as items to be monitored in the external perspective to ensure you do not forget these elements of the strategy as it is implemented and evolves.

EXERCISE:

Identify any uncertainties and risks in the picture. Note what they are, together with what trigger information or external predictive indicators might be available. Again, these become items to monitor in the external perspective.

CRITICAL DECISION POINTS

In describing a future there are always points at which decisions will need to be made, and other points at which there are uncertainties, assumptions and risks. The tangible future process helps you identify these. Make them explicit and available for use during the management and review of the implementation of the strategy. Critical decision points are where the organization will have some choice to make that is significant to how the strategy will evolve.

The manufacturing company needed to have gained sufficient credibility in its new markets to justify the investment in a new manufacturing plant. However, that meant that they had to create a critical mass of customers in these new markets in a relatively short time. To achieve this they needed to be really clear which new markets they could most effectively serve with their existing capacity and capability. This set the pace for their rate of expansion into new markets. If they failed to gain traction within this time, they believed competitors would have gained a significant foothold and it would be hard for them to develop a critical and economic market. So the decision point was dictated by the volume of the market they had developed by that critical point. Otherwise, they believed they would be relegated to a bit player. It was, for them, a crunch point.

You can see two decision points in their tangible future (Figure 5.4). There are usually several of these decisions or crunch points in a tangible future. Make sure you identify where your crunch points are.

EXERCISE:

Identify and make a note of any critical decision points in the tangible future. When do decisions need to be made?

DEVELOPING AND VALIDATING THE INTERNAL TANGIBLE FUTURE

Having reached a good state of development of the external view you can now turn to describing how the organization will respond to this external picture. On the inside you are describing what the company needs to achieve and will be like at particular points in time. The advantage of this approach is that it causes you to think about how the organization needs to change to respond to, or shape, the outside world. This approach causes the management team to look outwards and think through the consequences, timing and implications of various factors that might affect the industry and market.

The simplified example shows that the team concentrated on two internal themes: their position in the market and their offering. This is a simplification of the strategy map perspectives for the sake of this example, and yet it provides a useful view for this organization. In a more detailed version, you would use each perspective of the balanced scorecard laid across as internal themes: our financial performance, our customers' reaction, our products or service offerings, our processes, our capabilities, skills, knowledge, culture, and what we need to learn and grow as an organization.

Of course, the choice of strategy (of yours and of others) will also determine how the future turns out. So, developing a picture of the future is an iterative process: one that interacts with the strategy itself.

Eliciting the Tangible Future

The tangible future can be elicited in one-to-one interviews or during a group workshop. This is an example from an interview with a chief executive of a FTSE 100 retailer.

> *Whilst we were working with a large retailer, the chief executive expressed concern that 'They don't get the strategy'. So, in the interview with the chief executive, we started by saying, 'Imagine your shops in the future: tell us what they will be like – as if you were there'.*

> *His head rolled back, eyes closed and he started talking. He began outside one of the shops, in five years' time, and described what he could see, feel and hear as he walked inside and around the shop: its ambiance, offerings and customers. It was as if he were shopping there. With only a few prompts he was still adding detail and clarity to the image 25 minutes later.*

This chief executive had a very clear picture in his head of the future. However, it turned out that this picture was not in the heads of his fellow directors to anything like the same degree of detail. Neither was it clear how they were going to get there. We had searched the existing strategy documents before the interview, but this rich description was nowhere to be found, except in the head of the chief executive. In fact, the chief executive had recently visited a new flagship store and berated the team who put it together for not implementing it as he had seen it in his mind. The development of a tangible future that each of the team contributed to, and which was shared amongst the team, helped to bridge this gap.

AN EXERCISE IN FUTURE THINKING

Asking questions in the right way, as was the case with the FTSE 100 chief executive, and paying careful attention to the answers, means you can develop a far more detailed picture of the future than people realize they have. This helps individuals and the management team to understand in more detail what the future will be like. It also helps the quality of conversation amongst the management team and helps them explain their vision to the rest of their staff. To give you a feel for what it is like to develop a really tangible and specific description of the future, here is a simple exercise on future thinking I do with many of my clients. It is an exercise which you can easily repeat at any time when you want to do some future thinking, or when you want to encourage others to do future thinking. Usually I ask people to do this exercise in pairs, taking turns, but you can just as easily do it alone by talking or writing things down by yourself. The advantage of talking is that you say what comes into your head, which is often most useful.

The exercise is in three parts. Before you start, pick something you want to achieve in the future. Then pick a specific point in time in the future when you will have achieved that objective.

PART ONE: WHAT WILL IT BE LIKE?

Take around two or three minutes for each part.

1. Describe what it will be like to achieve the objective (make notes for yourself).
2. Now describe the problems you face on the way to achieving the objective (make notes for yourself).

Notice how you feel about the situation you are describing. Are you confident, apprehensive, clear, uncertain, sure, or do you harbour some doubts? Make a note of that as well. How do you feel about the problems you have to overcome?

PART TWO: WHAT IS IT LIKE, AS IF YOU ARE THERE?

Now do the same exercise again. This time, describe not what it *will be* like, but what it *is* like, 'as if you are there'. Imagine what it *is* like having achieved the objective. Ensure you use the present tense so that you talk 'as if you are there'. (If you are working in pairs, the person listening should pay attention to the tense you are using and encourage you to correct it if you drift from the present tense to the future tense.)

Describe also what you *see, hear and feel*, as if you are there. So, if you were describing a holiday, you might describe the feel of the warmth of the sand on your feet as it squeezes through your toes, the noise of the lapping of the waves on the beach and the colour of the sky and sea. Be specific and describe what you are experiencing and what it feels like. Some managers find it useful to think of the speech they are saying to their staff at the end of the year (whichever year it might be) where they are describing their journey so far, what they have achieved and the new challenges ahead. Whatever approach you take, take as long as you feel you need for this part.

1. Describe what the future is like (as if you are there).
2. Describe what you can see, hear and feel. Describe what others are thinking and feeling. Describe it 'as if you are there'.

Notice how the quality of the description has changed.

PART THREE: HOW DID WE GET HERE?

The third part of the exercise is helpful in overcoming the barriers you identified in part one. Stay in the future, using the present tense, as you do this part.

1. Now, from the future (as if you are there) look back and describe how you made progress and how you overcame the problems. Make sure you stay in the future and use the past tense to describe what happened on the way.

This part is useful to think beyond your objective. What will you want to achieve next?

1. Again, from the future, as if you are there, look forward and describe what you are planning to do next. For this part you can use the future tense, as it is the future relative to your current present.

Notice how you feel about the situation now.

USING THIS EXERCISE

Whenever I do this exercise with a group, the energy and enthusiasm in the room rises significantly between the first and second descriptions. Part one (speaking about what will happen) is a contrast to the second exercise and can be dropped once you have become adept at talking 'as if you are there'. Describing the future 'as if you are there' is designed to engage you and ensure you are assimilated into the situation, as if the future is now happening. Being assimilated into the future is a fundamental part of future thinking and creating a rich tangible future, which this exercise is designed to help you achieve.

People report that when they describe things 'as if they are there', it all seems more real. As a result the approach helps you validate whether you really want this reality. Quite often, what seems desirable from here seems less desirable when you really associate into the future and try it out. Of course this is only a thought experiment, but it does mean that you have at least tried it before betting the organization on the idea. It is a useful, simplified form of scenario thinking.

Associate into the future also exposes risks, and the assumptions and beliefs that the team, or individuals, have about the future. When these are explicit, the management team are more sensitive to changes in the outside world that might affect their strategy and so they know when they need to refine it. This helps with strategic learning and the refinement of the strategy.

The approach also helps you work out how to overcome the problems that you identified when speaking from the present. There can often seem to be obstructions in the way, obstructions we do not know how to overcome. Oddly, when a person describes already having achieved the objective and then looks back at how they overcame the obstructions, the problems seem to have shrunk in size. They are also able describe how they overcame them.

Don't take my word for this. Try it. A futurist for technology in a large oil company uses these techniques as a part of his strategy for assessing the application of new technology. He imagines having the technology in a real situation, using, wearing or experiencing the technology in the situation he is considering and what will happen when the technology is applied. Sometimes it leads to a realization that it simply won't work or it needs modification. Other times it provides him with a clear insight as to how valuable the technology will be and how best to apply it. In each case he imagines the technology 'as if he is there'.

When ambition is left vague, so are the targets. In the absence of clear, longer-term targets, the tendency is to incrementally move from where you are now and to react to what is happening at the moment. In contrast, working backwards from an ambition helps to identify where and how *step* changes could occur.

As you are probably on your own as you read this book, it will be worthwhile repeating these exercises with your team or colleagues. The same principles apply when working with a team. The reason I call the rich picture the exercises create a tangible future is that you get a very tangible sense of what the future *is* like. When people describe collectively what they see, hear and feel they build a far richer description. In an organizational context, anchor the future picture with numbers that describe the organization at that time (e.g. related to turnover, people, sales, customers, countries, competitors), as these will help make the picture more explicit and tangible.

Facilitating, Discussing and Agreeing on the Future

One of the main reasons for developing a tangible future is to create discussion, understanding and consensus over what the future might be. It also increases the understanding of the assumptions, uncertainties and expectations embedded within the strategy. It is the quality of thinking and conversation that matters. It is the mutual understanding of the assumptions, potential directions and ambition that is important. There will be areas where the management team disagree on the future or hold different underlying views of how things will develop. Good facilitation will bring these to the surface so they are discussed, shared and understood.

Two things often surprise me when I do this work. Firstly, how little the management team have discussed the broad picture of the future. It may be in some of their heads, and they may have discussed limited aspects of the future detail, but the broad picture is rarely discussed. Managers often describe the interviews as thought-provoking, with questions they had not considered in as much detail before. It is often the first time they have been asked to describe the future in as much detail and as tangibly as this. It is often the first time they have articulated the future outside their own heads.

On one balanced scorecard project we were told it was not necessary to interview the management team as they had done a large (and expensive) strategy exercise with a major consultancy. So, as instructed, we read the strategy documents which we were handed in a large custom-built box containing eight A4 folders. We dutifully went away for two weeks to review the documents. There was a lot about the strategy, finances and markets. But there was not an explicit picture or description of what the organization was to achieve through the next five years. It was only through the subsequent management team interview process and the following workshop that we were able to develop a complete picture. A picture one, two, three and five years out that the team had not discussed together before. Once they had a chance to see how each of them expected the future to develop, and the pace and extent of change, they were able to discuss their differing views and come to an overall consensus. From that picture we had enough agreement about the objectives for the future and had a basis on which to map out their strategy and the rate of progress they wanted to achieve. It quickly became apparent that not all the management team had been involved to the same extent in the strategy discussions. Some had more knowledge than others and were more engaged with it. It was necessary to backtrack, to create pictures of the future, to ensure a common understanding amongst the team of the size of the ambition, its timing and the implications.

Secondly, even though so little has been discussed, I am often surprised at how much a management team agree with the tangible future that has emerged from their collective minds. In part this is due to the future picture coming from them in the first place: it is their vision after all. Where there are disagreements, many of them can readily be resolved with a good quality discussion of the thinking behind them. Often it is questions of degree and timing that require a discussion of expectations. Sometimes assumptions of beliefs differ. Good facilitation usually resolves these quickly.

There are usually a few points of significant disagreement. These are often on topics which the management team have either never discussed or perhaps have stopped discussing. There can be a sense amongst the team that these topics will cause tension, and they are therefore avoided. Yet, at the same time, they are crucial to the strategy.

Sometimes these remaining issues can be resolved by a good facilitator bringing out the differences and finding common ground. Sometimes to inform or resolve the debate requires further information, external research, or others outside the core management team. These issues may need to be parked for a short period. On rare occasions it is just too early for the team to consider these issues. However, there will be a point when the management must come back to them. They cannot be lost, swept under the carpet or remain 'the elephant in the room'.

Conclusions

Developing a tangible future sets and confirms the pace of change for your strategy map. It also ensures that you have identified those changes in the external environment that might influence your strategy and that need to be monitored during implementation. The questions you ask and the quality of the tangible future will influence the quality and design of your strategy map. The quality of debate, discussion and thinking will ensure you leave the room as a team with the same view of where you are going. The detail in the tangible future provides the basis for developing the objectives in the strategy map and the level of ambition and speed of change that the strategy map (and balanced scorecard) need to represent. You also have a point of reference against which you can check off progress as you implement your strategy and your plans come to fruition.

III *Overall Design*

Part III is about making sure your strategy is communicated and implemented using the overall design of your cascade of strategy maps.

Chapter 6 introduces the powerful tool of strategic themes. Working across the perspectives, strategic themes communicate aspects of your strategy that work together to deliver the overall picture. They help you explain your strategy more effectively. They help you divide it into separate areas of attention and programmes of change. They can be used to break down organisational silos and create joined up thinking and working. They help you cascade and focus the strategy on various parts of the organization.

Chapter 7 will help you ensure engagement and implementation by designing the most appropriate cascade of the strategy through the organization. How do you get a piece of the strategy in every one's pocket? How do you ensure people are doing the right things, in the right way? This chapter will help you cut across organizational boundaries and also explains how you can engage support functions in the support of the strategy.

6 *Strategic Themes*

Strategic themes are fundamental to strategy maps. An understanding of how to use strategic themes will help you design a strategy map that explains your strategy more effectively. Strategic themes will also help you avoid destroying the cause and effect model which happens when practitioners try, incorrectly, to accommodate an aspect of their strategy as an extra perspective. Strategic themes act vertically across a number of the perspectives of a strategy map, dividing your strategy into separate aspects or themes. This chapter explains how you can use themes in your strategy, describes typical theme structures and explains how themes solve the problem of representing different aspects of strategy.

WHAT IS A STRATEGIC THEME?

A strategic theme is a set of objectives that cross perspectives to tell a part of the story of your strategy. Strategic themes work across, rather than in, perspectives. Any strategy, and the corresponding strategy map, will naturally be divided into a number of topics or themes. These themes are vertical and cross the horizontal perspectives of the strategy map.

If anyone suggests a new perspective, it is most likely a strategic theme. To test any any suggested new perspective, you should ask what the financial implications are, what the customer objectives are, what process objectives there are and what capabilities you need to learn and grow. Each perspective provides useful questions about the themes of the strategy, and the answers will lie in each of the existing perspectives. They are questions that uncover the cause and effect model between perspectives and can easily be applied to cost savings, revenue growth, innovation, quality or any other theme, as necessary. A strategic theme simply crosses the perspective rather than being a separate and additional perspective. Strategic themes are complementary and orthogonal to the perspectives.

Strategic themes work together with perspectives to create the whole strategy. Each theme has a cause and effect model. Sometimes these themes represent the evolution within the strategy, sometimes they represent different parts of the strategy and sometimes they act in tension to reflect the complexity of the strategy.

THEMES AVOID CREATING NEW PERSPECTIVES

Strategic topics such as innovation, environment or quality cause some practitioners problems. They understand that these topics are important but do not fit naturally into one of the existing perspectives. Their solution is to decide they needed a prominent label of their own, and so they are added as a new perspective. As a result many practitioners add new perspectives called 'quality', 'innovation' or 'environment' into their balanced scorecards and strategy maps. Unfortunately, adding extra perspectives has the effect of disrupting or at worst destroying the cause and effect relationship. If you do this, your strategy map will be destroyed and it will no longer tell a coherent cause and effect story. Fortunately, such concepts are easily handled using themes.

THEMES HELP TELL THE STORY OF THE STRATEGY

Themes help the organization tell the story of its strategy more effectively. For instance, one client was changing its emphasis from small customers who were expensive to service, to larger customers who demanded a different sales and servicing approach. Obviously it did not want to lose or ignore all its smaller customers until it had developed its new ones. They still provided revenue, so it was necessary to continue to service them whilst developing the newer markets and products. The two themes needed to operate in tandem. Using the themes, across the perspectives, communicated this important balanced in their strategy.

Themes are extremely important in describing strategy, communicating strategy and aligning the organization. They represent the natural tensions that exist in strategy. The strategy map should be used to represent these tensions, explain them to the organization and help you to manage them. A good strategy map will show these tensions and expose them for what they are: a real part of the strategy. In this chapter, we shall show how strategy maps are structured to explain some of the most common strategic tensions, and also how they are used to manage those tensions.

THEMES AND PROGRAMMES OF ORGANIZATIONAL CHANGE

A great advantage of themes is that they provide a structure for programmes of change, improvement and investment. Given that the themes of the strategy sit alongside each other and drive up through the strategy map perspectives, they naturally have different benefits for the customers and different financial implications. The projects that bring about the improvements in each theme can be managed as a separate programme of work.

Typical Theme Structures

This section provides some typical theme structures. Rather than show whole strategy maps, they have been reduced to the essence, showing the perspectives, relevant objectives in each perspective and the various strategic themes.

TYPICAL THEMES

Different strategies will create different alignment approaches and issues. No one approach is always right. In this section I have chosen seven of the most common and useful theme structures that are encountered when describing a strategy. This is not an exhaustive list. Thinking about the themes of the strategy in different ways creates different perspectives on the organization of the strategy and on the resulting programme of projects and change.

AREAS OF THE BUSINESS

The most basic arrangement of themes is where the strategy map is organized around existing functions, departments or processes. Some strategies and change programmes are centred on different areas of the business. For instance, the programme of change in sales may be separate from that in operations or customer service. This is effectively aligning the themes of the strategy around functional areas and is easily represented by focusing the themes on the process perspective. This is shown in Figure 6.1, where the process perspective dictates the shape of the strategy map. In this case the process perspective could either be based on existing departments or separate processes.

The effect of this is to focus attention within each of the functional areas. However, it often sacrifices the integration of the various parts of the organization and encourages any silo mentality that already exists. This can have an adverse effect from the perspective of the customer. From the customer's perspective, the parts of the organization may be operating separately. They will certainly be developing separate skills and capabilities to achieve their part of the strategy. We will see how to avoid this silo thinking and working later in this chapter.

The way this example is drawn, the values underpin all processes in a consistent way. However, you may have an organization in which different values are exhibited in different departments, countries or regions. In this example the organization is trying to unify the values, despite the development of separate processes and capabilities. Others may accept that different values may need the particular attention of specific parts of the organization.

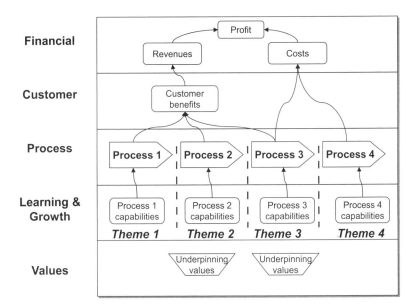

Figure 6.1   Themes based on departments or processes

A similar theme structure appears if the organization is working with processes rather than departments. In this case the themes are based around the definition of the processes rather than the departments that support them. If these processes span departments then they will have the effect of breaking down some organizational barriers. If the processes stay within functions or departments they are unlikely to create any change in behaviour.

EMBEDDED THEMES

The most effective way to represent a theme that transcends much of the organization, the strategy and the strategy map is to embed it into each objective that it touches, then show separately which objectives have a significant element of that theme in their descriptions.

Figure 6.2 shows a variation of the process-based strategy map with two themes embedded. The extent of each theme is indicated by coloured shadows attached to each objective to which that theme applies. In this case there are two themes, denoted by a light grey and dark grey shadow. In this example, the theme denoted by the dark grey boxes supports all the objectives that lead to the revenue objective. This might be a theme of quality or customer focus. The light grey boxes are all connected to the cost objective in the financial perspective, so in this case the theme might represent where cost savings are to be addressed. If we were to look in greater detail behind the strategy map we would expect to find in the detailed description or measures of each of these objectives a significant component that referred to the particular themes.

Of course you might have three or four themes, but you should avoid too many. Using this approach makes it easy to display each theme on a strategy map. You simply remove all the objectives on the picture that do not have the appropriate colour of shadow behind them, leaving behind those that are most relevant to the theme. This is useful when you want to check the coherence of the story of the strategy through a particular theme, and when communicating that theme to the organization.

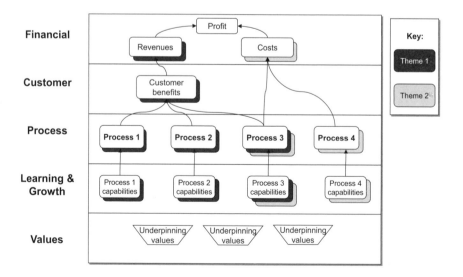

Figure 6.2   Themes embedded within the objectives

COST/REVENUE

Another simple arrangement is to divide the strategy map themes into one for cost reduction and one for revenue growth, as shown in Figure 6.3. These two themes are driven by the financial perspective, where the drivers of costs are treated as separate from the drivers of revenue growth.

This design is useful when management teams want to emphasize that growth and cost reduction are necessary at the same time. When a message of cost reduction and growth, together, gets misinterpreted it is like being in a car where a driver jumps from full on the accelerator to full on the brake and back again. There is no smooth adjustment from one extreme to the other. In contrast to the on/off approach of either growing or cutting costs, the organization may wish to reduce costs in some areas whilst growing its business. Presenting these two themes side by side on the strategy map makes explicit that both are required, in different areas, in different ways, at the same time.

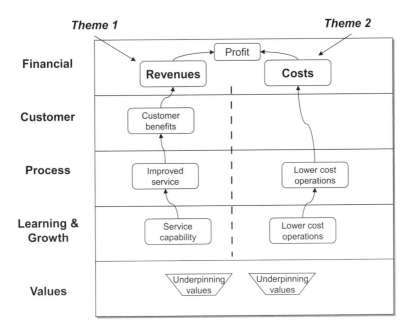

Figure 6.3   Themes based on cost vs revenue

CUSTOMER PROPOSITIONS OR GROUPS

If an organization has particular groups of customers with differing needs, then the themes of the strategy and programmes of work can then be organized around the groups of customers (see Figure 6.4).

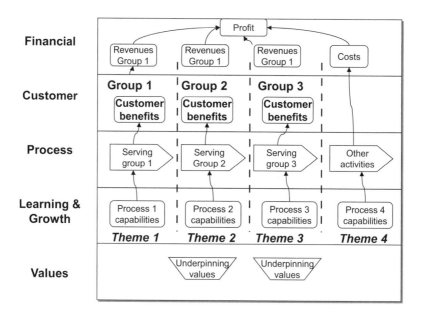

Figure 6.4   Themes based around customer groups

The differences may be caused by different age groups or other demographics. Typical examples of this kind of organization of a strategy may be to have a separate theme for business to business customers and for consumers. In local government, themes may be arranged by location or the needs of particular groups in the community. In commercial organizations, large multinationals might be served differently from those smaller organizations with only a local presence. The banking needs of a consumer are similar in many ways to the banking needs of a small business, but there are some distinct differences. The banking needs of a larger corporation will be quite different again.

The advantage of customer-based themes is that they serve to integrate the parts of the organization that serve particular customer groups, no matter where they sit in the organization. Well designed customer-focused and customer-themed strategy maps help to break down silos and integrate operations. Customer-based themes are useful where the programmes of change in the organization are quite separate or address distinct customer groups.

The tension in customer themes often comes from the conflicting needs of the client groups or from conflicting demands for resources or products. Whilst figure 6.4 shows customer groups with quite separate needs, there are often common needs with some distinct differences. It is this that pulls the organization in different directions.

EXISTING AND NEW PRODUCTS/MARKETS

A similar structure occurs where an organization has several product lines or is developing a new product to replace an old one. An example of this is would be a software company which is due to release a significant, new version of its software that will replace all existing versions. In these circumstances, the organization may want to ensure its sales staff continue to sell the existing product whilst the new one is still being developed, as they might be concerned that customers waiting for the newer product will delay revenue. However, once the new product has been released, the customers with the older version will need to be persuaded to migrate to the new one.

In this case, the strategy map is organized around new and existing products (or services) and the associated revenues, as shown in Figure 6.5. As this strategy develops, you can imagine the theme on the right increasing in dominance whilst the one on the left slowly recedes in importance.

The programmes of change will be organized around maintaining existing products whilst developing the new one.

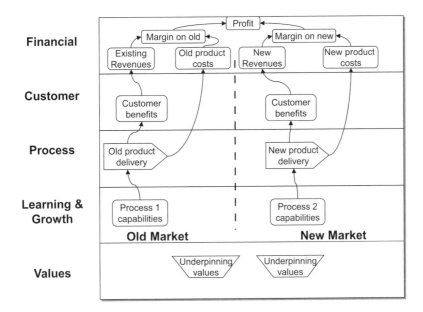

Figure 6.5   Themes based on existing and new products or markets

TIME-BASED THEMES

This example of new and existing products is also an example of time-based themes. In this case, the older products represent where the organization is focusing its attention today. The theme on the right represents where it will be starting to focus its attention in the near future and the tension is between existing and new products or services. There may well be another theme to the right of this one that represents further products and services coming down the line. These would emerge in the next phase of product release.

As organizations grow they sometimes merge with new organizations, divest parts or create alliances. These again can be the focus of the themes of the strategy. Quite often it is necessary to develop the strategy for the main organization and develop a theme separately that handles its plan for diversification, mergers or acquisitions. Having a separate strategy map for a new initiative is useful where you wish to avoid the management's attention being diverted from the operation of the business by the new, more interesting activity. In these situations it is often worth developing a more detailed strategy map just for this specific area.

CAPABILITY-BASED STRATEGY

In some cases an organization's programme of change will be driven by the capabilities it wishes to develop or the skills that the organization will need to compete or perform in the future: perhaps its ability to innovate or to understand its customers better. An example is shown in Figure 6.6.

The effect of this style of strategy map will be to create strategic themes that are based in the learning and growth perspective of the strategy map, yet transcend most, if not all, of the processes within the organization. For example, an emphasis on understanding the customer better may influence how marketing teams understand the markets, how sales teams interact with their customers, how customer service teams answer the phone and how development and operations instigate new products. A similar effect is created where the focus of change in an organization is its values. An example of this would be where teamwork and integrity are being emphasized.

An alternative to using themes for customer groups or capabilities is to use the themes to represent separate policy areas of the strategy. An example of this is where the police force uses different approaches to policing which are applied to different types of crime. These can include intelligence-based policing, local community street policing and targeting types of crime. Each of these different approaches to policing consists of both techniques and underlying capability, and they may create a different level of change programme within each policing region to which they are applied.

The tension in these themes is how the capabilities compete to influence the processes and deliver the benefits. The challenge of management is to communicate

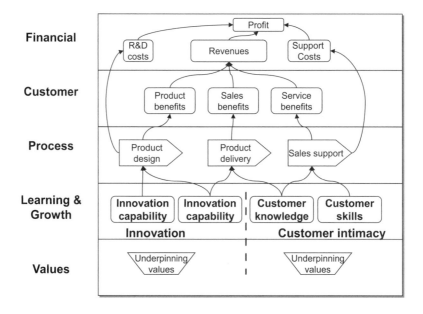

Figure 6.6   Themes based on organizational capability

the new behaviours and ways of thinking and working, so that people understand what they mean for them. Introducing cultural change can be a long process in an established organization. The tension will often be between the existing and the new culture and behaviours. Introducing too many areas of new cultural emphasis and behaviour can serve to create confusion and 'change overload'. By being specific as the strategy maps cascade, you are better able to explain how changes will manifest themselves in different parts of the organization.

SUMMARY OF THEMES

This section has carried across the earlier discussion of strategic themes to the design of programmes of work. Each programme is designed to support a theme, or themes, of the strategy. This provides a way to structure the understanding of the strategy and make it easier to start designing programmes of work, or to align projects to the strategic themes. This approach helps with the essential stage of choosing the shape of programmes of work, into which projects will later fit.

Just as you can have too many objectives on a strategy map, you can have too many themes. In the early days of theme development, I was involved in a project that ended up with eight themes in the corporate strategy map. Each of these themes was developed into a programme of change. To be frank, we got carried away and went too far. The strategy map had more vertical slices than horizontal perspectives. Consequently, it was a messy strategy map that lacked integration between the themes, even though the client loved it. The strategy map was also hard to read and there was no richness of detail in any of the themes. Each theme consisted of single objectives in each perspective. I think we fell into this trap partly because of over-enthusiasm for a new idea and partly to try and break up the strategy into programmes of change. So be warned. Use themes to show the distinct parts of the strategy and the tensions within the strategy without creating more silos and divisions within the strategy.

The choice of themes is a judgement call. You need a clear understanding of the strategy and how themes work together, and you need to consider what might make a sensible structure for the programmes of change. Thinking about how you plan to communicate and cascade your strategy is part of the judgement that goes into the choice of themes on your strategy map.

Using Themes to Join up Organizations

Organizational structures naturally divide up an organization into pieces: divisions of labour. This is good from the point of view of efficiency and responsibility. However, it becomes a problem when the parts of the organization are introspective, operate in isolation, or think and work in silos.

In functional organizations, the objective is control of the business units. Management processes encourage managers to operate as functional specialists, the organization tends to be more analytical and it concentrates on regular events and meetings. The emphasis is on drilling down into detail, with the result that information is viewed more in isolation. A business unit may try to optimize its own outcomes, resources and activities at the expense of others. Budget allocation becomes a zero sum game where one wins or loses against a fixed pot. The culture encourages isolation and separate units. The frustrated customer sees the organization as a series of parts that don't talk to one another.

One solution is to find a new structure or organizational shape that optimizes the parts so they work better together. Of course, reorganizations consume time and resources, cost money and distract the organization from dealing with its customers. Typical reorganizations also take many months, or even years, to plan, communicate, implement and bed down. The reorganization rarely solves the original cultural or relationship problems that underpin the thinking. Often they simply create different silos and problems.

Rather than reorganizing, a quicker, cheaper and more effective way of working is to improve the connections between different parts of the organization. When based on processes this is often called 'business process re-engineering'. When based on customers it is called 'customer orientation'. When based upon relationships and connections across departmental, functional, process and organizational boundaries, it is called 'joined up thinking and working'. Rather than reorganizing, the joined up approach establishes connections between people in existing structures. Rather than using a functional breakdown, the approach might ask, 'who needs to work together to make the biggest contribution to this customer and their experience?'

Good strategy map theme design helps you ask the questions that start to create these connections. If a functional breakdown is used, it will further encourage and embed functional practice. If a more collective, joined up approach is used it can develop joined up thinking and working. This is about responsibility and contribution. In joined up thinking, responsibility for delivering the objectives is often shared amongst a team. Despite collective responsibility, it is common for members of a management team to each have objectives for their own area. They may have some common objectives combined with the individual ones. Joined up thinking would have several directors jointly owning an objective. An individual director may own several objectives, each shared with different fellow directors. This means they have to cooperate together in various combinations to achieve the overall goals. Their focus is not just individual responsibility or whole team responsibility, but combinations of the team to achieve particular ends.

Themes are Fundamental to Strategy Maps

A strategic theme provides a story of your strategy across the objectives in each perspective of the strategy map. The choice and design of the themes will affect how the story of the strategy is told. It will also affect how the story is cascaded and told through the organization. The themes explain the tensions and apparent contradictions within the strategy. In other cases, they will explain how the organization needs to act collectively, break down silos and join up as an organization. In further cases, the themes reflect the different programmes of investment and change that are planned.

Many balanced scorecards are ruined by replacing perspectives with themes, because in doing so you are replacing the cause and effect model with a simple taxonomy of measures of objectives. In contrast, keeping the cause and effect model and asking how the perspectives apply to the various themes usually reveals the underlying drivers of the themes and whether there are different capabilities that drive the different themes.

Your choice of themes in your strategy will also affect how your strategy will be cascaded through the organization, as we shall explore in the next chapter.

These example themes have been chosen to open up your eyes to the possibilities of themes and how they should be used. The warning about copying strategy maps still applies. Think through your strategy and what you wish to represent, achieve and communicate. This will inform your choice of themes.

7 *Designing the Cascade of Strategy Maps*

In addition to thinking about how the themes of your strategy work together to tell the story on a strategy map, it is important to think through how your strategy will be cascaded through the organization so that each part of the organization has its own part of the overall strategy.

How you design your cascade through the organization will affect the communication of the strategy in each part of the organization. It should help each team focus on what they have to achieve. It should help them understand what you are doing and why you are doing it. It should also help them understand why they have to achieve their objectives as part of the overall strategy, providing a golden thread from the team through to the organization's overall objectives. It will provide the framework for the subsequent alignment of resources, investments and initiatives: the 'how you do it'. In this chapter you will learn the various ways in which strategy maps can be cascaded through different organizational structures, and so you will be able to plan the cascade of your strategy into your organization.

Why Cascade your Strategy?

Why do a cascade of the strategy map at all? There are two reasons: what we gain from the process of cascading, and what we gain from having the cascaded strategy maps and scorecards in place.

VALUE FROM THE CASCADE ITSELF

The first role of the cascade is to create manageable pieces of the overall set of strategy maps. The strategy map at any level of management only contains 15 to 25 objectives and can be represented on a single page. This can be repeated all the way through the organization. This creates manageable pieces, with a clear sense of what each management team has chosen to focus on, and what they wish to delegate. This separates the detail from the overview. If they were to try to put all the detail in one strategy map it would quickly become overwhelming and too operationally focused.

The second benefit of the cascade is to provide a line of sight (sometimes called a golden thread) from a team or an individual to the overall objectives. This communicates intent. It helps teams to work out how they can contribute to the wider picture and provides clear objectives for each team. Going further, the effect of cascading a theme of objectives from across the perspectives is to provide a balanced view of the team's contribution to the cause and effect relationship. Not only how we fit in, but how we contribute and how we make a difference.

VALUE FROM THE PROCESS OF CASCADING

The process of cascading should create debate and conversation about the objectives, as a team develop their strategy map based upon the work of their leadership team. To do any cascade, the leadership team will need to explain their thinking, communicate their objectives, and will want to create a debate amongst their staff to help them understand the strategy. Cascading also allows the lower team to express their views and 'step up to the plate' of discussions about the strategy, the direction and what needs to be done about it. The process creates debate, understanding and ultimately ownership.

The process of cascading has a second benefit. It allows the leadership team to validate their thinking amongst the teams beneath them, and to check that their view of how to implement the strategy is correct and to gather their more detailed thoughts. This allows for a certain amount of iterative design between the two levels of strategy map, so that the higher one may be refined once more detail is available below.

How do we Cascade?

How you cascade will depend on your existing organizational structure and also what you wish to achieve with your strategy. It depends on the structure of the organization because ultimately the strategy has to find its way to teams of people who are to implement the strategy for you. It also depends on the strategy, because the different choices you have made will have different implications for the organization and how it moves forward. A market-focused strategy will have different effects on the organization to one aimed at cost reduction or repositioning the capability of the organization. Different organizational structures will be affected by the strategy in different ways, depending upon your strategy.

The tool for describing your cascade is a strategy cascade map. A strategy cascade map is quite different to a strategy map. A strategy map is created for a single management team. The strategy cascade map is created for an organization, and shows how the individual strategy maps fit together. It shows the line of sight from an individual team through to the overall organizational objectives.

In this chapter we look at the four main ways that structure affects the cascade, how to use strategy maps in each case and the implications for those strategy maps. We cover a typical functional hierarchy; a cascade to identical or similar operations; a cascade where themes have been used that do not match the organizational structure; and finally a cascade to a support function such as IT, finance or HR. As Figure 7.1 shows, these may apply in combination across your organization. We will also set out the main principles that apply when detailing a cascade.

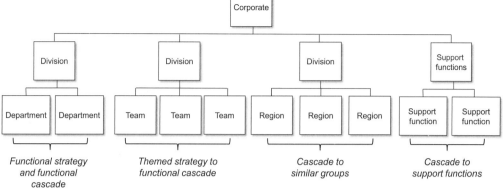

Figure 7.1 Typical organizational structure with a variety of approaches to the cascade

A FUNCTIONAL EXAMPLE

Using the example of an organization based upon a simple functional hierarchy is the simplest way to describe the basic approach to cascading a strategy map and its strategy. Many organizations have a hierarchical organizational structure where the corporate body is divided into, say, divisions, which are further broken down into teams, departments or regions. Each function is usually the responsibility of a single member of the management team.

If the corporate strategy map is structured around the organization's functions then the functional cascade will be very simple. The objectives in the process perspective at the higher level will be associated with the main functions or departments at the next level down. The lower level strategy map will simply expand on these functions in more detail. In this situation the scope of each lower strategy map will be the same as the scope of each of the process objectives that represent the functions in the higher strategy map. Figure 7.2 is a strategy cascade map that shows how two of these functions of processes could be expanded into their more detailed strategy maps.

It is not just individual objectives that are cascaded. In both cases they take the whole of the theme associated with that process objective, ensuring they address the related objectives in each perspective. The whole cause and effect relationship across the perspectives is cascaded to ensure that the cause and effect relationship is maintained. If we were doing a cascade simply using management by objectives (Drucker 1954), the objectives in each perspective would be individually broken down into those sub-objectives that applied to the sub-function, department or team function that we were dealing with. The drill down would be within an objective to more detailed objectives in the same perspective.

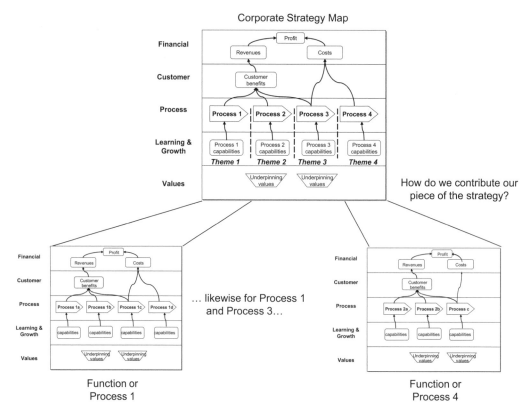

Figure 7.2   Typical functional or process cascade

Figure 7.3 shows a single theme from a higher level strategy map, which is expanded into the more complete lower level strategy map shown in Figure 7.4. In this case it is the bid process from a technology company's overall strategy map. It shows how the objectives in a single theme can be expanded into a complete strategy map at the lower level that would be the responsibility of the bid team.

The bid process strategy map provides a much richer cause and effect relationship between the objectives in different perspectives than the theme description from which it was derived. As you cascade further into the organization, the cause and effect relationship becomes more specific and more detailed.

CASCADING TO SIMILAR LOCATIONS OR OPERATIONS

The second common type of cascade is where there are a number of similar functions under the higher level strategy map. Many organizations will have multiple sites, offices, operations, functions or services that perform the same, or a similar, task. Banks and retailers have multiple branches or outlets. Multinational companies may operate HR and finance departments in many countries, all doing similar roles. A manufacturer may work with many distribution companies in different countries. A franchiser will operate many franchises. In this case there is a collection of similar operations in many locations, so you would expect to see essentially the same strategy and therefore the same strategy map

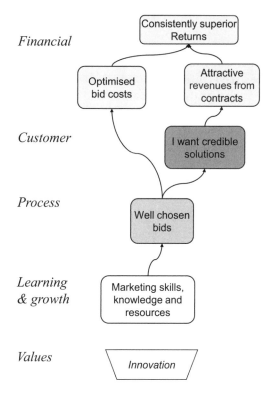

Figure 7.3   A theme of a strategy map for the bid process

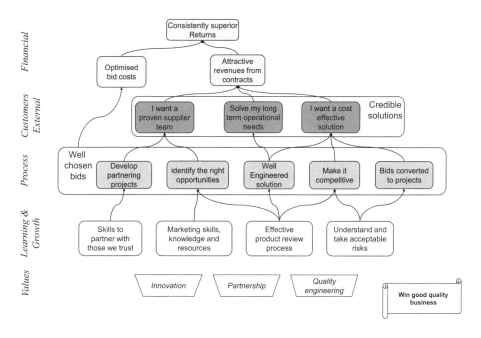

Figure 7.4   The bid process expanded into a full strategy map

structure, objectives and measures. The targets might be different in different locations; the objectives that need most attention might be different. In this case, the strategy cascade map shows that the cascade to the lower level strategy maps is a copy of the higher level strategy map (see Figure 7.5).

There are three variations of this replication of the higher level strategy map that you might meet: each a subtle variation on the theme that might cause the details of the cascade to the lower strategy maps to vary.

If the units are all very similar, with similar circumstances and context, then you would expect each lower strategy map to be identical, and their balanced scorecards to have the same measures. This would be true in a large retailer with hundreds of outlets around the country. The targets for each shop may vary, and local circumstances may dictate local performance levels. For instance, a bank branch in a city location will have a different customer profile from one in a location with a predominantly elderly population, and again from one in a small town or rural location. Demographics and the context of the unit will affect performance and execution of the strategy. This may

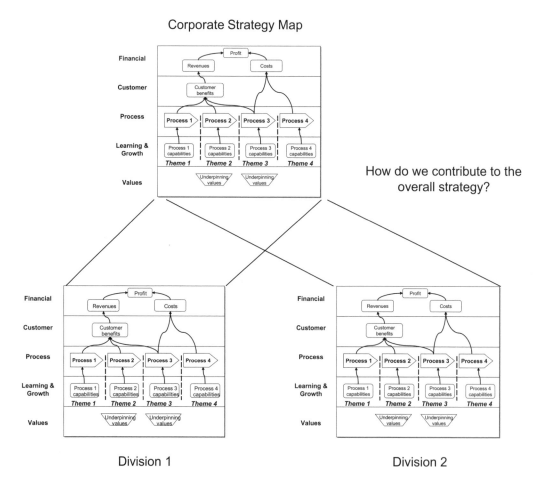

Figure 7.5   How can we contribute? In a group structure the overall strategy is refined in each division

alter the targets associated with the various operations. Some outlets or branches may add local objectives, measures, actions and initiatives to their particular strategy map and scorecard, depending upon their local need. Overall, however, the strategy maps and scorecards would be identical (which would simplify aggregation), and you would be able to compare across the various units easily.

A second variation is where there are again large numbers of units, but there are differences between the types of units. For instance, one retailer we dealt with had around 2,000 stores ranging from simple pharmacies to shops serving 20 categories of product that could either be in high streets or situated in out-of-town retail parks. In this case some of the retail outlets would only be able to deliver part of the strategy, whilst others would be delivering a wider offering to their customers. The overall strategy map in this case would have a small number of variations to accommodate the various types of outlet. There would be common objectives amongst these alternatives, but some would only apply to particular types of store. This approach allows easy comparison across similar types of operations as well as the overall aggregation. It ensures that each type can make their contribution to the overall strategy as far as they can.

A third variation is where you are dealing with business units that are following the same overall strategy, but the strategy has a different emphasis in each business unit. This tends to happen where you have a smaller number of similar functional units that have more variety amongst them. Typically the reason for the variation in strategy is where that unit is positioned now relative to its peers. For instance, a set of distributors across a range of countries might be in different places if some are mature and others have only just started up. The emphasis of their strategies may be different. In these cases the themes and objectives of each strategy map will be broadly similar, having being inherited from the same overall strategy, but there will be a different emphasis in themes and individual objectives. So the strategy maps might vary, with a consequential impact on their scorecards.

An example of this was used with an international engineering consultancy associated with the technology group example earlier. The company had recently acquired five similar, but complementary, businesses in different countries. Whilst they were all engineering consultancies, they were not performing quite the same services and had different strengths. The main UK office was strong in project management and innovation. A UK subsidiary was strong on commercial contracts and innovation, but in a niche area. Germany was strong on sales and engineering skills, but needed more project management expertise. In this case the strategy map for UK operations provided the overall template for all the other business units in the different countries.

The strategy maps for each of the subsidiaries had a similar structure of themes and objectives that reflected their overall strategy and their contribution to the corporate objective, but they omitted some objectives and added others, depending upon their circumstances, emphasis and capabilities. The main mechanism of the cascade was the structure of the themes rather than the detailed objectives. Some objectives were renamed to provide local ownership (even though they had the same meaning and contained similar measures). The software tracking the objectives had to keep track of the various different names used and ensure consistency.

In each of the three variations of a cascade, the lower units are adopting the parts of the overall strategy that are most relevant to their circumstances. In each case the team in the lower unit are asking, 'how do we contribute to the whole of the overall strategy?'

There is a large degree of conformity between the overall strategy map and scorecard, and the lower strategy maps and scorecards, making comparison easier. Also, the external perspective is used to provide a context for each unit, to help explain variations and similarities.

One great advantage of this approach is that you can compare relative performance and relative improvement. In Figure 7.6 the runners represent the starting position of, say, five different regions. You might think of the picture as showing their times to run a set distance. Clearly the lowest runner is starting from further back and has more potential for improvement. So a 50 per cent improvement by the slowest runner might reasonably be expected. In contrast, a 5 per cent improvement in the fastest runner might be considered excellent. In both cases it depends on their starting position and relative performance today. It will also depend on the context in which they are operating. A region operating in a slow market may have less potential to improve than one operating in a more favourable environment. These characteristics should be captured for the external perspective. The strategy map for each of your teams, regions or subsidiaries should provide you with a picture that allows you to assess where they are now and assess relative improvements. It also provides the potential for sharing lessons and approaches amongst the runners, in this case, so that the teams can learn from each other, rather than seeing it as a simple competitive race where the fastest always wins.

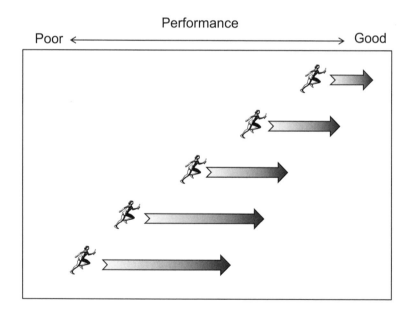

Figure 7.6 Comparing the relative performance, given where each unit has started

THEME-BASED CASCADE

The advantage of choosing strategic themes that cross functional boundaries is that it allows you to express your strategy as a whole strategy for the organization rather than as a set of smaller, functional strategies that add together to make the whole strategy. This helps with joined up thinking and working that can act to break down existing functional silos. You may be doing this to get people in existing functions to work together better, or this may be a precursor to a more radical change of structure within the organization.

When doing a theme-based design that ignores existing functional structures, it is often useful to break down the top level or corporate strategy map and its themes into more detailed strategy maps that still ignore the existing functional structure and allow you to develop the themes in more detail. This will have the effect of defining the joined up thinking and working more explicitly at a lower level in the organization.

You can vary the degree of joined up thinking you use, depending upon your strategy. The modular building company used a corporate strategy map in which the process objectives deliberately overlapped the functions of sales, design, manufacturing, logistics and after sales, so that they joined up at their interfaces. You can see this in the overlaps between process objectives and departments shown in Table 7.1.

Table 7.1   Example of process objectives and the departments that own them

Process objective	Departments responsible
P1 Convince people of our expertise and solutions	Sales and Marketing (Finding customers) Design team (Having flexible designs) Manufacturing (Demonstrating the facility)
P2 Effective propositions for building solutions	Sales and Marketing (Preparing bids) Design team (Creating flexible designs)
P3 Quality designs that balance price and performance	Design team (Designing for customers and manufacturing) Manufacturing (Ways to maximize building performance)
P4 A flexible operation that delivers for our markets	Design (Designing for efficient manufacture) Manufacturing (Having a flexible operation) Logistics (Flexible inventory management, delivery and installation)
P5 A consistent installation process	Logistics (Consistent installation and sufficient capacity) After sales (Ensuring quality during installation) Design (Designing for easy installation with clear instructions)
P6 Excellent after sales support	After sales (Managing any in-life issues) Design (Building in lifetime support)

In contrast, at a city council, a more radical approach was taken to break down the six departments that operated as silos. The corporate themes were taken from the customer objectives and the process objectives linked directly to these. Consequently three separate directors became responsible for safety in the city. The environment director became responsible for the design of safe environments, the community services director for issues such as drug safety and links to social services, and the contract services director's teams were on the streets cleaning up graffiti and reporting back issues to the others. This joining up caused the three directors' teams to have to start working together in a way they had not before. This was without the need for, or great expense of, reorganization.

At some point you have to convert from the theme structure to a structure that suits the individual teams, units, departments or functions that are supporting the overall strategy and its themes. If the new themes are a precursor to a restructuring of the organization, then the new theme-based strategy map will become the basis for the new organizational structure. If the themes do cross existing organizational boundaries and there is not to be a restructure, then at some point in the cascade you have to make a link between existing teams, functions and departments and the overall themes of your strategy. At some point a team have to know which objectives they need to support. You move from theme-based strategy maps to strategy maps that are owned by existing departments, functions or teams. It is here that you make it clear how objectives are shared between functions and where joined up thinking and working is made explicit.

At this point you have to know how a particular business unit, function, team or department supports the corporate strategy map and its themes (Figure 7.7). You then approach the unit's strategy map in a very similar way to how you would if you were doing a functional cascade. The primary question is 'what are we responsible for?' You will also ask, 'how can we contribute to the wider picture and objectives?' and 'what local strategies and proprieties should we adopt?' These lower unit strategy maps may adopt the themes structure, or may show it partially while they adopt their own functional structure to make it easier to cascade to those strategy maps below the unit. If done in this way, it is important to show how the functions or processes support the various themes of the corporate strategy map and its objectives.

Theme-based structures give you the choice of not only following a functional approach, but following an approach that crosses organizational boundaries and joins up parts of the organization. As we have seen, these structures could be organized around the customer so that the organization collectively acts to serve that customer group's needs. Other arrangements may support existing product ranges and future product ranges.

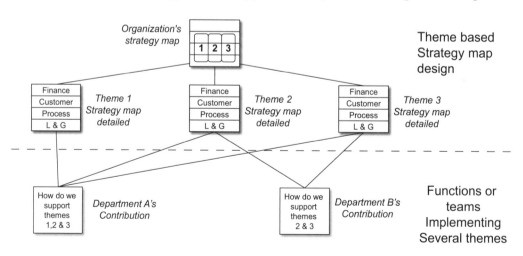

Figure 7.7 **In a cascade, themes are ultimately translated to departments or teams**

Both theme- and function-based cascades will start and finish in the same place. All will have a corporate or top level strategy map. All will finish at the level of an individual, team or unit, who will be able to clearly see their contribution to the strategy. The two options will take a different route through the structure of strategy maps and therefore communicate a different message and imperative about a strategy.

It is important to be able to trace a theme's objectives across the various functions that may be supporting it and be available through the management information system. The themes and functional view provide alternative ways to drill through the organization. The functional cascade provides each division or department with their version of the strategy. The theme-based cascade ensures that they contribute to the themes, and acts to join up the organization. The main difference is that when the strategy map cascade follows the themes of the strategy it asks at each level, 'who is contributing to it?' I sometimes think of the view of a theme working across many functions as being represented by a knitting needle threading through a set of cards, finding the appropriate objectives and pulling them all out together as a set. The main difference is one of perspective. In functional strategy maps you are asking, 'for this function, which objectives do we own?' In a theme-based strategy map you are asking, 'for this objective, who contributes to it?'

Your strategy will determine the extent to which you wish to break down organizational boundaries and create joined up working. It will also determine the precise way that you wish this to be done. This can be captured in the choice of themes and the design of the cascade of strategy maps and scorecards, as they move from the overarching organizational strategy and themes down to individual functions and teams.

Cascading to a Support Function

These approaches also work when you are cascading or working with support functions. Support functions have a different relationship with the corporate strategy map and its cascade. Whilst you will find many of the objectives and deliverables for the functions of IT, HR and finance from the learning and growth perspective, their strategy maps do not simply come out of this perspective.

Generally, support functions do not directly interact with external customers. They support the capabilities of the primary functions, which in turn support external customers. Support functions help other departments deliver the service. Support functions' customers are therefore internal customers. Support functions tend to interact with their internal customers at the internal customers' learning and growth perspective. The processes within HR, IT and finance help to deliver the competencies, capabilities, knowledge, skills, technology and support that the primary functions need, as shown in Figure 7.8. A department such as HR will contribute to the capabilities of a number of primary functions at the learning and growth level of their strategy map. Likewise an IT department will ensure the availability of technology, make information available through reports and deliver the new systems necessary to improve the operation of the front line functions.

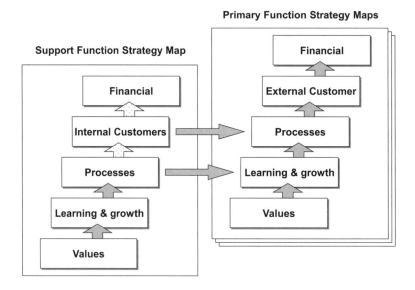

Figure 7.8   **A support function will tend to support the learning and growth perspective of a first line process or department**

The primary customers of a support function are internal customers. To represent this the customer perspective of a support function's strategy map is split into two layers: the lower immediate internal customers and the ultimate external customers. This clearly links the support function to both the internal and external customer needs. It provides a view from the support function's activities through to the organization's end customers and so shows how the support function adds to the organization. An example of an IT department strategy map showing both internal and external customers is provided in Figure 7.9.

Developing a support function strategy map is carried out in two phases. The first stage is to work out where the support function contributes to the rest of the organization. The customer layer of the strategy map for the support function contains the aggregated set of objectives for all its *internal* customers. The second phase is to assess the processes and capabilities, at what costs, that the support function needs to deliver. What is the strategy for the support function to support the rest of the organization in delivering the overall strategy?

As you would expect, support functions' costs are shown in their financial perspectives. Do be careful with these as sometimes the support function costs are embedded within the operating budgets of the line functions, especially where there are devolved finance and HR functions, or budgets for IT projects funded by customer facing departments.

The strategy map for a support function should describe the strategy which that support function will use to deliver its services to the rest of the organization. The processes perspective should contain the process objectives that are necessary to deliver the function's strategy. The capabilities should be those that will allow the function to learn, grow and deliver its strategy.

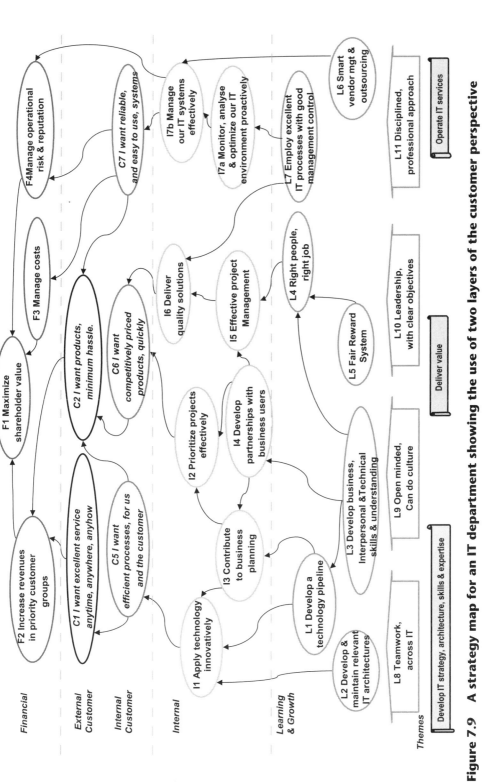

Figure 7.9 A strategy map for an IT department showing the use of two layers of the customer perspective

You will encounter the exception of a support function that has some direct interaction with the external customer. Web services and IT point of sales systems will be used directly by customers and supported directly by IT. IT may even provide customers with technical helpdesk support. In these cases you can easily represent these additional links by bypassing the internal customer perspective and linking directly from the customer objectives to the objectives in the process layer of the support function. If there is a direct revenue source then this is simply shown as a driver of revenue in the financial perspective.

The great advantage of including both internal and external customers is that the strategy map will provide a direct line of sight from the support function's values, capabilities and activities, through the delivery of its services inside the organization and onwards out to the support function's contribution to the organization as a whole.

Detailing the Cascade

When developing a strategy map at any level in an organization, be sure to understand the context as well as the detail. Remember that a strategy map is for a team. You therefore need to be clear about the extent and limits of responsibility of that team. That way you will ensure you include the correct scope of objectives. I once worked with a retailer whose managing director had responsibilities for developing a new market overseas. However, his overseas activities were explicitly ruled out of scope of the balanced scorecard, as we were looking at only the UK retail strategy. The strategy map concentrated on the UK retail operations. If they had wanted to include the strategy for the overseas expansion, we could have developed that strategy map separately. On another occasion, I worked with a technology company whose team explicitly excluded the search for further acquisitions, wanting to concentrate on getting the synergy from the existing acquisitions. Another company had a significant part of its profits originate from its property portfolio. It was decided to include this as it was such a significant part of their business model. In each case you need to be sure of the scope of the business or organization you are dealing with and what might be ruled in or out. In the case of a technology company, the people who supported the bids were not just the sales team. Bid teams were drawn from project and technical staff. What appears to be a straightforward cascade might not be in every case. It pays to check.

When starting from the top, make sure you understand the scope of each of the next level strategy maps and the part of the organization you are dealing with. Think through the cascade as a group of strategy maps before you start detailing the individual ones. This will ensure you are clear of their scope. Refer up to the strategy map (or maps) that sit above and beside the individual map you are working on. Sketch out detail in the level below where that helps clarify a situation. In some cases, you may need to develop at least first cut lower level strategy maps to provide enough information to populate the higher level meaningfully.

FOUR QUESTIONS DURING THE CASCADE

There are four questions to ask as the strategy maps cascade and when working out which objectives should be supported by a particular function. These are:

What are we responsible for?

What can we contribute to?

What does this mean, locally, for us?

Do we have a clear strategy and story, consistent with the overall strategy?

Ask, 'what are we responsible for?' As you cascade the top level strategy map you need to ensure that you pick up all the objectives that a particular unit is responsible and accountable for. These are the objectives or sub-objectives that they must focus on to ensure they make a contribution to the overall strategy. This means that you are making cause and effect relationships within the higher level objectives and contributing towards other higher level objectives. Responsibility will cover all the perspectives, so you should ask the question for the objectives in each perspective. Once you have identified these you can expand and detail the objectives that apply from the higher level to the next level of strategy map.

Ask, 'what can we contribute to?' 'Where can we make a significant difference or contribution to others?' These are useful questions because they encourage teams to look at the strategy maps of others to see how they could be helped. Ask yourself, 'how does this part of the organization contribute to the strategy map at the higher level, or the strategy maps of other units?' The contribution question is powerful in that it seeks to join up parts of the organization so they are actively looking to work together. Do be careful of bottom-up justification. Some functions, especially support functions, may use this question to justify their existence and suggest that they make a contribution to everything. For example, there could be a legal component to almost any transaction or business activity. Of course the legal department should be involved, but from the perspective of the overall strategy their contribution would be small, although important. Where you could contribute and where you could make a significant contribution are two completely different questions.

Ask, 'what does this objective mean for us, locally?' This is similar to the responsibility and contribution questions, but comes at it from a different angle. When dealing with a financial objective, say a reduction in working capital, the question can be interpreted as, 'what can we do to make a difference to the working capital?' This then creates a discussion about how the unit influences working capital and where it could make a difference. This applies equally to objectives in any perspective. For instance, given a set of learning and growth objectives in the corporate strategy map, the unit would ask, 'what do these mean for the way we work and the development of our skills, knowledge and capabilities?' As an example, if at the corporate level there is an objective of 'making time to do the right things', then this raises the question, 'what should we stop doing and how can we make the time to do the right things within our unit?' There will also be local imperatives and priorities that will be added to the unit's strategy map. This adds detail as the strategy cascades and represents what is strategic at a unit's level, but what may be more tactical at the next level up. Some of these imperatives may not be so important or visible at the higher level. You are choosing what is strategic at one level and tactical at the level above.

Finally, as with any strategy map, test the story. Rather than just looking at the strategy map in isolation, test it with a cascade test to check that the local lower strategy map makes sense against the story of the higher strategy map. Does it explain how we contribute to the overall strategy? Does it explain where we fit in? Does it show a golden thread and give you a line of sight? Does it work as a part of the overall strategy?

ITERATIVE DEVELOPMENT

Whilst the preferred way of developing a cascade of strategy maps is from the top down, this does not mean that the high level strategy maps need to be completely developed and signed off before any work can be started on the lower level strategy maps. In fact, the opposite is true. It is often helpful to dive into the next level of strategy maps and outline their structure as a part of the process of developing the strategy map you are currently working on.

Iteration helps to validate the higher level strategy map and helps to confirm that it is addressing sufficient detail and content. This is especially true when developing new themes for a strategy, as an extra level of detail sometimes helps to clarify what is meant amongst the team. It is also true when doing a simpler, more familiar functional cascade.

Dropping down into the next level, iteratively, is also good for ownership. One good reason for taking this iterative approach is that the teams involved in the next level of strategy map do not feel they have been given a *fait accompli*. Rather, they feel they have a chance to shape and develop the strategy at their level, within the overall framework and guidance provided by the higher level strategy map. This way the iterative development process becomes a conversation between the layers of management about the strategy, its assumptions, directions, pace of change, and how it can best be implemented.

I have worked in some large organizations where the cascade was done bottom-up. The functional teams across the organization were tasked with building their own strategy maps to implement the strategy as they understood it. This was done to create ownership and invite them to 'step up to the plate', to show how they would support the new strategy and save costs. Once the strategy maps for the first iteration were complete, they were then evaluated as a complete set across the organization. There then followed some refinement to further develop each into an appropriate scorecard. This of course made creating the overall strategy map a little harder, and also required that a certain amount of preparatory work was necessary to ensure everything joined up. It did, however, have the effect of creating much more of a sense of empowerment and ownership across the various functions with their part of the strategy. Of course, this would only work where there was a clear enough imperative for change and the organization had already communicated the intent and direction of the strategy. However, in this organization's case it still worked.

CASCADING VALUES

It is normal to place the values of the organization on the lower level strategy maps, as these are expected to underpin the organization's behaviour, no matter where in the organization they might be.

When dealing with the values perspective of a department or support function you may encounter two different situations. In one, the values of the function should be the same as those of the organization as a whole. They may be at a different level of adoption and embodiment within the support function; if so, they will be acting to bring the support function more in line with the rest of the organization.

Occasionally you will encounter a situation where the values of the lower department or support function are different from those of the rest of the organization. This seems counter-intuitive, but does happen. Perhaps the function is outsourced. Perhaps it is behind or ahead of the rest of the organization. Perhaps it is out of synchronization and has specific problems. In each case, explore the underlying causes. It is more natural, and better from an organizational alignment perspective, to have the same values in support functions as you have in the rest of the organization.

WHEN TO STOP CASCADING

One question that often comes up is how far to cascade. The answer is, when the strategy is communicated well enough, people have objectives they can own and the strategy maps have served their purpose. A more practical explanation would be, when you have reached the groups or teams who are going to take responsibility for the delivery of the strategy on the ground.

Sometimes strategy maps are used to establish the strategy at a high level and only rolled out to major departments or divisions. Other times they are detailed all the way down to individual teams. In each case the explicit decision is about the natural team or unit size and the clarity of the strategy for that team. You should not stop cascading the strategy because strategic thinking has become too difficult to think about at a particular level. You can stop when individuals within a department can own a small set of objectives from the strategy map and feel they can directly contribute to them. If these individuals directly own or feel they strongly influence say three or four of the process objectives, you are probably at a low enough level to allocate objectives, measures, targets and responsibilities to individuals. They then have a piece of the strategy in their pocket, can see how they contribute to the strategy and have a clear line of sight to the corporate objective, to their impact on the customers and to the strategy as a whole.

CHECKING THE STORY

As a final check, make sure that the set of cascaded strategy maps still communicates the strategy. Placing the maps together and reading across the various strategy maps should show a consistency between them as well as completeness across and within the set of cascaded strategy maps. They should still tell the same story of the strategy as the higher level strategy map told, yet in more detail.

Final Points on Cascades

As soon as you start to design the top level strategy map you are starting to design the cascade. How you structure and represent the strategy at the top level will influence how it is rolled out. Various cascade approaches are possible. Many organizations develop their strategy maps through functional cascades where each department owns its part of the strategy. The functional cascade is the simplest, as it follows the existing structure of the organization, ensuring that each function is clear what it is responsible for and how it contributes to the whole picture. Many organizations will use standard strategy maps across similar divisions, functions or geographic locations. A theme-based cascade can be used to join up the organization and demonstrate how the parts of the organization contribute to the various themes. Front line functions will be ensuring their activities and capabilities directly affect the customers they interact with. Support functions sit one step back from these customers. They need to establish how they will improve the capabilities, skills, knowledge and culture of their internal customers, and be clear how that filters through to the external customers, as well as being clear about their impact on finances. Most organizations will use a combination of approaches, depending on the structure of the organization and the purpose of the strategy.

Whichever approach to the themes and the cascade you adopt, you are creating the framework for programmes of change. You are also designing how you communicate the strategy through the organization, the message that you wish to communicate and how people will organize themselves and own their part of the strategy. Cascading your strategy aligns the organization's resources and ensures that people know how they contribute to the strategy. The design of the cascade of your strategy will ensure that you preserve the cause and effect relationships as well as the themes of the strategy. Having these principles of themes and cascades in mind, and knowing the implications of your choices will make designing an individual strategy map far easier and more effective.

IV Detailed Design

Part IV explains the detailed design process that applies to all the perspectives of the strategy map and how you develop your scorecard beneath it.

Chapter 8 is about asking the right questions in the right way. Facilitators will find this particularly important as it contains precise questions that will help you navigate through an executive interview and develop the strategy map objectives correctly. This chapter will also help executives to think through why they believe their strategy is correct and where those beliefs come from. What are the few things that will make the biggest difference, what is the performance gap and why do we believe that the chosen way is the best way to close it?

Chapter 9 is a fundamental piece of the thinking. Get this wrong and the whole approach will collapse into operational detail. Developing objectives before measures is fundamental. It is too easy to jump straight to measures and omit the valuable thinking that objective development provides. It will also help you avoid the performance management problems of measure mania and the tyranny of targets.

These two chapters set the overall context for the development of objectives in each of the perspectives.

CHAPTER

8 *The Questions to Ask when Developing your Strategy Map*

This chapter is about how the management team's thinking about the strategy is captured for a strategy map and the types of thinking you may encounter. It provides the overall approach to strategy map development and gives you the questions you need to ask and the reasons for those questions. It explains why precise questions, phased in specific ways, are used to elicit the strategy at each level of the strategy map.

The questions in this chapter will help you develop your objectives in each perspective and help you to navigate your way through the cause and effect relationship of your strategy map. These include questions to establish the objective, find the performance gap and identify the few things that will make the biggest difference to closing that gap. They also ask what stops you closing the performance gap today. They check to see which aspects of your strategy will make the biggest difference and what to focus on. These questions will ensure your strategy map is about your strategy and change, and that it does not try to become a complete picture of the operation of the organization.

These questions ask you as managers what you believe about your strategy. This leads to the question, 'how do you know?' *How* have you developed your understanding of your strategy? *Why* do you believe it will work? Understanding the answers to these questions helps the executive team to appreciate where they are using evidence, assumptions and beliefs. This will help you refine those assumptions as your strategy is implemented. It helps facilitators understand the source of management thinking and how the strategy was developed, knowledge which can be used in the design of the strategy maps and in the communication of the strategy.

The chapter concludes with tips for facilitators to think about, to ensure the integrity of the strategy map, as they are asking the questions and tracking your responses.

The Overall Sequence of Strategy Map Development

The sequence is to identify and develop the objectives in a perspective and then, once you have these well defined, to ask questions about the drivers from the next perspective down.[1] So, the overall sequence through the perspectives is:

---

1   The financial objectives, as you will recall, have links from both the customer objectives (for revenue) and process objectives (for costs), so you will need to ask about both these lower perspectives.

1. Identify the set of objectives in the perspective. Detail the objectives, desired states and performance gaps and how to close them.
2. Establish the cause and effect relationship: what objectives do you need in the lower perspectives to drive your change?
3. Iterate down through each perspective (steps one and two), detailing the objectives as you go and establishing the underpinning objectives.
4. Check the overall story makes sense. Validate the cause and effect relationship across all the perspectives.
5. When all the objectives are available in each perspective, and only when they are all available, return to ask,
    a. What is the best way to measure these objectives?
    b. What other activities do we need to align the organization against these objectives?

For the five steps listed in the sequence above, there are three sets of questions you need to use. For step one you need a set of questions to develop the objectives and detail them. For step two you need a set of questions appropriate to navigating between perspectives. Step three is simply the iteration of steps one and two as you work through the cause and effect model. The two sets of questions for steps one to three will be detailed in this chapter.

Step four checks the story through the cause and effect model. Chapter 20 will explain some of the more subtle messages it also contains. Step five has questions that move you from objectives to measures and the overall alignment of the organization. The next chapter will explain how to develop objectives into measures. Chapters 17 and 18 include questions to help you align the organization's resources and projects.

Always develop the cause and effect relationship from the top of the strategy map downwards. You start with either the purpose and financial objectives, or the purpose and customer objectives, and move from these, through the process perspective, towards the learning and growth and values perspectives. Only once you have sufficient detail of the objectives in the current perspective should you start to identify the few objectives that will make the biggest difference from the next lower perspective. Part of the art of interviewing is to track the thinking of the interviewee within and across perspectives whilst teasing out the few things that will make the biggest difference and will implement the strategy.

Six Questions to Develop Objectives in each Perspective

In each perspective you need to ask a sequence of questions to identify the objectives for that perspective. These six questions are asked for each perspective, and are:

1. What do you want to achieve? (Objective)
2. How well do you do that today? (Current state and performance gap)
3. What are the few things that you will have to focus on, to make the biggest difference? (Focus and choice)
4. What stops you doing that today? What do you have to do differently to overcome this? (Underlying reasons and what has to change)
5. If you do that, will it achieve your objective? (Validation)

6. How do you know? (Confirmation)

The process of developing the strategy map takes an executive team iteratively through this sequence, detailing it further and further as the strategy maps are developed. Later we shall add further questions that help with strategy implementation, asking about the resources needed, and how projects and budgets are aligned. These questions ensure your answers will be about change and provide focus. They will help you to understand the thinking behind the strategy and develop a strategy map that is about the few things that will make the difference.

You must be precise about how you state and frame the questions when you ask them. For example, asking 'how well is that objective achieved today?' will give you a completely different answer from, 'how well is that objective achieved today against your strategic ambition?'

These open questions are designed to elicit a wide range of responses that will give you useful information about the objective, what is done well and what problems there are. You may get quantitative information about the problems, targets and performance gaps. Asking these questions against a fixed point in the future will elicit a more explicit response.

Question One: What do you Want to Achieve?

How do we establish the objectives in each perspective? A simplistic view of the strategy map perspectives might lead someone to think that you simply ask questions that generate the objectives in each perspective, in isolation. They might ask what the organization wants to achieve, in each perspective, for instance: what are our financial objectives? What do our customers want? What do we have to do well? What do we need to learn and grow? Using these questions would be a mistake. These questions will give you answers that focus on each perspective individually, not the links between them. The value of the perspectives comes from the cause and effect relationship *between* objectives in adjacent perspectives. This cause and effect relationship requires answers about how your strategy will drive change; how change will ripple through across the perspectives; how improvements in your capability will bring changes in the way you operate that will affect your customers and the market, and the consequential impact on the financial results of the organization.

To derive the objectives in each perspective and to navigate your cause and effect relationship (step two), you have to ask about the relationships between objectives in adjacent perspectives, starting from the top. This means that, if you were to start with your financial objectives, you would ask the five questions below to develop each objective and ensure it is linked to the objectives below it. These questions are about the relationship between objectives in the perspectives and the objectives within a perspective. After the first question, the subsequent questions are asked for each objective in the perspective:

1. If we succeed, how will we look financially? (Given purpose, what financial objectives do we have?)
2. To achieve this financial objective, what customer needs must we satisfy?(Customer requirements derived from revenue expectations)

3. To satisfy this customer objective, what do we have to do well? (Processes derived from customer needs)
4. To achieve this process objective, what do we have to learn and how do we have to grow as an organization? (Learning and growth, from process)
5. Do our values underpin our learning and growth objectives?' (Learning and growth to values)

Notice earlier I said, '*if* you were to start with the financial perspective'. There is a myth in balanced scorecard circles that you have to start with the financial perspective because it is at the top of the cause and effect chain. The myth continues on to say that having the financial perspective at the top is a sign that the balanced scorecard is more interested in financial results than customers. This is not true. Whilst you are interested in the financial consequences, they will only result from serving your customers' objectives. You have to satisfy your customers to create revenue. The customer perspective is the most important one, even though it lies in the middle of the cause and effect model. You have to understand who your customers are and how you will satisfy them before you can establish what revenue they will create, otherwise you will just be making up the numbers. Having established the customers and their objectives in the customer perspective, you then establish the revenue implications that come from satisfying those customers' needs. Consequently, you do not have to start with the financial perspective. In fact, it is better not to start with the financial perspective. It is better to start with the customer perspective and have that as your point of emphasis, iterating between the customer and financial objectives to check they tell a consistent story. To emphasize this point, you will find the chapter on developing the detail of the customer perspective is before the chapter on developing the detail of the financial perspective. In reality you will iterate between the two. Starting with the customer perspective creates a simple modification to the first two questions:

1. To succeed as an organization, what customer needs must we satisfy? (Purpose linked to customer needs)
2. If we satisfy these customer needs, what will be the financial consequences? (Financial implications of satisfying the customer needs)

The other questions are the same. Choosing either of these perspective routes is equally valid. I usually choose the one the client prefers and use both routes to help them validate their story. What you must not do is start with any lower perspectives (process, or learning and growth). Starting lower down will create operational strategy maps that justify your capabilities or operations. You must start with one of the top two perspectives and validate them as a pair, before moving to the objectives in the lower perspectives that support them. So the first step is to decide which perspective you will start in, financial or customer, and then ask questions to derive the objectives in these two perspectives.

Question Two: What is the Performance Gap?

Once you have statements that describe the individual objectives in each perspective you need to establish the performance gap for each objective. There are two related and complementary approaches: quantitative and qualitative performance gaps. I recommend you use both.

QUANTITATIVE PERFORMANCE GAPS

In the financial and process perspectives especially, you are likely to receive a quantitative description of the objective and its associated performance gap. For instance, you may discover that the majority of the revenue growth is expected to come from new commercial contracts associated with the growing international business, whilst the existing core domestic business is expected to remain at a constant size. Financial objectives are usually quite easily quantified. In this case the two financial objectives appear to be, 'maintain and protect existing revenue' and 'grow new international revenue'. However, it is worth exploring the other qualities of existing and new revenue growth. For instance, what sort of quality of new revenue are you looking for? Are they safe contracts or innovative ones? Is the new revenue from new or existing customers? What about the cost of sales? What about potential repeat customers? These are all characteristics of the new revenue stream. What about the existing revenue stream? Is that certain or does it need to be protected and maintained? Does it have quality issues? These characteristics are expressed in the objective rather than the quantified measure.

You may find the same when you are dealing with process objectives, where explicit measures and targets may be quoted. For instance, you might get, 'we only convert 35 per cent of our bids into contracts'. In this case the objective might be, 'we bid for contracts that we are likely to convert to projects'. You will have to convert this to a performance gap to understand what percentage of bids would be a desired conversion rate. However, the reason for this poor conversion rate could be a number of factors, especially if the contracts that you do win are the least profitable ones. This illustrates the dangers of diving into measures too early, and this stark figure does not reveal the additional important subtleties behind the bids that are won. Whilst you can ask for measures and targets, the problem is that you will then only be dealing with part of the objective: that represented by the measure. So, capture these quantitative performance gaps and return to the objective, in this case the bid conversion rate and the growth in revenue, and explore the qualities and characteristics of the objective.

Make sure you have the objective, its characteristics and any quantitative performance gaps that you are provided with. To gather more about these objectives, there is an alternative approach that is very effective.

QUALITATIVE PERFORMANCE GAPS

To get a richer description of the objective and the performance gap I have found that the most effective way is to use what appears to be a qualitative measure: to ask for current performance as a score out of 10. You simply ask:

Overall, giving a mark out of 10, how well is that done today?

Using the 'marks out of 10' question (0 being the worst score and 10 being the best) quickly establishes, from that person's perspective, how well the objective is performing and the size of the performance gap overall. The follow up questions provide a rich picture of how the person is thinking about the performance gap, what stops them closing it and what it will take to close it.

People are often surprised that this approach is used. However, it is extremely effective. This approach works because it gets managers to talk about what they believe, as well as what they know. The important part of this approach is to elicit the objective and tangible thinking behind the *apparently* subjective score. Once you have this, you can compare that thinking with others and have a quality conversation.

What appears superficially to be a simple question requires a significant amount of mental processing to come up with an answer. To answer the question, 'giving a mark out of 10, how well do you do X?' requires that they first assess what constitutes a 10. They have to construct an ideal situation. They then have to assess where they are now. This means they are rating what they already have against that perfect situation. They will construct in their mind the gap between where they are now and the ideal situation. This means they must have some idea of what it will take to close that gap. The really important part is that, having asked a simple question, you can now ask about any aspects of this: the perfect situation, where they are now, the gap, what it will take to close it. All this information is now available.

What seems at first sight a simplistic question actually creates extremely rich thinking which provides a very holistic view from that person's perspective. It will include evaluations and assessments that specific measures often omit. It provides an honest assessment that can be built upon. Used alongside the other information, it is a useful perception of the objective.

In imagining what a 10 looks like, the person may use several approaches. They might have an ideal. It might be a desired state. It might be a state they have been in before. With one client the question was about the diversity of the workforce. When asked how he worked out what a 10 was, he described how, in his mind, he reviewed the diversity of a number of organizations he had experienced and then compared how well his organization did to the others. With further questioning he was able to articulate some of the characteristics of the other organizations that he admired and whose aspects he would like to see in his workforce. This took him all of two to three seconds. This is quite a rich picture to construct from a single, apparently simple, question, but it is typical of the richness that the question can create.

When you are dealing with an area that has not been discussed before, there may well be no measures. Asking for measures of 'well chosen bids' may elicit the reply, 'I have no idea how to measure this'. If there are no measures, there are probably no targets to set levels of performance. So you will end up in a discussion about lack of information. In contrast, using marks out of 10 allows somebody to describe the whole of the issue in whatever words and constructs they like. The question does not restrict how it is answered. Rather, you can get a rich and useful conversation amongst the team about how each of them scores the objective, what constitutes those scores and what each believes is needed to close the gap. This rich conversation helps to clarify different perspectives and build a common understanding.

Question Three: Strategy is about Choice and Focus

Having elicited the performance gap, either with the 'marks out of 10' question or via some other means, the next step is to ask what it will take to close the performance gap you have just identified for that objective. The question is:

What are the few things that you have to focus on to make the biggest difference?

This question is about strategy as choice and focus within an objective. As explained previously, this question is fundamental to strategy maps and makes them different from other ways of modelling the organization. Rather than being complete maps of the organization, they focus on the parts that will make the biggest difference to implementing the strategy. We do not want a list of thirty different things that might all contribute to closing the performance gap. We want to concentrate the management's attention, and the organization's attention, on the few things that will make the biggest difference.

If you have used the 'marks out of 10' approach, you can now add, 'what few things will make it a 10?' If you have used a quantitative approach you might ask, 'what few things will raise the new revenue to £130m?' (Or an equivalent question appropriate to your objective.)

The emphasis on the few things that you have to focus on to make the biggest difference embodies the ideas of choice, focus and differentiation that are deeply embedded in strategic thinking theory. It applies in the market, the organization's value proposition and the organization's internal activities. It particularly applies to the extent of change the organization chooses to undertake, as too much change can overwhelm an organization. Again it is about focus. What few changes will have the biggest effect on the organization?

With so many aspects to strategy: choice, focus, differentiation and change, we need a way of asking questions about the strategy and teasing out the thinking, without being specific about the particular model used. The 'few things/biggest difference' question provides that openness. You can always ask specific questions about choice or focus or change later, once you have the answer to this initial question. You can also vary it to ask about specific perspectives. Be careful with the answers you get at this point. Sometimes you will get answers in the same perspective. At other times you will get answers that indicate the response is from a lower perspective.

When you ask this question, depending on the original score, you will get two or three things that will make a difference and improve the situation. You might think that in asking this question you would get a list of 30 things that could potentially close the performance gap. This tends not to happen. If it does happen, you may have asked the question with the wrong emphasis. Put the emphasis on the *few things* that will make the *biggest* difference.

If you are asking this question with a group you will find the varied comments provide a rich view of the characteristics of the few things that need to change. If you do get an excessively long list you *can* follow up with one of:

What are the few, most critical things that will close the performance gap and make it a 10?

What one or two things will make the biggest difference?

What are the one or two things that will make it a 10?

It is this attention on the few things, the one or two, that will make the biggest difference that creates the focus of attention in the strategy map at each level.

Question Four: What Stops you?

You might wonder what has stopped this organization making these changes in the past. If they know these changes and improvements will make a difference, why have they not implemented them before? It is useful and important to find out what has held them back from achieving this in the past. There is a pair of questions you can use at this point. These are:

What stops you doing that today?

and

So, what do you need to do differently to achieve your objective?

Asking 'what stops you?' helps you identify the *underlying* reasons an objective is not being achieved. This question sometimes gets you an answer in the same perspective, though you are likely to get an answer from a lower perspective and particularly the learning and growth perspective.

These questions work because sometimes managers will find it easier to explain what has held them back than immediately describe what they should do about it. Asking, 'what do you have to do differently?' helps them think through what has prevented forward movement, change and improvements up until now, and what alternatives will make a difference. These two questions can help you to avoid the trap of 'if you always do what you always did, you'll always get what you always got'. After all, strategy is about change.

You can ask this question in any perspective, looking for answers from the perspectives below the one in question. In the financial perspective, asking, 'what stops you getting revenue from new sources?' might elicit the answer, 'not concentrating on the right bids' (process perspective) or even 'poor sales and marketing skills' (learning and growth). You can now check their logic by following the problem back up the tree, whilst turning the negatives into positives. In this case you might say, 'so, you believe that your poor sales and marketing skills stop you choosing the right bids to follow up on. This stops you getting revenue from new sources. So, if you could improve your sales and marketing skills, it would have a big effect on your choice of bid and therefore revenues from new clients. Is that the case?'

Both questions, 'what stops you?' and 'what will make the biggest difference?' are likely to give you some answers that are in the same perspective and others that are in a lower perspective. As you listen carefully to the answers, be sure to be clear which you are receiving and capture them appropriately.

Question Five: Validating the Answers

It is important to validate the answers you have been given. At this point you may not be sure whether you have an important leverage point or not and whether the answers will close the performance gap. There might be others that are more significant in the person's mind. There is a simple test for this. Repeat back what they have said will close the gap and ask:

Will this make it a 10?

You are likely to be closer to a 10 than the original score, though you may get the answer, 'not quite' or 'that would make it an eight'. If so, you will have to ask, 'so, what else is needed to make this a 10?' With this new answer you can again check that this will close the performance gap and produce a 10. If it is now nine or 10 out of 10, you know that you have the main contributors to the change.

Sometimes this approach uncovers a deeper issue that has not been addressed. The problem may be in the management team, the culture, the skills or the behaviours. These deeper issues usually reside in the learning and growth perspective, so probe deeper to see what may lie there. Knowing when to stop is, of course, a skill of rapport and facilitation.

This stage identifies the elements that will fill the performance gap. It is likely that there are a number of such elements, each of which contributes to part of closing the gap, and they may well work together to have a multiplying effect. The combination of, for example, marketing knowledge, skills, the process and the relationships with partners will make the whole difference.

By repeatedly asking the series of questions involving, 'what stops you?' and, 'what will close the performance gap?' you are helping people to identify what needs to change. It is these questions that distinguish a strategy map that is focused on change and improvement from an operational map that simply documents the activities of the organization, many of which may already be performing at nine or 10. You are focusing attention on the few things that will make the biggest difference in closing the performance gap.

Question Six: How do you Know?

Having worked through the first five questions, we have one question remaining. It is one that can cause controversy during strategy map development:

How do the directors and managers know which few things will make the biggest difference?

Broadly there are four schools of thought: the hypothesis and evidence school, the best practice school, the analytical school and the judgement school. You will encounter a combination of these as you work through the strategy map questions. Let us look at each school in turn and then assess the implications for practitioners tasked with developing a strategy map and its balanced scorecard.

THE 'HYPOTHESIS AND EVIDENCE' BASED SCHOOL

Quite often the management team will have a number of hypotheses about the strategy that they will have tested with research, modelling or other techniques. This 'hypothesis-based' approach is often used by strategy consultancies to test the viability of and evidence for alternative strategies, so that the management can select the one with the greatest likelihood of success, based upon the information available at the time. As a result, the management team may have commissioned market research; talked to customers; analysed successful and unsuccessful work; looked at the financial models; examined their processes and practices; assessed the skills, knowledge and capabilities of their staff; and conducted cultural surveys. They have sought evidence and from this they will have made choices about their strategy.

A strategy is a hypothesis rather than a theory, because a strategy cannot be repeatedly tested and therefore cannot be proven to be true. It can never be executed twice, in exactly the same context and circumstances, to see if it was a good strategy executed poorly or a bad strategy executed well. A strategy is not a repeatable, testable theory: it is only a hypothesis. However, if it has been researched well, and bears up to the scrutiny of that research and evidence, then it might be a sound strategy to execute. If the limits of the research are also tested, perhaps through scenario planning, then the strategy could be seen as robust in changing circumstances.

This 'hypothesis and evidence' based approach usually informs the customer and financial perspectives and the links between them and the lower perspectives. The strategy map documents this and makes this thinking explicit.

THE BEST PRACTICE SCHOOL

Sometimes the choices within the strategy map are based on practice elsewhere. This most often applies in the process, and learning and growth perspectives.

External benchmarks may be used to establish the level of ambition. Experienced managers will bring practices they know to have worked from other organizations. Consultants may be brought in to provide systematic practices that they have implemented elsewhere with success.

Whilst it might be called 'best practice', it might be merely common practice or only good practice, depending on the state of the organization. For example, where project management practices are failing, introducing an industry-wide accepted project management approach will probably make a big difference, but it will only be good practice. Where a bid process is failing, introducing a bid qualification process with gateways and reviews may make a significant difference. Where partnerships and alliances are not creating revenue, conducting a best practice alliance review will highlight where things need to improve.

Whatever the source, or extent of improvement, the best practice school will expect these practices to improve their capability, ensure their processes perform better and that this ripples through to their customers and financial results. Again, the strategy map is capturing and communicating this.

THE ANALYTICAL SCHOOL

When considering value propositions and external markets, there is a strong school of thought that is very analytical and looks for evidence to find and prove strong causal relationships. Retailers, for example, spend an enormous amount of time testing product design, positioning and shop layout to create evidence to prove that particular arrangements will increase sales by certain percentages. In the same way, detailed web analytics are used to analyse browsing patterns and shopping activity, and influence purchases on websites. Davenport and Harris (2007) provide a five-stage road map towards competing using analytics.

The analytical approach looks for quantifiable, explicit relationships between actions and results, and uses this evidence to choose what to do. It will use existing customer information and business intelligence systems to analyse the data that is available to them. The approach is intended to provide information to test the strategy prior to its use and monitor it during execution.

This analytical approach is extremely effective in the customer perspective and between the customer and process perspectives. However, the analytical school sometimes gets carried away and some practitioners like to argue that you need analytical evidence across the whole of the strategy map. They want evidence that particular skills will improve the performance of a process and therefore increase customer satisfaction and revenues. This link between skills and performance can be hard to come by. The time and effort necessary to prove this is often too great (not to mention the need to acquire a suitably large sample size). The analytical school is extremely valuable with large volumes and patterns of data that persist over time, for instance with a large sales force or large numbers of retail outlets, but a small number of staff in a variety of roles does not satisfy this criteria.

The analytical approach is useful and has its place, but do not be tempted to force every relationship on the strategy map to be proven in this way. Sometimes relationships are simply the management's judgement.

THE JUDGEMENT SCHOOL

The judgement school relies on management to make choices and decisions based upon their view, judgement and perception of the situation. It asks questions of the team, individually and as a group, such as, 'what do you *believe* will make the biggest difference?' Of course, you can ask for evidence but it is unlikely to be a statistically provable relationship. The team's answers are likely to refer to experience and their observations about what they have seen and heard from around the organization and in the marketplace.

This operates on the basis that managers are intelligent, rational, experienced people who are making judgements and decisions all the time. The role of the strategy map is to capture and document their decisions, so they can be communicated and turned into action. From a consultant's, or facilitator's, perspective it is most respectful of the management's experience and knowledge. One way to acknowledge this experience is to ask the question, in a way that refers to the person's extensive experience, 'with all your experience in the sector, what do you believe are the few things that will make the biggest difference?'

The great advantage of respecting experience and discussing beliefs is that it encourages discussion amongst the team, often about how to implement the areas they agree on as well as differences of opinion. It encourages individuals to provide evidence, anecdotes or the rationale behind their thinking. It opens up the underlying thinking and improves the quality of conversation about all aspects of the strategy.

Using this approach, the strategy map then represents the management team's judgement and beliefs about their ambition for the organization, how to change the organization and how to deliver the strategy.

IMPLICATIONS FOR FACILITATORS AND PRACTITIONERS

Most strategies, and therefore strategy maps, use a combination of these sources of information in their design. Management teams will hold beliefs and make choices and decisions from a variety of sources. The judgement school reflects the experience of the management and their collective view. The evidence school will look for hard facts. The best practice school will refer to external experience and practices to provide a quick solution that saves reinventing the wheel. The analytical school will have detailed evidence from buying patterns. In fact, the management will use their judgement about which approach to use. Each can play an important part in developing the strategy map and identifying where focus and effort need to be applied. Judgement and evidence should work together.

When you ask why people believe a relationship exists, you may get various types of response. The strategy map needs to reflect these judgements and experiences, as well as what is measurable. Various managers will have different beliefs about what are the most important things to focus on. You may even have two managers who may believe the same thing, but for different reasons. They may have the same facts and choose different actions as a consequence. Much of the art of strategy map facilitation is to bring these different beliefs to the surface, have them discussed and resolve the contradictions. In doing so, you are improving the quality of conversation and mutual understanding amongst the team.

As a facilitator, you should be sensitive when you ask, 'how do you know?' If you have not earned the right to ask it, it *may* be seen as a cheeky, rude or even impertinent question. Choose carefully how you frame the question, as it will make a big difference.

Do not get stuck in any one school of thought. All are valid. All are useful and all will be used individually and in combinations. Be aware of the sources of decisions and why people believe what they do. Collect that information and the evidence to support the thinking as you elicit the design of the strategy map. Be aware of differences of opinion and belief, and be prepared to facilitate discussions where managers have different views of the strategy, and to encourage conversation that raises, if not resolves, any issues and differences.

Finally, respect the managers for who they are: experienced managers who understand their market, who have been thinking about their strategy and now wish to articulate it. Your role is to help them. On the way, if they need a little help refining or clarifying their strategy, then so be it. However, I counsel you to start from a position of assuming they know what they want, or at least that the information is in their heads.

Managing Scope, Perspective and Detail

At any stage of the questioning it is vital to be aware of the scope, perspective and level of detail you are dealing with. This is especially important if you are the facilitator interviewing and helping the management team develop their strategy map. In the example of the bid process, the growth relied on both existing markets and new market extensions. When you are asking questions in such a situation, be sure to frame the question so the context is clear. You might separately frame questions about the existing market and the market extensions, by asking:

For your existing markets, what revenue objectives do you have?

and

For your new markets, what revenue objectives do you have?

MONITOR WHICH PERSPECTIVE THEY ARE THINKING ABOUT

As you listen to the answers it is absolutely crucial that you keep a mental track of which perspectives the answers refer to. All the time you need to be tracking the answers to check their scope, their perspective, the level of detail and any other information that is emerging. If you are working in the customer perspective you might ask, 'what objectives do your existing customers have?' This should elicit information about the customers' objectives. However, if you receive an answer about how the customers' needs are served by the organization, you can be sure, somehow, that the interviewee has moved their thinking into the process perspective. The answer has become about what the organization does, rather than what the customers want. You will need to ask the question again in a way that emphasizes the customers' perspective.

Likewise, if you have asked, 'what do you have to do well in the bid process?' you expect answers in the same (process) perspective. If you receive an answer about developing bid process capability or knowledge, you know the thinking has moved into the learning and growth perspective.

LEVEL OF DETAIL

Sometimes you want to explore the detail of an objective, remaining in its perspective. For instance, in the process perspective you may have an objective around 'well chosen bids', so you might ask 'what does identifying the right opportunities involve?' This information will be useful for the characteristics of the objective. Again, be sure what is important here. Where is the core problem? Are current revenue sources performing well, or is the real issue how to grow? Is it the whole of marketing that is broken, or just one or two aspects? Are all sales skills a problem or only specific ones? Is it all areas, or just one division that is the problem? In each case make sure you are clear about the objective, what it is a part of and the part or sub-objective that you need to concentrate on.

DOCUMENTATION ALONGSIDE THE STRATEGY MAP

As you work through these questions you will pick up a rich variety of information. All the answers you will receive during the interviews and discussions are useful and important information, even if they are about something you did not expect.

It is important that these 'side issues' are acknowledged, recorded and tracked. They are obviously important to the person answering the questions, and so will undoubtedly come in useful later. You can always come back to them. You want to be sure that you have covered the detail sufficiently before you move on.

Make sure that you capture any actions, initiatives, improvements and changes that are mentioned along the way. Whilst they might be a detail at this stage, they will prove useful later when you are reviewing the objectives to ensure that the actions and initiatives are addressing the changes believed necessary to achieve the level of performance and improvement.

Conclusion

This chapter has given you the precision questions that you need to ask, during interviews or a workshop, to work your way through a strategy map and ensure you get the right sort of answers.

It has provided the overall sequence to follow and the questions that you need to ask. It has covered identifying the performance gap and eliciting the few things that will make the biggest difference to that gap. It has explained how to establish that the performance gap will be closed with the validation question. The 'marks out of 10' question allows you to get a rich answer and a deeper understanding of somebody's thinking without going immediately to measures. This chapter has also increased your awareness of the different ways that directors and managers may have come to believe or know things, and the implications of the various approaches.

These questions will work in both one-to-one situations and in groups, though you would clearly support the approach with further facilitation methods when dealing with a larger team. The principles are the same.

9 *Objectives before Measures*

The previous chapters have been dealing with the structure of strategy maps and the identification of the objectives in those maps. The emphasis has been on objectives, rather than measures. This is because the objectives in the strategy map are the framework within which the scorecard part of the balanced scorecard is developed. The principle of developing and detailing the objectives, before any measures are chosen, is fundamental to modern balanced scorecard design. It avoids many problems such as measure mania, the tyranny of targets and feeding the beast, which are caused by a design process that leaps straight to measures, bypassing the development of the objective.

This chapter first explains the reasons behind the 'objectives before measures' principle. It then explains how to develop the characteristics of an objective, so you can then develop the detailed measures, actions and responsibilities to support that objective. Finally, it explains how to avoid the most common and damaging mistakes that are made when objectives are defined. Overall, this will help you develop better measures that you can communicate more effectively, so avoiding problems like measure mania and the tyranny of targets.

The principles in this chapter apply equally to the objectives in each perspective. Having the techniques from this chapter clear will help you apply the more subtle aspects of the development of objectives specific to each perspective that are detailed in the following chapters.

Collecting Existing Measures

The whole approach to measure design in this chapter is summed up by, 'do not start with measures: don't look at measures until you are completely ready'. The emphasis is on the development of the objectives, before measures are considered.

It would be foolish to completely ignore the existing measurement regime. It is therefore useful if you have already done an exercise to gather the existing measures, but only for reference as you develop the objectives. As your set of strategy maps develops you can place these existing measures against the objectives at various levels in your strategy maps to identify gaps and areas of overemphasis. There will inevitably be some existing measures that are valuable and will serve well. Others may act as an indirect measure or partial measure of a characteristic. Some characteristics will be completely omitted from the existing measures. Some measures will be useful as surrogates until better ones are developed. The trick is not to prejudge which should be in and out. Rather, wait until the stage of choosing how to measure to see where measures are available and where there are gaps to be filled.

The Framework

In the previous chapters we developed strategy maps by identifying the objectives in each perspective. The strategy map describes the cause and effect relationship between objectives across the perspectives. The scorecard details each objective and how it will be achieved. To develop the scorecard we need additional detail. This consists of:

> The objective. What is to be achieved? A short name that summarizes the objective, appropriate to its perspective.

> Its characteristics. What are the characteristics of success and what will show we are making progress? The overall detail, characteristics and qualities of the objective.

> The measures. How will we know we have succeeded and are making progress? What you choose to measure the characteristics.

> The targets. What level of ambition do you have for the measures, and when do you want to have achieved them?

> The projects and actions. What needs to be done? Those actions necessary to deliver the objective, which may include both major projects and small tasks. What investment in change?

> Responsibility. Who has overall responsibility for the delivery of the objective?

Using this overall framework to develop an objective and the scorecard detail behind it means that, when evaluating the objective, you can: assess and describe progress towards the objective, qualitatively; back that up with facts and evidence (the measures); assess progress against the target or ambition; examine trends in the measures; show and explain the status of actions and tasks against the objective; show and explain progress with projects; and provide a judgement score to supplement the evidence. This detail is also helpful when you are developing the scorecard. When reporting progress on the scorecard you will need a different format. It will also need an overall assessment that includes: an assessment of the progress towards the overall objective, an assessment of progress with each measure within the objective, and assessments of projects and actions designed to support the objective. You will also need the actual measures: their current state, how the measures are changing, how the target for each measure varies over time and any remedial actions you intend to take, including timescales and responsibilities.

The Benefits of Objectives before Measures

AVOID PREMATURE MEASURE CHOICE AND NARROW MEASURE DESIGN

Developing objectives before measures prevents premature measure design. There is a tendency for people to leap straight to measures instead of defining more clearly what they want to measure. In doing so they are assuming a whole host of rules about what a measure should be. As a result, they end up managing only that which they think they can measure, rather than choosing measures for that which they want to manage. In this situation you are dictated to by the measures, and end up managing what you can measure, rather than finding ways of measuring what you want to manage.

It is common practice, but poor practice, to decide *how* to measure before it is clear *what* you want to manage and measure. Unfortunately these decisions are often taken at the same time. This limits the thinking about measures to only that which the person thinks they can measure: usually limited to those things that are very tangible or quantifiable (money, activity, outputs and physical deliverables). These quantifiable measures are useful, but they are also a narrow view of the organization and how to measure it. This narrow thinking associated with premature measure choice encourages greater numbers of financial and process measures and leads to the imbalance that the balanced scorecard sets out to address.

You want to measure progress towards your objective. However, this often gets interpreted as 'all objectives should be measures'. If that were the case, why distinguish between an objective and a measure? They would be the same. In fact, this is a mistake many practitioners make. Thinking that all objectives should be measureable leads to the mistaken idea that all objectives should be measures. This is clearly inappropriate and nonsense. Your conception of what an objective might be should not be prejudiced by what you think you can measure.

Far better is the process of deciding what you want to measure before you think about how to measure those characteristics. This approach enables you to identify measures that you might not have thought of had you leapt straight to measures. It allows you to be clear about the difference between the objective and its measurement, allows the use of surrogate measures and indicators rather than direct measures, and helps you to describe your strategy rather than simply to measure it.

CLARITY OF THINKING AND COMMUNICATION

Developing the characteristics of objectives encourages a far richer conversation within the team about what you are trying to achieve. There is less likely to be an assumption about what a short, three word objective means when it is backed up with a thirty word description of its characteristics. This is especially true when the characteristics have been discussed and developed as a team. Of course, if people want to quantify the objective in a conversation then let them, but also gather the characteristics and qualities of that objective. A statement like, 'we want £500m of revenue', still requires clarification as to the quality of the revenue, its sources and whether it is substitute revenue or from new customers.

When it is time to communicate to the rest of the organization, having the rich story of objectives and their characteristics alongside the measures makes communicating what you really mean far easier. If you communicate just the measures and targets, people have to work out what the objectives are. I call this 'the measure mind-read'. This is further described in Chapter 20. When you communicate objectives and measures together, you raise the level of conversation from measurement to an achievement which you intend to measure.

MORE HOLISTIC – LESS DIVISIVE

This approach of objectives before measures is also more holistic. One of the underlying causes of the dysfunctional behaviour experienced in performance management is where individual measures and targets look at only specific parts of an organization in isolation. As a result, staff are asked to achieve targets that are locally optimal, but dysfunctional in the big picture and wider system. If, instead, they are asked to achieve an objective which has a wider context, and is detailed by a set of measures and targets, they are provided with a more complete picture of what is required. This is a far wider picture that is less likely to be misinterpreted.

EASIER TO REFINE AND REVISE MEASURES

In the absence of objectives, people designing performance management systems often compensate for problems with measures, by adding more measures in the hope that they are communicating and covering all the aspects. Unfortunately this leads to measure mania, which is characterized by overload, confusion and unnecessary detail.

In contrast, objectives set direction: this is what *we* want to achieve. By defining the objective and its characteristics first, you have a basis for choosing measures of that objective. You can then ask, 'what should we measure for this objective' and then, 'what is the best way to measure this?'

This approach makes measure design, and redesign, both simpler and more systematic. It means that when looking at the measures of an objective you can always check to see how complete a picture they provide of the objective and its characteristics. You can tell how well they inform progress against the objective. You can tell how well they cover all the characteristics of the objective. You can tell if they are true, fair measures of an objective, or surrogates used to get a feel for the situation in the absence of better information.

A significant benefit of having objectives from which measures are derived comes when you find that one of the measures is not fit for purpose or not functioning well. When you have an objective, and its characteristics, you have a point of reference against which to choose a better measure. When a poor measure is used temporarily, it is clear that it is merely an indication of the objective rather than a true and accurate measure. It is also easier to eliminate the less effective measures and bring in better ones. When a new measure is introduced, people can see why the new measure is better than the old one when they also have the objective and its characteristics as a point of reference.

Developing Objectives and their Characteristics

When you are developing the objectives, and the balanced scorecard behind them, you use the same basic approach in each perspective. This section explains the overall approach, so that the subsequent chapters can concentrate on the refinements and subtleties in each perspective. No matter which perspective you are dealing with, the approach to developing the objectives in that perspective is fundamentally the same. The basic sequence to choose and design measures for an objective is:

1. Have a clear statement of the objective
2. Detail the characteristics of the objective
3. Choose the most important characteristics of the objective to measure
4. Then, and only then, choose how best to measure those characteristics of the objective.

STEP ONE: IDENTIFY THE OBJECTIVE

The first step is to identify the objective. The questions in chapter eight will have helped you to do this. At this point you want a simple statement of the objective, appropriate to the perspective you are in.

They are called perspectives because they look at the organization from a particular viewpoint, or perspective. Each viewpoint is different. This idea of distinct perspectives sounds obvious, but when people are developing the objectives in a strategy map they often forget this. When you are clear that the perspectives are quite distinct, you can start to state objectives, develop their separate characteristics and be clear what the relationship between them is.

No matter which perspective you are in, first obtain a short description of the objective, then detail its characteristics.

STEP TWO: DETAIL THE OBJECTIVE'S CHARACTERISTICS

The approach to developing the objective is fundamentally the same, no matter which perspective you are in. The question to ask is, 'what are the characteristics (or qualities) of this objective?'

I use the expression 'characteristics of the objective', but 'qualities of the objective' is just as effective, as long as you do not confuse qualities with quality.

A director had responsibility for 'quality measures' in his organization and wanted ways to define what quality meant for his organization, as 'quality' tends to be intangible, indefinable and difficult to measure. I asked him to choose something for which he had difficulty defining quality. He chose the care that his staff provided for the people with learning disabilities that they supported. So, I asked him to tell me what were the qualities or characteristics of those staff who did an exceptional job. He then started to describe their characteristics. They listen well, spend time with the people they support; they put themselves out; they talk to the person's circle of support, their family and friends. They encourage the person they support to express themselves and give them opportunities to try new things. They make time for the person. Of course, they do the basics well, look after the person's health, cleanliness, food, drug administration, money, care, welfare and basic needs, but the best care workers go much further.

These were the characteristics of 'excellent care', the phrase from my original question. Notice at this point we were not trying to measure these qualities. Rather, we were trying to express and define them. Once we had these qualities, we could then think about which to measure and then how to measure them.

This example shows how easy it is to start by describing the qualities (or characteristics) of high performers. If I had asked the director to think how to measure high performers we might have been there all day. The thinking that was exposed here would never have been articulated. He would have had to have thought about the characteristics and then articulate a measure, using whatever filter he had in his head to design and select each measure. Asking for characteristics obtains a far richer conversation. This example also shows how easily the characteristics of an objective can be developed.

There are two approaches you can use to capture these characteristics. You can simply list the characteristics as a piece of text. Alternatively, you can use a more structured approach that splits the characteristics of any objective into two parts. The first part describes what is necessary to make progress towards the objective. The second part characterizes what it will be like when the objective has been achieved. You will notice that the second question, 'how will we know we have got there?', is similar to that used when developing the future thinking. You may well have gathered some of this information already in the earlier stages of development. Using the characteristics of both progress and the end state is not only richer in its description than simply listing the characteristics. It is also more useful for later when we come to look at measures of progress as well as the end position. This more structured approach is most easily captured and recorded using the framework shown in Table 9.1.

Table 9.1   Objective development framework

Perspective: Objective:	
How will we know we are making progress? (Lead)	**How will we know we have got there? (Lag)**
Projects and actions:	
Issues:	

At the top of the framework we write the relevant perspective and the short summary phrase that describes the objective. Having the name of the perspective next to the objective reminds people which perspective they are dealing with. That way, should topics arise that fit in a different perspective they can be put aside to be included in a more suitable objective.

The main part of the framework is divided into two sides. The right hand side describes 'how you will know that the objective has been achieved'. Here you describe the characteristics of success (not the measures yet). The left hand side describes 'how you will know you are making progress towards the objective'. Again, do not put measures here, rather include the characteristics, activities and behaviours you want to encourage. These should be the characteristics you are expecting to see that will help you move towards the achievement of the objective. Characteristics that came from asking questions about closing the performance gap.

As you do this, make sure you are clear of the difference between the characteristics of achievement of the objective and the characteristics of making progress. The characteristics of 'how do we know we have got there?' provide potential lag indicators for the objective. They tell you that you have already succeeded. The characteristics of 'how do we tell we are making progress?' provide potential leading indicators. The word 'characteristics' is deliberately chosen to move people away from measures. 'Qualities' works as well. What *characteristics* or *qualities* will tell you that you are making progress?

As this framework is completed it will inevitably raise ideas, issues and discussions. The lower portion of the framework is a place to capture these, so they can fit into other parts of the overall balanced scorecard. You may pick up information about the volume of activity, number of staff, problems with the process, or impediments to achieving the objective. You will hear about initiatives and actions that are designed to bring about the objective. You will also hear about measures and even targets: some will be associated with the process, others with the objective. Some items may be put aside so they are addressed later. Some will be noted and addressed in the discussion. The two sections at the bottom are used to capture these as they arise. All this information is useful and may eventually be needed for the subsequent scorecard details. Take care not to lose any of this.

A common mistake is to have characteristics in one perspective that should be in a different perspective. A common example is to let process statements get into the customer perspective or to have customer statements in the 'how do *we* know *we* have got there?' part of the process perspective. It is also easy to let learning and growth pieces drift up into the 'how will we know we are making progress?' part of the process perspective. There are two ways to avoid these mistakes. First, filter them out as the issues arise: this requires the facilitator to spot them when they appear and mark them to be moved into other perspectives. Second, review the completed information to make sure it is consistent and makes sense as a complete story.

This framework works perfectly well for each perspective, and can be used unmodified for the process perspective. However, it is useful to refine it slightly when you are dealing with each perspective.

In the customer perspective you have to change the wording of the questions to ensure you are looking from the customer's perspective. It is also important to note from which customer's perspective you are talking. So the framework becomes, 'how will I know (as this customer) *I* am making progress?' and 'how will I know (as this customer) that *I* have got there?' You can see how this works for an example in Table 9.2. In this case, there are three parties relating to the customer: procurement, project delivery and operations. Therefore characteristics are included for each separate party.

Table 9.2   Example of objective development from customer perspective

A customer objective and its characteristics	
Customer: Procurement team **Overall objective:** 'I want a cost-effective solution': 'Before I sign the contract, I want to be sure that this will be a cost-effective solution, using proven technology, delivered on time to budget and quality, and that it will provide long-term, low operational costs.'	
How will *I* know *I* am making progress? (Lead) (The customer says...)	How will *I* know *I* have got there? (Lag) (The customer says...)
Procurement I expect the proposals to represent value for money against my budget. I want proven technology. I want evidence that they have done this before.	**Procurement** I want a thorough business case from a proven supplier. I want to see the technology in action. I want others to confirm the technology works.
Project delivery I want a supplier that will deliver on time. I want to be sure the project will run on time.	**Project delivery** Evidence of project delivered on time, and of cost and quality. Evidence of the figures. Costs we can validate. I want to talk to suppliers who have done it before.
Operations I expect low operational costs. I need to be convinced that disposal and decommissioning costs will be low.	**Operations** A guarantee. A cap on operating costs. A disposal solution built in.

With the financial perspective, you would expect to see aspects of financial characteristics in both parts of the objective. In this case you may well be looking at predicted income versus actual income, and predicted margin versus actual margin. This is usually how the lead financial indicators are compared with the lag financial measures. In this example, the two aspects of the objective, the revenue and the margin, have been separated out in the characteristics. This is often useful when you want to ensure that the whole of the objective description is covered in the characteristics.

When using the framework for learning and growth objectives, you will need to be extra careful of projects. Whilst these projects will improve capabilities, skills and knowledge, it is the improved knowledge, skills and capabilities that should be in the characteristics, not the projects.

No matter which perspective you are working in, you will still be defining the lead and lag characteristics of the objective. You simply adjust the titles in each framework to suit the perspective you are working on. I strongly recommend that you do not move on to measure selection until you have completely defined the characteristics of all the objectives in each perspective of your strategy map. This will ensure that you are clear on all the objectives within each perspective and also between perspectives. When dealing with characteristics, it is easy to put the same, or very similar, characteristics in two different objectives. A little rationalization is often needed, and it is best done before you start to think about measures.

STEP THREE: CHOOSING WHAT TO MEASURE

Once you are sure that the characteristics explain the objectives properly, you can start choosing which characteristics you wish to measure. You can now ask, 'which of these characteristics would be most useful to know about?' In other words, 'what would be best to measure?'

The simple way to choose which characteristics you want to measure for any objective is to choose the two or three characteristics in each objective which best communicate the intention of the objective. You must do this without regard for how you might measure them. How you will measure them is a separate question. What you are looking for are the few characteristics that best encapsulate the objective. I tend to encourage the client to choose at most three: one or two from each side. Sometimes this results in four characteristics being identified. Sometimes it results in only two. What is more important is that you are picking those that are most important in driving behaviours (lead) or defining outputs (lag) and what is the intended outcome for that objective in that perspective. At this stage simply circle the characteristics you have identified.

In some cases the client wishes to have many more than three or four measures of the characteristics. This will depend upon the granularity of the objective. For instance, the example used earlier of the characteristics of high-performing staff contains a very wide range of characteristics. In part this is because the objective is very wide in its scope, and so you might want to look at measures for each aspect of the characteristics. For example, the characteristic, *'they listen well, spend time with the people they support; they put themselves out; they talk to the person's circle of support, their family and friends'*, actually contains at least four characteristics that the client might want to encourage and could potentially measure in some way.

Your list of characteristics is not constrained by the question, 'how would I measure that?' The emphasis is on, 'what would be best to measure?' Once we know this we can work out how.

STEP FOUR: CHOOSING HOW TO MEASURE

Now you have chosen the characteristics that you want to communicate, emphasize, measure and manage, you can start to think about how best to measure those characteristics. Extend the framework so that you can place possible candidate measures beneath the characteristics, by extending Figure 9.1. Then you can select from the candidates the preferred measures for the most important characteristics.

You will typically find that this approach has opened up a set of characteristics that are not being measured within the organization at the moment. I usually find that between 30 and 50 per cent of the identified characteristics, ones that the management team would like to measure, are not being measured at the moment. So some measure development will be needed.

Even where they are being measured already, it is well worth checking that the existing measure is a true representation of the characteristic that you want to be measured. Quite often you will find that a measure is similar, but not exactly the same, and some

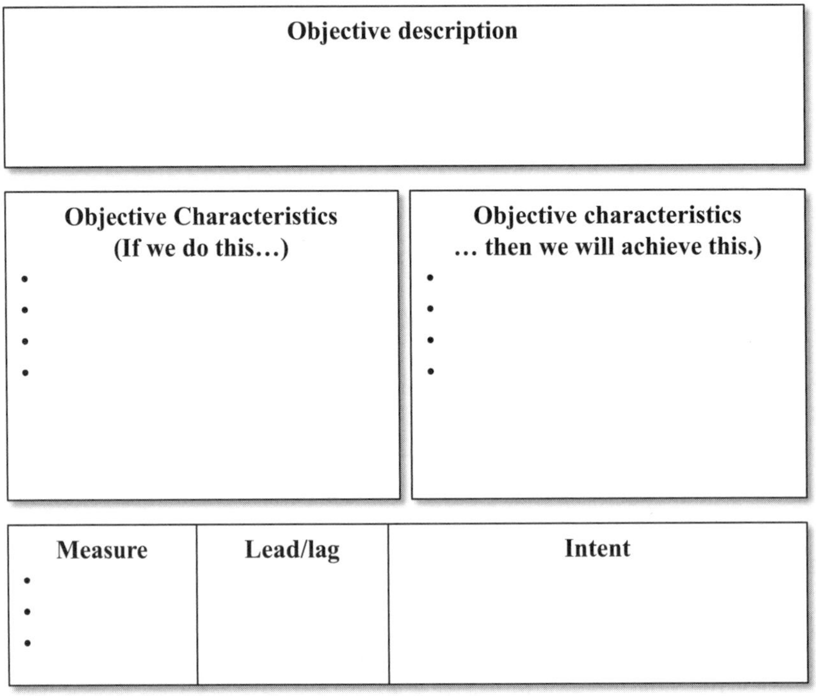

Objective description		

Objective Characteristics (If we do this...)	Objective characteristics ... then we will achieve this.)	
• • • •	• • •	

Measure	Lead/lag	Intent
• • •		

Figure 9.1 Extending the objective framework to include potential measures

refinement or clarification will be necessary. Perhaps the measures are not as well defined or specific as the characteristics that have been chosen.

It is useful at this point to make a clear distinction between measures and indicators. Unfortunately the two words are used interchangeably, when they are really quite different. Imagine a table in a room. A measure of the size of the table might be, 'it is six feet by three feet'. An indication of the size of the table might be, 'it will seat six people'. 'Six feet by three feet' measures its size using indisputable units. 'It seats six', indicates its size using units we can understand, but are merely indicative of its size. An indication is clearly not the same as a measure. There is also the question of usefulness. To a carpenter, being asked to make a table that will sit six people is pretty useless. To a restaurant owner thinking about the people that the restaurant can seat, knowing that a table seats six is very useful – far more useful than knowing it is six feet by three feet, though knowing it is six by three might help in planning the maximum number of tables that would fit into the room. The question is, 'is an indication (indicator) useful, or do we need a more useful measure?' It is a question of usefulness.

Sometimes you might be willing to accept a surrogate for the measure you would really like. It may not be a perfect measure, but it may be a useful indicator for the moment, until some better one can be developed. This is often the case with customer measures. Be clear about where you are using a surrogate, its limitations, and when a better measure or indicator can be put in its place.

Both qualitative and quantitative measures can be useful. Use both, and do not focus on only quantitative measures. As we have already discussed, judgements from people can be as revealing as the quantitative measures, and together they help build judgement backed up with evidence.

There is also the difference between monitoring and measuring. You might monitor progress, by looking at and paying attention to how things are done, as well as measuring activities and outcomes. If you let your staff know you will be paying more attention to a particular activity, measuring it as well may not be necessary. This can be a useful approach where a measure is poor or not yet available and where you wish to make clear the intention of the objective.

When there is the need for a new measure, you can use Table 9.3, which provides a checklist of aspects to think through when developing and introducing a new measure.

Table 9.3   Checklist for the development of new measures

Aspect of measure	Description
Strategic objective	The name of the objective
Perspective	In which perspective
Measure	The name of the measure
Measurement intent	Measuring which characteristic. Why selected?
Frequency of update	How often it is to be calculated
Units of measure	The units in which it will be reported
Measurement formula	The formula for calculating the measure
Assumptions	Identify any assumptions that underlie the formula
Measure availability	Currently available. Available with minor changes. Not available
Data elements and sources	The data required to calculate this measure and its sources
Next steps to report	What has to happen to report the measure
Target setting approach	Source of target or target setting approach
Target setting responsibility	Named person
Accountability for meeting the target	Named person
Reporting responsibility	Named person or team
Measure availability	When will the measure and targets first be available?
Targets	What targets are to be set

Words of Warning

How you word your objectives will have an influence on the understanding of the objectives and of the whole strategy map. The clearer the wording, the more effectively it will communicate the meaning and the easier it will be to work out how to measure it. There are many common mistakes that people make that undermine an objective, and ways in which you can improve an objective's wording. This section provides ways you can word your objectives more effectively.

ELIMINATE VAGUENESS IN THE OBJECTIVE

A very common mistake is to use the word 'management' or 'manage' in the description of an objective. Phrases like 'manage customers better', 'well managed projects' and 'a well managed marketing pipeline' are quite vague and leave great room for interpretation. Where an objective is vague or the objective is being described as an activity, you can ask questions related to how the activity affects each perspective to tease out what is really meant.

It is helpful to ask questions that make the phrase far more precise and actionable. You might ask, 'what is the precise purpose of this activity/process?' or 'what specific part will support the strategy?' In the 'management' example above, it is useful to ask, 'what aspect of the management of this objective needs to be improved?' This moves the improvement from a general need to a more specific need that others will be able to interpret and act upon. For instance, 'a well managed marketing pipeline' might be about control and information being available. It might be about more effective following up of marketing initiatives. It might be that no one is actually managing the marketing process, as opposed to the sales process. Depending upon the circumstances, a better version might be, 'higher sales conversion', 'improved visibility of marketing' or 'the right sales and marketing skills'.

By being specific, the objective acquires greater clarity. It becomes much more obvious what actions are needed to achieve it. It is helpful to ask, 'what specific aspect of management is the issue here?' In some cases it may be the management process. In others it may be the capability of the management to deliver the process. This only becomes clear when less general and more specific words are used. Being specific allows you to communicate what you really mean and saves people having to guess.

THE RESULT, NOT THE ACTIVITY

Sometimes objectives are confused with activities. For instance, 'selling' is an activity or process, not an objective. If you have an objective that is initially stated as an activity, then restate it as the end result rather than the activity. Instead of 'selling' the objective might be 'a systematic sales process that wins high margin business' or 'a compelling sales proposition that engages customers'.

This use of activities instead of objectives occurs frequently in the learning and growth perspective. You may have statements such as 'more sales training', but again this is an activity not an objective. The objective might be 'improved sales skills', 'a high quality network', 'a deep understanding of the customer' or any other aspects that could be developed to support the sales process. It is the end result in each perspective that will have an effect on the objective in the higher perspectives.

OBJECTIVES, NOT PROJECTS

As you work through these objectives you will encounter many projects stated as objectives. Whilst you have to deliver the project, the objective is not simply to complete the project, but to deliver the benefits of the project. You will need to restate the project as the eventual benefits of the project, rather than the project name. For instance, the project to implement a customer relationship management system might be about delivering the objective, 'understand our customers better'.

The way to identify these is to recognize that projects have a beginning and an end. Delivering the project is merely an interim objective en route to something bigger. Train staff, implement the new IT system and reorganize the department are examples of projects that have a finite duration: they are not persistent objectives, but short-term actions. The purpose of the training, once it is complete, is to develop skills so you have a capability that persists in the organization. The purpose of the new IT system, once it is installed, is to improve operations within the area in which the system will be delivered. The purpose of the reorganization, once everyone is in their new role, may be more effective working, customers served better or reduced costs. In each case, the project has a beginning and end, but the project is merely a part of the way to achieve and develop capability within the organization.

To get from a project or action to an objective, ask, 'what capability is this project helping to develop?' Supplementary questions such as, 'is this a short-term project or a persistent objective?', 'what is the real purpose?' and 'what difference will this project make?' will also help you to identify the sustainable and persistent capability that the organization is trying to develop. No matter how intense and important the project may feel at the time, remember that the project is a means to the end, not the end in itself.

THE OBJECTIVE, NOT THE MEASURE OR THE TARGET

Avoid objectives that are stated as measures. The disadvantage of an objective that is a measure is that you are prejudging what the measure will be and limiting your ability to refine it later to produce a better measure of the objective. This happens most often when you are dealing with objectives in the financial perspective, as there is often a direct relationship between the financial measures and the objectives. Usually there is richness in the objective that the measure alone will not communicate. Increases in revenue or profitability are often about the *quality* of the revenue as much as the *quantity*. Simply saying, 'increase revenue by 20 per cent' does not explain where and how that will come about, where it will come from or the margin associated with that revenue. The source of the revenues or costs savings can also be important. Does the revenue come from new business or from cannibalizing existing business? Where do costs savings or working capital improvements come from? To move from financial measures to the financial objective, ask, 'what are the characteristics of this improvement in the financial measure?' and 'why is it important?' It is useful to have the revenue target, but also build in the description and its characteristics.

The same is true in other perspectives. Stating objectives as measures often happens when people apply the rule that all objectives should be measurable. This does not mean that all objectives should be measures: that is quite different. Deciding whether you can measure the objective when you conceive it is prejudging and narrowing what you might think of as an objective. All objectives become measureable once their characteristics have been defined.

When a measure is mentioned in discussions, always acknowledge it and record it, but place it on one side for later. It may well be a useful measure of the objective (but it might not be). When you encounter measures, translate them into objectives before they reach the strategy map. To get to the objective behind the measure, you can ask:

What does measuring this tell you?

What does knowing that give you?

How does knowing that help you?

If you are being given specific targets (e.g. increase sales by 10 per cent, train 30 per cent of the staff, or reduce errors to < 0.5 per cent), you can ask similar questions to move to the objectives. For instance:

What does achieving that target do for the process/customer/finances?

How will striving towards that target make a difference?

How will achieving that target make a difference?

Where does that target contribute to the strategy?

In each case you are seeking the underlying objective that the measure or target is communicating.

OBJECTIVES AND RESPONSIBILITY

Sometimes you will receive suggestions for objectives that are statements about responsibilities. For instance, 'we have to complete compliance reports' or 'we have to be open seven days a week'. These are useful because they will help with the scope of the objective. To convert a responsibility into an objective, you ask:

What does this team have to deliver/achieve?

If you are successful, what difference do you make to the organization… to the customers… to the finances… to the strategy?

What is the most significant thing that you have to achieve next year?

What difference do you want to make to the team?

In each case, also be clear whose responsibility it is, as this will help you with the scope and context of the strategy map and tell you if you are wandering.

SUMMARIZE THE CHARACTERISTICS OF THE OBJECTIVE

When you have all the characteristics, revisit the short summary of the objective to see if you can improve it and make it clearer. Look for an adjective associated with the objective.

This gives you an indication of the qualities of the objective so, subsequently, you can know how the objective is being achieved. Phrases such as 'simpler processes', 'higher quality revenues', 'appropriately skilled people', 'clear leadership' and 'trusted staff', with all the detail behind them, help to communicate what it is about the noun that you are trying to achieve. In each case, what you are trying to achieve should be obvious from the short phrase and the more detailed characteristics.

If you are struggling with a name for an objective and you find that different people in the group are describing the objective differently, it is highly likely that they have different interpretations of what the objective actually means. They are in danger of developing a vague label that hides what we really mean. Rather than trying to resolve the name from two conflicting versions, drive into the detail and get both parties to describe the objective in more detail. As soon as you do this it will start to become apparent where the agreements and where the differences lie. Then the differences can be resolved and you can reach an agreed wording for the objective. Trying to get to the wording too early will turn the whole strategy map into a set of vague jargon statements in which people have unresolved, different interpretations of what the objectives mean, that will never be understood or implemented.

Conclusions

Having an objective before you start specifying measures is fundamental to strategy maps and any balanced scorecards that want to get beyond a collection of measures in a table. However, merely having a short phrase is only the first part. The better you can detail, characterize and define the qualities of the objective, the easier it becomes to choose what will be best to measure. Then you can choose how.

This approach of developing the characteristics of the objective before you decide what to measure and how to measure, has several benefits. It means that you can be clearer which are measures of progress and which are measures of the end objective. You can also easily check whether the set of measures covers the whole of the objective, and communicate the characteristics of that objective. You can be clearer which are measures and which indicators of the characteristics. If a measure does not work, then it is easy to drop back a step and find another, more appropriate measure. Your targets and incentives will have a context, and so you can avoid inappropriate and narrow targets that tend to create dysfunctional behaviour. Having established these general principles, the following chapters explain how to think about objectives in each perspective.

V *Detailing the Perspectives*

Part V is the most detailed part of this book. It provides you with the specific approach to developing the objectives in each and every perspective of your strategy map. It will help you ensure each perspective provides a unique perspective. A perspective that is linked to others objectives, in other perspectives, to tell the overall story of your strategy.

Executives will find that each perspective captures a particular view of the organization's strategy that builds up to an overall story. A story that, when captured, will make it far easier to communicate your strategy to staff and engage them. It will also make it far easier to manage the execution of the strategy and refine it should that be necessary as you learn from the implementation. Practitioners will find detailed guidance on the subtle differences between the approaches in each perspective. This will help you ensure all aspects of the strategy are captured and communicated as an overall coherent story. From this story your scorecard can be developed.

A Note On Framing Your Strategy Map

When you are developing your strategy map, place your organization's purpose or mission statement at the top of the strategy map. Then place your organization's values at the bottom of the strategy map. I put these statements at the top and bottom of every strategy map I create. It has several advantages. It makes clear that the strategy is part of the overriding purpose of the organization and is supported by the organization's values. It provides a test of coherency between the strategy, the organization's overall purpose and its values and they complete the story of the strategy when read from the strategy map. It also tests whether there are any omissions between the purpose and the strategy as stated.

The purpose and values also provide pivot points for cascading the strategy map. As the strategy is cascaded to each business unit, they are emphasised on each strategy map. Each unit should be thinking about how it contributes, through its strategy, to the overall strategy, purpose and values. If a sub-unit has a local purpose or mission statement it can be placed underneath the overriding one, as this will ensure consistency and make any inconsistency between them immediately apparent. They will need to say, 'our overall purpose is to... corporate mission statement... and to support this as a department we need to ensure we... local mission statement'

10 *The Customer Perspective and Customer Objectives*

Perhaps the most important perspective in strategy map design is the customer perspective. Having the right objectives in this perspective makes all the difference to the rest of the strategy map.

The most important feature of customer objectives is that they are written from the customer's perspective – otherwise, why call it the customer perspective? If you take nothing else away from this chapter, take this one point.

This chapter builds upon the value chain analysis you used earlier, whilst also considering different ways to develop your customer objectives. One way is to derive your customer objectives from generic models of competitive advantage, or customer value propositions. These provide useful checklists, but can lead to quite generic customer objectives and other problems with the strategy map. A wider value chain approach that looks at the customers' processes in detail can give you a much richer and more useful view. It makes it easier to develop the customers' objectives and can lead to more insights about their behaviours and needs. It makes it easier to identify measures for your customers' activities and reactions, and to explain the story from their perspective.

The purpose of this perspective is to represent the needs of your customers, so you can describe how to satisfy them (as objectives in your process perspective). You also want to receive a financial return (as defined by your financial perspective).

There are three steps to developing customer objectives:

1. Identify customer layers, groups and types
2. Develop objectives for each type of customer from each one's perspective. This involves:
   a. Understanding the customers' value chain or processes
   b. Understanding their needs and identifying their objectives (from their perspective)
   c. Detailing their objectives (from their perspective)
3. Check you will deliver your strategy by addressing these objectives of your customers.

The Biggest Mistake in the Customer Perspective

There is one serious mistake you can make with the customer perspective that will undermine your strategy and strategy map. It is unfortunately very common. It is to believe that what *you* produce for the customer is what the customer wants, then to state your objectives as if they were your customers' objectives.

This mistake occurs widely in organizations, who then translate this error on to their strategy maps and their scorecards. It is even more common in balanced scorecards that omit strategy maps, because measures are developed without a context. Without explicit customer objectives, it is easy to drift into this thinking.

The consequence of this mistake is that you put *what you deliver* into the customer perspective. For example, 'provide excellent customer service' is an objective often placed in the customer perspective. Who is the subject of this sentence and who is the object? The subject is the organization, '*We* provide excellent customer service...' The (unstated) object is the external customer, 'we provide excellent customer service *to these customers*'. This is clearly not an objective from the customers' perspective. If it were, they, the customers, would be the subject of the sentence. They might say, 'I want excellent customer service (from whoever can provide it for me)'. This analysis of the subject and the object of the sentence that describes the objective is the easiest way to identify this common mistake.

If you populate the customer perspective with what your organization delivers, your organization's activities and processes move into the customer perspective. This then moves the capabilities you need to develop (the learning and growth perspective) into the process perspective. Suddenly, the strategy map has been reduced from four to three perspectives, because the customers' perspective has been lost. The story of the strategy is undermined because the customers' view is missing.

The solution lies in how you ask questions about the customer perspective and how you word the customer objectives themselves. Over the years, I have seen many strategy maps and even more balanced scorecards that have made the mistake of losing the customers' view. Fortunately, it is easy to correct, once it is realized. It is even easier to avoid. Asking the question in the form, 'If you are the customer, what specifically do you mean by "excellent customer service"', will get you a different answer from a different perspective. You are asking the person to think as if they are the customer *and then* to respond *as if they are* the customer.

I encourage clients to include either 'I' or 'me' in every customer objective. Often it is helpful to start with 'I want...' There are variations with the same effect: 'I need...', 'Tell me...' and 'Help me...' It does not matter which you use. They add variety and emphasis, as long as they have the first person singular as the customer. This simple change to the first person ensures that you are positioning objectives *from the customers' perspective* rather than your organization's perspective. It forces the person stating the objective to first choose a customer before they answer as that customer. This might seem like linguistic trickery, but customer objectives should be written from the customers' perspective; otherwise, why call it the customer perspective?

Despite this 'I want...' approach, you will often come up against corporate speak. For example, 'I want... a product that is differentiated in the market and provides a sustainable solution'. Let's be frank: customers do not usually use this sort of language. It is yet another reflection of what the customer wants being what the company provides. To avoid corporate speak, it is useful to express the need colloquially, as if in a conversation with a human (Levine et al. 2000). The earlier sentence might be better stated as, 'I want something that makes me look smart and will last'. If you have direct quotes from your customer research, use them. They will help you move away from corporate speak to what the customers really say, and it will help your employees speak the language their customers actually use.

These techniques ensure you are looking and speaking from the customers' perspective. They add dramatically to the emphasis when you tell the story of the strategy. You can see how this works in the various examples from the customer perspectives of different strategy maps. The technology company's customers say, 'I want a credible solution that addresses my long-term operational needs'. The retail customers are saying, 'I expect expertise from you' and 'I want convenience'.

As well as looking for 'I' or 'we', a further test ensures you are thinking about things from the customers' perspective. Look at the existing customer measures. Are they measures of what you produce, or what the customers actually do and feel, as expressed by the customers themselves?

It is important that the objectives in the customer perspective relate to the organization's purpose or mission, because this is where you will add detail and bring it to life. So, as you work through this perspective ask questions which link the customer groups to the purpose, such as, 'Which customers does our mission serve?' and 'What need of our customers do we address as an organization?' You should of course have this answered in your strategy. The clearer you are with these relationships in your strategy map, the better you will communicate and implement them.

Identifying Customer Types and Groups

The next stage is to know which customers to include in the customer perspective. Always identify customers before you start developing any customer objectives. First you need to ensure you understand the layers of customers, then identify discrete groups. Finally you need to ensure you include other groups such as regulators or other stakeholders.

MULTIPLE CUSTOMER LAYERS

You need to take care when identifying customers. Many organizations serve multiple *layers* of customers, and the structure of the customer perspective should represent these layers. How do we do this? The answer is that we have done much of this thinking already. We created the value chain, the context of the organization and the tangible future. These are ideal sources for checking the layers of customers, describing the value chain and developing *the structure* of the customer perspective.

An organization that sells through distributors will have a chain of customers. For example, a car manufacturer will have both their dealers and car owners as their customers. If they are also serving hire or lease companies, both the lease company and the end user are customers in the chain. Moreover, these are distinct customer groups with quite different needs.

For a construction company, the customers might be the contract manager commissioned by the developer to manage the build, the architect commissioned by the developer and the developer themselves. If the developer sells the building on, or leases it, they may also have longer-term commitments to the eventual end user, under warranty.

In public sector examples and charities you also get multiple customer layers. A charity's money, grants and services may actually be routed through intermediate beneficiaries before they reach the eventual beneficiaries. For instance, the funds may help the carers of those in need. The funds may help to fund other bodies, such as hospitals, which actually deliver the services to specific groups of patients within the hospital. A cancer charity may fund research, which is eventually used to help cancer sufferers. In each case, there are layers of beneficiaries.

A similar thing happens with franchises. A company that runs franchises has both the franchisee as a customer and end customers. Even though the company may never deal with the end user directly, the story of the strategy would not be complete unless both the franchisees and the end customers were included in the picture. Both have needs, and the strategy map is likely to have to reflect both sets of needs.

Several manufacturing companies I have worked with have had their parent company as their main customer. The parent company was building or developing something larger and all the manufacturing company's output went to the parent company. These organizations are not in an open market, but have a single customer with a transfer pricing arrangement. Their product does eventually reach end customers, still has to be competitive and has to serve those end customers' needs, but the relationship is more with a parent organization rather than an end user. In these cases, you need to identify needs of end customers *and* any parental needs along the way. So, refer to the value chain you developed previously to ensure you have a clear view of the layers of customers that you need to develop objectives for.

IDENTIFYING GROUPS OF CUSTOMERS

Even when you have identified the layers of customers you still need to identify discrete groups of customers within each layer, and the needs and objectives within each group of customers. Identify specific groups that you have amongst all the sets of customers you are dealing with.

You may find that these groups have some needs in common and others that are distinct to a particular group. Perhaps they are associated with new products and existing ones. They may be completely different, as in commercial customers and end consumers.

Even within the same customer organization there can be quite different requirements amongst the individuals. The purchasing department may focus on cost, whereas operations may concentrate on delivery reliability and quality. Meanwhile, the customers' R&D team or managers may value the interaction and sharing of ideas to develop new opportunities.

For a retailer, there might be customer segments with particular needs. For instance, an online retailer may recognize that business customers and end consumers have different needs, purchasing patterns and support requirements.

How you choose to segment your customers will be determined by the strategy. If your strategy is to move from one customer segment to another, it makes sense to identify these distinct segments. If your strategy is to move up or along the value chain, then knowing the characteristics of customers in different parts of the value chain will be important. If your detailed strategy for a particular area is interested in the distinctions amongst a group, then show those distinctions at that level in the strategy map cascade.

The choice of customer groups will also be determined by (and will influence) how you structure your financial perspective. Perhaps you recognize that some customer groups are more service intensive and cost more to serve. Your strategy may be to charge more for service or move away from over-expensive, less profitable customers. Be sure to recognize these as different customer groups.

Whatever strategy you have, use your value chain analysis and context diagram to detail the separate groups, to identify their common and differing needs.

REGULATORS

When considering the value chain and context we included regulators, and so we need to include their objectives. You can choose to put these in the customer perspective, but bear in mind that they do not usually give the organization revenue (though in some cases they approve capital investments). Alternatively, you can create a separate perspective specifically for regulators, alongside the customer perspective. This emphasizes their importance as a part of the landscape of the organization. It is simply a question of clarity.

Examples of regulation include where an insurance company needs to comply with regulations coming from the Financial Services Authority (FSA). The FSA may say, 'I want to see a compliant sales process' or 'I want to see you are treating customers fairly'. A pharmaceutical company will have to comply with drug research, pricing and testing regulations, so their regulator may say, 'I want you to demonstrate ethical drug testing'. A mobile phone regulator may want to ensure fair pricing exists within the market.

As with any customer objective statement, ensure that you use the regulator's words and express the objectives from their perspective. Using regulators' objectives communicates the importance of regulation to the organization. It also raises the question in the process perspective, 'So what do we have to do to satisfy the regulators' needs?' As the regulators often ask for strategy documents, it also sends a positive message to the regulators that delivering their requirements is an important element of the strategy.[1]

OTHER GROUPS YOU WISH TO INFLUENCE

You might also seek to influence politicians, or the media in a lobbying organization, or investment analysts in a listed company. These groups will have objectives and needs in exactly the same way as customers. They will not give you money as a result, but may positively affect others or the perception of the organization. Do not overuse this and include everyone who places demands upon the organization. You do not list all potential 'stakeholders'. Many will have nothing to do with the strategy, but some will.

A water company included both investors and the regulator in its customer perspective, because they wanted to improve the quality of briefings to their investment analysts to influence the share price (in the financial perspective).

Several charities that I have worked with included both politicians and the media in their customer perspectives. One charity sought to lobby and influence politicians, in various countries, to change perceptions and gain support for the people they were trying to help. They also worked to get their message out through the media, to gain the media's backing and thereby to influence the perceptions of the wider population. Another charity sought to influence politicians to introduce positive policies and to fund activity in the sector. The money did not go to the charity, but to provider organizations who served the same community that the charity were helping.

---

[1]   It is not a good idea to have, 'keep the regulator off our back', as a process objective, especially if the regulator sees it.

Deriving Customer Objectives from Value Propositions

Now we have identified the customers, we need to develop their objectives. This section looks at the underlying thinking behind the customer objectives. It provides a generic technique that is useful, but that also has limitations. So an alternative approach is suggested that gets wider and more informed responses and a richer, more useful, customer perspective.

A popular way to develop your customer objectives is from the organization's value proposition. Porter's model of competitive advantage is a popular choice (Porter 1985: 12). This model suggests that an organization must choose whether to have a narrow or broad focus. The organization must also decide whether to compete on costs or through differentiation. This leads to three generic strategies for achieving above average performance in an industry: cost leadership, differentiation and focus. Focus can take two forms: cost focus and differentiation focus. This approach presupposes that Porter's model of competitive advantage and customer needs (Porter 1985) applies in your market. This is no bad thing, but you do need to be aware that that is the model you are using. You also have to be clear that it is a model to obtain above average returns in the long run from 'a *firm's* positioning in a market'.

Take care, because this is not a model of what customers want. It is a model of the *organization's* positioning: a subtle but important point. They are position statements *against competitors* for a customer's needs. They say, 'we are more focused than a competitor' or 'we differentiate more highly than a competitor'. It is from this that we believe we can serve this customer group better and therefore get superior returns in the long-term. What this means in strategy map terms is that cost leadership, differentiation and focus are choices of the organization, *not the customer*. Therefore these choices should be represented in the process, and learning and growth perspectives of the strategy map.

Kaplan and Norton use a variation on this approach in *'The Strategy Focused Organization'* (Kaplan and Norton 2001: 86–98) and *'Strategy Maps'* (Kaplan and Norton 2004). They list three different value propositions that are used by organizations to differentiate themselves in the marketplace, based on a model from Treacy and Wiersema (1995). They suggest that your customer objectives should be derived from these generic value propositions, and you should identify the one in use by the customer and the organization. The three generic propositions are:

1. Product/service attributes: price, availability, quality, selection and functionality
2. Relationship: service, partnership
3. Image: brand.

It is useful to have a generic value proposition when you want a checklist to validate the needs of customers and to check for consistency and completeness of the customer perspective and customer proposition. However, I find this framework far too generic and it still comes with warnings.

Whilst Treacy and Wiersema's model provides the basis for objectives within the customer perspective, it is as much a model of competitive positioning and advantage as it is of what is provided for the customer. You have to be clear whether this is what the customer wants *or* whether this is what you believe they want and where your organization is choosing to compete. Unfortunately, I have seen strategy maps that have copied such a framework into their customer proposition without actually testing that it is both what the organization believes and what the customers want. They used this generic model directly from the book and placed it, complete, into the customer perspective. This is usually a symptom of a lack of understanding of strategy, their own strategy, a lack of understanding strategy maps and the scorecard model, or of an isolated team that has no contact with the strategy or management team and therefore have to guess the strategy.

Finally, be warned that thinking has moved on from Porter's view. McKinsey & Company suggest you need to compete on several of the fronts whilst excelling in at least one. Kim and Mauborgne (2005) suggest you should not position yourself against your competitors, but find clear blue ocean in which to operate in. Coyne (2000) of consulting firm McKinsey & Company suggested 'new-game' strategies as a way to change the rules which were written about as far back as 1980. When Hambrick and Fredrickson (2005) ask in their paper, 'Are you sure you have a strategy?', they are taking a much wider perspective and suggesting these views are merely one part of the five aspects to having a strategy. These include your vehicle to deliver as well as the economic logic and alignment of the organization. So, whilst these models that inform the customer perspective are useful, they should be used thoughtfully and with some care. They are useful frameworks and checklists, but they are not a substitute for thinking. Also, there are many cases (regulators, public sector, charities) where such a commercial model would not apply. We need a more widely applicable model that is more robust, flexible and insightful: one that does not presume a particular camp of strategic thinking.

Deriving Customer Objectives from their Processes

Whilst these models of generic customer needs can be useful, their application can be limiting. To develop specific and meaningful customer objectives, it is better to look for specific customer statements that reflect your customers' specific needs: statements your customers would recognize if they saw them. Go further and test them out with your customers. Levine et al (2000) says, 'To learn to speak in a human voice, companies must share the concerns of their customers'. To have really meaningful statements requires that you understand the customer's business, their processes and their needs within those processes. Starting with the customer's needs allows you to explore how and why your proposition works for each customer (assuming it does). It also allows you to examine whether the proposition changes in different parts of the customer organization and for different customer groups. This clarity makes it easier to explain the proposition to your own organization. It also makes sure that you are not relying on a generic sales model.

Understanding your customers' specific processes and needs is a generative tool. That is it provides insights and ideas. It helps you to explore where else you might find value for them (or they might get more value from you). From that you may well end up with a more incisive and intimate competitive strategy. The best way to explore the needs of your customers is to first look at the processes they are going through, starting with the value chain work you did earlier and diving deeper into the processes that individual customers, or groups of customers, follow.

Your customers will have processes that they are following which use your products and services. For example, with the technology company, the customer perspective reflected the key parts of the customers' buying cycle. You would expect there to also be customer needs that extend before and after project delivery. You can see this with the wider process perspective shown in Figure 10.1. The wider perspective of the client includes establishing the need for a new plant, detailing their requirements, procuring the plant, choosing a partner, the build and implementation process, getting the plant commissioned and then its long-term operation through its lifetime. Finally, there is the decommissioning phase.

For this strategy map, the management team chose to concentrate on the client's process from procurement through to commissioning. They did consider the wider stages, which led to insights about getting closer to clients during the specification stage, ensuring the plant was easy to commission and operate, and taking into account lifetime costs of ownership and commissioning. They even considered offering a 'design, build, operate' service, which would include managing the plant through its lifetime. Taking this wider perspective helps to open up opportunities, and explore where the clients might have problems and where opportunities lie. This strategy map was focused on the project delivery theme, with wider aspects considered in other aspects of their strategy. This sent the clear message to their staff to focus on converting bids to projects and delivering the projects well.

Make sure you do not simply mirror your process in the customer processes. For instance, it is possible that their buying process is similar to yours, but you can be sure that they have stages where they agree their requirements and evaluate the tender. If the customer process you draw up is identical to your own, you need to be sure that you are not simply imposing your process on your customer's process.

When developing each customer's needs it is useful to ask, 'what is their process?' 'What do they do at each stage in their process?' 'What needs do they have at each stage of their process?' These questions provide the opportunity to think about what value you might add and could add to other parts of their process, to make things fundamentally better for your customer. The strategy positioning and value proposition models can help here, but there is no substitute for listening to real customers' needs.

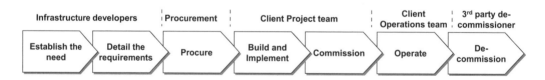

Figure 10.1 Developing the customers' processes for the customer perspective

WHAT EACH CUSTOMER SAYS THEY WANT

When developing the specific needs of a customer or group of customers, I find it helps if people use an archetype. Go further and specify the actual person you are thinking about. This helps your thinking to become specific, so that you think 'as if you are that person'. It also means you can always, later, test it by actually asking them. In the case of the procurement officer, I would say, 'think of a procurement officer (politician, customer, end user or whoever) that you know. Say specifically who you are being, when you are talking from their perspective'. Now what do they want? Now choose another one and see if they would say the same thing, or something different.

It has been suggested to me that this is stereotyping, with all the negative connotations that word carries. However, you are looking for common characteristics to serve, and archetypes help you understand these individual and common characteristics. It does not mean that you have to treat every customer the same. It does mean that you are thinking about specific individual needs in detail, without generalizing. An archetype helps you with this. You only stereotype if you treat all your customers as if they were in a very limited set of archetypes, and did not ask them to verify what they thought. As Levine et al say (2000: xii), 'Markets consist of human beings, not demographic sectors'. This approach is also far better than generalizing from a large population to the expectations of individuals.

Once you understand a customer's process you can then ask, which particular needs are there? Objectives at one part of the process may be different from other parts, especially if you are dealing with different roles and people. For instance, if at one stage in the process you are dealing with your customer's purchasing officer who acts as the corporate Rottweiler, driving supplier prices down, then you will need to demonstrate value for money. However, the production people may be looking for quality of product and its long-term durability. The sales staff may be looking for a trusted supplier in order to use the supplier's reputation to help sell their product through to the end user. These are quite different needs, value propositions and objectives in different parts of the customer's process.

In the technology company, there were quite different client needs at each stage of the client's process. Figure 10.2 summarizes each different customer's objectives at each stage of the overall process. Figure 10.3 converts these into objectives on the strategy map. Notice how the client specifies different cost objectives at different stages of the process. During procurement, there is a cost-effective solution. During operation there are lifetime costs. During decommissioning, there are no hidden costs. These might appear to be the same but they may not to the separate customers, and it is important to establish this. If

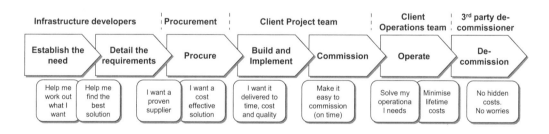

Figure 10.2 Developing objectives for each step of the customers' processes

Figure 10.3 The customer objectives as shown on the strategy map

those procuring the solution are only looking at implementation costs, then lifetime and de-commissioning costs may not be important to them. However, there may be others in the client organization for whom these are important considerations. This situation is typical when you are developing client objectives. It is vital you are sure whether you are dealing with the same things, or different things. They may be expressed the same way or differently in various parts of the customer's organization.

This approach is useful even with consumers in the public sector and with donors and beneficiaries in charities. A consumer example would be the process people go through when dealing with music. Apple have recognized that for their consumers of music, it is not just about playing music but buying it, organizing it, sharing it, learning about the artists, commenting and buying tracks by similar artists. Their proposition reaches the whole process, what you might call their 'music experience'. A patient in a hospital is not just an individual with a disease. They will have had a history of illness and of visits to various parts of the health service, seeing several doctors and nurses. They will have had care outside the hospital when discharged and will have been seen by other health professionals as well. The doctors do not see their patients as a series of diseases hosted by people (as one healthcare professional described the old attitude to healthcare service). The patient is a person, possibly with multiple diseases and symptoms, who experiences a relationship with the whole healthcare service.

Approaching customer needs from the perspective of customer processes tends to get a richer answer than starting with customer propositions. Use the customer propositions as well, as they provide a useful checklist against which these customer needs can be checked.

Having gone through this process, you can now return to the customer value propositions and validate that the needs that they have correspond with the value propositions you offer.

Representing the Customer Objectives

Once you have these objectives within the steps of the process, you can choose a number of ways to represent them in the customer perspective. I find that, in most cases, the best way is to show different customer groups, their processes and the individual and joint objectives within these processes. This exposes the thinking and shows how different groups are thinking through their processes.

However, this does take up space, especially in the top level strategy map. Sometimes this level of detail is reserved for lower level strategy maps, and the higher level customer objectives in the top level strategy map summarize the main customer groups and their main objectives.

Remember that the point of the strategy map is to both capture and communicate the strategy. Having captured the strategy, the question becomes, 'what is the best way to communicate it?' If this is best done through the cascade of strategy maps, then so be it.

I find that putting the customer groups and their processes in the customer perspective places the customer objectives in a context, which makes them easier to explain. It makes an explicit link between the customer groups and their needs. This is particularly important where there are multiple groups with overlapping and differing needs. If there are major differences between the groups, this is all the more important. If the differences are more subtle, then the distinctions may only become apparent at lower levels of the strategy map. For instance, marketing's strategy map will contain more detailed customer objectives for different customer groups compared to the less detailed top level strategy map.

The technology company used a similar approach, in order to consolidate the customer objectives for their top level strategy map whilst using far more detail in their lower level strategy maps. You can see how this detail was summarized in Figure 10.4.

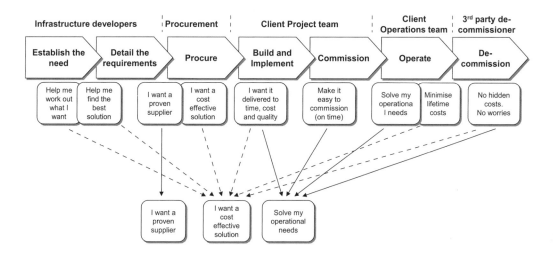

Figure 10.4 Sometimes it is useful to aggregate multiple objectives into common themes

Be careful in using this approach not to lose clarity and the detail. I find that clarifying the customer's process is so powerful that it is worth explicitly including it on the strategy map. It is particularly useful for widening the perspective of the organization to the broader context in which their product or service sits. It also causes the organization to think less about their own process and more about their customer's process. In turn this helps with joined up thinking and working.

The technology company worked on the assumption that UK customers and international customers followed broadly the same buying process. As their strategy maps cascaded into different regions, to different sub-companies and into different themes, the distinctions and different points of emphasis were provided. It is important to recognize and capture these distinctions as your work develops. They may not be material at the top level but may well be important as the strategy map cascades through the organization.

Before we detail the characteristics and choose their measures, you first need to validate the customer objectives with some test questions.

Validating the Customer Objectives

As you work through the customer perspective, developing a model of your customers and developing their objectives, you will eventually have to ask a set of questions to validate your strategy. There are five questions you can use to validate your customers' objectives:

1. Is this really a customer need?
2. Will satisfying these needs deliver the revenue you expect?
3. Can you satisfy these needs (and do so economically)?
4. What do we have to do well to deliver this customer's needs?
5. Are you doing anything that distinguishes you from your competitors?

IS THIS REALLY WHAT THE CUSTOMERS WANT?

First, is this really what the customers want? Is it a real need? How do you know? You are looking for evidence that there is a need there to be satisfied. It might also be prudent to consider whether the customers would want to buy from you.

In the retailer example, they had an immensely detailed customer segmentation and analysis programme which helped them target different types and groups of purchasers. The technology company was relying on its knowledge of the market and its success in opening up opportunities with new customers.

WILL THIS CREATE REVENUE?

It is only so much use knowing your customers' needs; you have to be able to make money serving them. Your revenue predictions need to add up. Between the financial and customer objectives, you have to check:

Will delivering this customer need create revenue for us? If so, how much?

What are the most important needs that will create this revenue?

What is the timing?

These questions will ensure you have a coherent story about how revenue is generated between the customer objectives and your financial objectives. You also need to consider the costs.

CAN YOU SATISFY THESE NEEDS ECONOMICALLY?

You have to be capable of satisfying the customer objectives, and of doing so economically. An element of the service of customer objectives is, 'what will it cost?' This will be reflected in the processes that you need to develop and operate, and the costs of those processes.

WHAT DO WE HAVE TO DO WELL?

From each customer objective ('I want' statement) you need to create links to the objectives you need in the process perspective (see Figure 10.5). To do this you need to ask:

To satisfy this customer objective (naming the objective), what are the few things we have to do well?

This question will allow you to elicit the process perspective objectives and make a clear link to them from each customer objective. Supplementary to this question you can ask:

Is it something we can deliver?

Is this proposition credible for us?

What are the few things we have to focus on to make sure this customer need is satisfied?

What will be different?

Where should our emphasis be? What should change?

Does it create value? For us? For the clients?

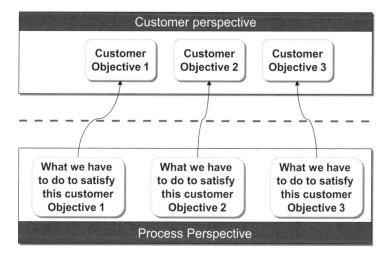

Figure 10.5 The process perspective supports the customers' objectives

IS IT A COMPETITIVE PROPOSITION?

Finally, you can ask whether this is a competitive strategy. Are you doing anything different from your competitors? Could they easily copy this from you? It is at this point that the competitive advantage models play an important role. Are you choosing a strategy that positions you in the market to make above average profits? Is it also a defensible position that means that your above-average profit stream is sustainable?

It can be very insightful to develop your competitor's strategy map. That is, the strategy map from their perspective, the one they would create in the same market. When operating in the same industry you may well have the same customer groups, processes and needs. The top halves of your strategy maps may well be very similar.

The bottom half of their strategy map, which describes how your competitor delivers their strategy, is likely to be different. This is a useful way to raise awareness of overlaps and true differentiation, and to clarify the uniqueness, competitiveness and sustainability of your own strategy.

Detailing the Customer Objective

The characteristics of the customers and their needs are documented in the description of the objectives' characteristics that sits behind the strategy map, in a variation of the standard framework. You can also include additional detail in the description to refer to research, explain timescales and add all the other rich information that sits behind the objective. This becomes useful when the strategy map is explained and also helps others when the time comes to cascade the strategy map and the objectives within it. Once you have developed the objectives and characteristics you can then work through to the measures of the customers' needs being satisfied.

Summary

The key with the customer perspective is to know who your customers are, to develop the objectives from each customer's perspective. This will rightly give you the customer perspective. State their needs as an 'I want…' statement from their perspective. Do not make the mistake of projecting what you do as being what they want.

Be clear who your groups of customers are, and even use individuals as archetypes to help you develop the statements of their needs and objectives. You are looking for statements from *their* perspective, understanding the processes that they go through. You can use a generic value proposition. Better still, identify their processes and the specific needs within those processes, and think through how best you can meet these. Test how well you position your organization to serve these needs against your competitors.

Once you have this information you can check that serving these needs will lead to the revenue objectives you have set. You can also start to develop your process perspective and the objectives you need to deliver to meet your various customers' objectives.

11 *The Financial Perspective and Financial Objectives*

This chapter helps you to think through and develop the structure and content of the financial perspective and its objectives, so that it reflects your strategy.

The chapter explains the overall structure of the perspective and the questions to ask to link that structure to the tangible vision. It provides you with ways to define the most common financial objectives, revenue, costs and profit (or surplus). It also explains how to capture financial issues such as cash flow, risk and compliance, and triple bottom line accounting. It will also warn you of some common traps to avoid along the way.

A standard framework is used, from which to develop your particular financial objectives. There are also specific questions to navigate from the financial perspective to objectives in the customer and process perspectives.

Work with the Management Team and their Financial Model

It is assumed that you understand the finances of the organization before you start. If you are a member of the executive team, this should be taken as read. However, if you are facilitating this work for that team, make sure you are familiar with the accounts, the sources of revenues and their relative sizes, the main cost drivers and where the overall value of the business comes from. From the work on the value chain and the tangible future, you should also understand the major changes to the financials that are expected over the time horizon of the strategy. Most importantly, talk with, and work with, the finance director and the finance team. They will have financial models of the strategy and how they see the finances developing as the strategy evolves. They will also know why it changes as it does and what should happen to drive these changes.

The financial perspective is not trying to replace a detailed financial model of the organization; rather, it should highlight where most change is required. The detail will be in the financial models, the budgets, the investment cases and in the lower level strategy maps. You are capturing the financial consequences of your strategy.

Common Mistakes with the Financial Perspective

The financial perspective represents the financial outcomes of the organization's activities. Using the financial perspective to represent financial outcomes may create some misconceptions about how the strategy map and scorecard work to describe and manage the finance functions and budgets. Here are three common mistakes and a misconception:

1. The mistake of putting only financial measures in the financial perspective
2. The mistake of failing to link financials to other perspectives
3. The mistake of confusing financial capability with financial outcomes
4. The misconception that you need financial inputs at the bottom of the strategy map.

MISTAKE ONE: USING ONLY FINANCIAL MEASURES IN THE FINANCIAL PERSPECTIVE

Some organizations simply put financial measures from their budgets and revenue expectations into the financial perspective of the strategy map. They do not use an objective statement at all. You can almost get away with this, except that you never get the richness of the description in the perspective if you only use financial measures. As the examples in the chapter on objectives before measures explained, it is useful to establish the quality of the revenue, as well as the quantity. Just as budgets only tell part of the story of how the organization operates and little of the thinking that went into them, having an objective and a description of the qualities helps tremendously when communicating the whole story. This is true for any of the potential financial measures and objectives.

MISTAKE TWO: FAILING TO LINK THE FINANCIALS TO THE OTHER PERSPECTIVES

I occasionally see financial measures and targets without an explicit link to the other perspectives. This is most common where only a scorecard has been used. This assumes that there is a link between the financial objectives, measures and targets and the other objectives, measures and targets, but leaves that link as implicit. In contrast the strategy map demands an explicit explanation for changes in financial outcomes.

It may be explicit through other mechanisms such as budget statements and project benefits statements, created during the planning and budgeting processes. It is hard to conceive that an organization might have a strategy that reflects changes and improvements, but does not also account for the investment necessary to make those improvements, but this does happen. I have seen plans that show a reduction in costs or improvement in performance but no description of how it will come about. Even when these elements start aligned they can drift apart. One problem with the budgeting process is that emphasis on the collection of budget data can often omit the underlying explanation for the changes that will bring the financial improvements about. With a strategy map there has to be an explicit relation between the financial outcomes and the organization's activities, its objectives and its strategy for change. There should also be links from the strategy and scorecard to the budgets (inputs), and revenue and costs (outcomes). This is the minimum level of integration that should be carried out to ensure that the two mechanisms of control, the budgets and the performance management approach, are linked and work together. This is covered in more detail in chapter eighteen.

MISTAKE THREE: MIXING FINANCIAL CAPABILITY WITH FINANCIAL OUTCOME

There are times when you might want to put into the strategy an objective that reflects an increased financial capability. Perhaps the organization needs a greater awareness of costs, or is implementing a new investment appraisal approach. Perhaps you are moving to rolling budgets. The strategy map will need to reflect this improved capability, whether it be in the finance department or spread through the parts of the organization. It should contain the financial activities you wish to focus on and the capabilities that you need to develop within the finance department.

These items often first get mentioned when the financial perspective is being developed. As a result, some practitioners try, incorrectly, to put this financial activity or capability in the financial perspective, because it appears financial. You certainly need to explain how the financial outcomes are derived, but the processes that bring about financial results, and the underlying capabilities that need to be learnt or developed, lie in the process or learning and growth perspectives respectively. They must not go in the financial outcomes perspective. Just as with any theme, a cause and effect relationship exists that should bring about changes in the eventual financial outcomes. The trick is to capture the thoughts and return to them once the appropriate perspective is eventually reached.

Similarly, projects associated with financial initiatives should also be lined up against the process or learning and growth objectives. Placing them in the financial perspective acts as a useful interim parking place when you are first eliciting the financial objectives, but do not let them live there permanently. They will occur either inside the finance department (and therefore in their strategy map) or perhaps in other departments, as a sign of the need to increase their financial capability (in the relevant department's learning and growth perspective). Having financial projects aligned with objectives in the financial perspective will create an odd set of projects that appear to be disconnected from others, not to be owned by any functional area (or only the FD) and not directly affecting any part of the organization.

Financial capability and financial initiatives should always only be aligned with objectives in the process or learning and growth perspectives at some level of the strategy maps. Set them aside temporarily, but move them to their proper place at the appropriate time.

A MISCONCEPTION: WHY AREN'T FINANCIALS AT THE BOTTOM OF THE STRATEGY MAP?

Occasionally, I meet someone from finance who wants to put the financial perspective at the bottom. Their argument is that it is the funding that drives everything else above, and so putting the finances at the bottom of the cause and effect model represents this. Sometimes they want an additional financial perspective; sometimes they want it instead of the one at the top. They are right, in identifying the need, but also wrong in their use of the model.

They are right in that the allocation of financial resources does provide the funds to pay for the capabilities, investments and processes, and that they need that money to deliver the strategy. This is precisely the model we shall use in chapter eighteen.

The financial perspective is at the top because it captures the intended financial outcome of the organization's activities, *not its planned financial inputs*. It represents the predicted end costs, revenues and cash flows that result from the activities that cause them. It represents the answer to the questions, 'were we able to deliver services for an appropriate price? Did we generate the revenue? Were we able to attract funding as planned?' These are the predicted (eventual) financial outcomes, not the allocated (input) budgets, as they are sometimes misconceived to be.

The cause and effect model for the strategy map deliberately puts the learning and growth, and organizational values perspectives at the bottom. If you were to put financials at the bottom, it would suggest that the organization's value is driven only by, or fundamentally by, its ability to fund activity. It is true that funding enables activity. However, capability and capacity drive improved performance.

So how do we accommodate the truth in this question? The anticipated cost of operating the business, investing in change and delivering the results for customers is the aggregated budget that results from the drivers of the change. As we shall see, these are derived from the operations and investment in change, as expressed in the strategy map, to create a budget for the strategy. These predictions sit beside the strategy map and scorecard, rather than in another perspective beneath the others. Once aggregated across objectives, themes and strategy maps, they are a part of the financial model, and the anticipated outcomes are then placed within the financial objectives at the top of the strategy map. We shall cover this more thoroughly in Chapter 18.

Asking Questions about Financial Objectives in the Right Way

Having got over these misconceptions and potential pitfalls, how do we proceed? First, position the organization's purpose or mission statement at the top of the strategy map. (For the purpose of this section, treat the organization's purpose and mission statement as synonymous.) I put such a statement at the top of every strategy map I create, as it has several advantages. It makes clear that the strategy is part of the overriding purpose of the organization. It provides a test of coherency between the strategy, as expressed in the strategy map, and the organization's overall purpose. It completes the story of the strategy as read from the strategy map. It also tests whether there are any omissions between the purpose and the strategy as stated.

Next we develop the objectives in the financial perspective. The financial perspective describes how the major elements of the organization's finances will evolve as the strategy develops. How you ask the questions about the financial objectives will critically determine the quality of the answers you get.

STARTING WITH THE PURPOSE OR MISSION

When starting from the mission or purpose statement, the financial objectives derive from that statement, and the work you have already done in bringing it to life with the tangible vision. A good starting question is therefore, 'in order to achieve your ambition and deliver your strategy, what do you have to achieve, financially?' This question is explicitly about your strategy and the financial implications. Were you, instead, to simply ask, 'what are your financial objectives?', you would get responses about *today's* financial objectives. The reason for using 'ambition' and 'strategy' as the reference points, is to highlight the differences that will occur between today's financial position and those of the future. It is the financial objectives that contribute to the ambition through the strategy.

WHEN YOU ALREADY HAVE THE CUSTOMER PERSPECTIVE

When you already have customer groups and objectives in the customer perspective, you could start with the previous question. You can also cross-check the revenue objectives against the customer objectives by asking, 'so, in delivering your strategy and achieving these customer objectives, what will be your financial objectives?' Of course, if you have multiple customer groups or quite different customer objectives that will create quite different revenue sources (and potentially different costs), in which case you may need to ask this question for each customer group or objective.

The trick here is to keep strategic and operate a pincer movement on the financial objectives, ensuring consistency between the customer objectives and the overall mission to ensure consistency between the three.

What to Use as the Highest Financial Objective

With any financial perspective one overall financial objective sits at the top. How do you choose what this should be? For commercial organizations there are several alternatives, each with different implications. The most common are: profit, shareholder return, cash generated, or perhaps company value.

PROFIT

Perhaps the most common approach with commercial organizations is to use profit as the highest financial objective. The improvements to the financial objectives (revenues, costs and cash flow) will bring about the change in profitability. This will come from the combined effect of, for example, increasing existing sales, the introduction of more profitable lines, lower sales costs, dilution of fixed costs, and better cash flow and use of capital. In not for profit organizations, surplus is used in exactly the same way to denote the difference between income and expenditure. Using profit works well; however, this is not the only approach one can adopt for commercial organizations.

SHAREHOLDER RETURN

Rather than linking their financial objectives to profitability, some organizations put shareholder value or shareholder return at the top of their financial perspective. Shareholder return consists of the increase in both the value of shares and the dividends received from that holding. It is a higher level objective than profitability, and it expresses the creation of the company's value beyond its mere profit.

Using shareholder return is useful to raise the horizon, but does have some disadvantages. For listed businesses, shareholder value or the total return to shareholders on their investment consists of movements in the stock price as well as dividends distributed. A company can be making a good profit, yet be subject to stock market fluctuations, or bids, which are outside its control and which lower its share price (and those of all the other companies in its segment of the market). So you might improve, but the market might move against you. Likewise, the dividend distribution strategy can also play a significant part, the choice of which is more often than not determined by the cash generated by the business. On the other hand, executive incentives might be based upon an increase in shareholder return. I have used shareholder return with some organizations, but I would caution you if you do so as it places some of the results outside the management's control. You can use it: just use it with care and be aware of the consequences.

CASH GENERATED

Whilst some companies put 'shareholder value' at the top of the strategy map, I have worked with several companies who defined their overall value in terms of their ability to generate cash. This usually happens with a company within a group where cash generation is an objective of the group as a whole. Using free cash flow is also popular[1] and is often used for company valuations. I like cash generated and free cash flow because they also address the issue of working capital, the build up of reserves and the potential distribution of profits to owners or shareholders via dividends.

COMPANY VALUE

If you are dealing with an unlisted company the owner of which is planning to sell, or perhaps they are planning to raise capital through a listing, it is not uncommon to have an overall financial objective that reflects this, such as, 'a valuable business'. Clearly, how a company is valued will depend on the industry, the perceptions of the market when listing, or the value that a potential acquirer sees when they assess its value. The statement about the value the company has will need to be made more specific to reflect the value of the business to a potential purchaser or investor. This might include: future cash flows, access to customers, brand, market penetration, customer loyalty, specific processes, core technologies, intellectual capital, knowledge and quality of management.

Whichever you choose as the highest financial objective, be sure it reflects the nature of the organization and its overall objectives. Each approach communicates a different message. Each one will be driven by the ownership structure and, potentially, how the management team are incentivized. In the following sections, for simplicity, I shall use profitability in the examples, but any of these highest level objectives will provide a similar framework.

Overall Structure and Content

The objectives in the financial perspective should capture where your financial emphasis lies. A typical framework of objectives in the financial perspective is shown in Figure 11.1. There is no single correct financial model for all organizations. The choices made will reflect what your management team believe are the most important aspects and what you need to concentrate on. The question is not, 'what is the financial model for the

---

1   There are various ways to calculate free cash flow. One is: Net Free Cash Flow = Operation Cash Flow – Capital Expenses to keep current level of operation – Dividends – Current Portion of Long-Term Debt – Depreciation. See http://www.analystforum.com/samples/schweser/CFA_Level%202_Book%204_Reading42.pdf

business?' Rather it is about which financial variables you believe you need to pay most attention to – the ones that need to change most significantly as a result of the strategy.

The financial perspective of a commercial organization's strategy map will typically contain statements about revenue and cost, cash flow and risk. What you are looking for is where the large and significant changes to the financial model will occur, and why they will occur. This movement is represented in Figure 11.2.

You will have the basis of this from the work you have already done in developing the tangible future, which will already have provided you with the expected significant financial changes, what will have brought these about and their timing.

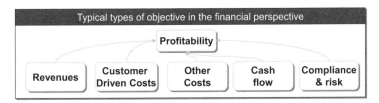

Figure 11.1 A typical structure for objectives in the financial perspective

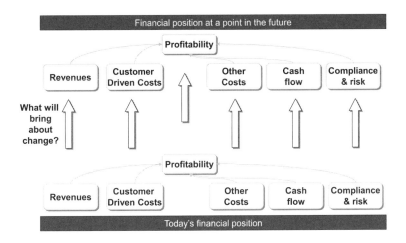

Figure 11.2 Changes and improvements in the financial objectives

REVENUE AND CUSTOMERS

To discuss revenue, you need to understand the customers, which is why we spent so much time on the value chain and the various customer groups. If you understand your customers and how you add value to them, you will understand the thinking behind the revenue objectives. As has been made clear previously, whilst developing a strategy map appears to be a top-down approach, with the financial perspective above the customer perspective, you typically develop the customer perspective first and then iterate between the financial and customer perspectives, asking:

What revenue targets do you have?

Where do your revenues come from (i.e. which groups of customers)?

Which groups will be providing which revenues?

How and why are they changing?

The organization may be protecting existing revenues and may also be seeking to grow new revenues. The retail example shows how new revenues can be grown at the same time as existing revenues protected. The retailer was maximizing value from their core offer (typically represented by like for like sales), whilst separately growing new revenue through innovative areas. In contrast, the technology company was concerned with optimizing the cost of sales whilst growing turnover in both new and existing markets. The management believed increased turnover to come from existing services expanded into new markets. In both these cases, the examples include new markets *in addition* to the existing sales. New products may act *as a substitute* for existing products, so revenue from existing products and customers may need protecting whilst the new product revenue is being developed. As the types of revenue have different characteristics, they would be shown as separate objectives representing existing and new revenue. As you develop the revenue objectives, constantly refer back to the customer objectives and how they are expected to bring about changes in revenue.

COSTS

The financial perspective always contains some cost elements. There are often two distinct cost elements, reflecting changes to both the direct and the indirect costs of the organization. Direct costs are associated with activity levels (for instance, the cost of sales is directly related to sales and production activities). Indirect costs are usually fixed or change little with the volume of activity, for example factory overheads, research, capital costs and costs of support functions often vary little with sales volume. Whatever the case, we need an explanation of the changes to the cost base over the specified timescale and what will cause these changes to happen.

How these costs objectives are represented will vary from situation to situation. A retailer may wish for costs and complexity to be minimized. A technology company might want its costs 'optimized'. A manufacturing company may want to minimize the costs of production, with associated objectives covering working capital and investment. Within each of these cost objectives there should be further detail as to how the costs will be optimized, minimized or controlled.

CASH FLOW

Whilst profitability comes from revenues less costs, it is of course not the whole financial picture. Many organizations will have objectives to improve cash flow or reduce working capital requirements, each requiring a relevant financial objective in the financial perspective. The cash flow ambition would be reflected in a financial objective. The improvement in cash flow may come from a number of places, such as reducing work in progress or stock, improved credit management or better management of the cash itself. How these are achieved will be contained in objectives within either the process or learning and growth perspective.

RISK AND COMPLIANCE

Sometimes a financial risk objective is needed. This represents the costs associated with regulatory compliance or the financial implications associated with its breach. Many organizations have to comply with legislation, ensure compliance, adhere to reporting standards, and ensure they satisfy the regulator's requirements for prudence, solvency and transparency. In banking and insurance, this will often involve capital adequacy requirements and reserves.

There are also financial risks and exposures. For instance, companies trading internationally may well have various currency dealings and will also seek to mitigate the financial risk associated with currency fluctuations, interest rate changes or the commercial risk of default. A company seeking to profit from its currency trading is also creating a risk rather than mitigating one. Mitigating and taking advantage of financial risk can also appear in the financial perspective.

Triple Bottom Line

There is one other type of financial element that is having increased prominence. That is the financial costs of the social or environmental impact of the business, often referred to as Triple Bottom Line accounting. You can include these costs in the financial perspective, but they do need a special treatment. The financial consequences of the social and environmental should be considered alongside the immediate social and environmental impact, considered in Chapter 12.

Financial Objectives in Not for Profit Organizations

There are some extra considerations when dealing with public sector and not for profit organizations. Not for profit organizations do not always talk about revenue, but they still need sources of funding. It is just that the funders are not usually paying by choice (if a taxpayer), not paying directly for a received service (when government funds a public service) or not paying with an expectation of a benefit to themselves (if donating to a charity).

These funds often come with conditions. Donors or funders may not get a direct service, but they do put expectations on the use of their money. Public sector bodies may receive an allocation of funding based upon activity or population served (e.g. hospitals or a city council), and are set an expectation about their level of performance and activity. Donors could be thought of as groups of people who need influencing to provide funding in response to the messages provided. In each of these cases there is a revenue element that, although not precisely the same as revenue in the commercial sector, relies on the influence of the population they serve.

Pure revenue is also appropriate in the not for profit financial perspective. Some public sector bodies receive central funding and also charge for some of their services, whilst charities sell Christmas cards and other products to raise income directly. They may also obtain additional funding by competing for discretionary grants.

Any of these situations is easily accommodated using small refinements in the strategy map perspectives to reflect each particular situation and the variety of sources of funds or income.

The public sector and not for profit organizations also use a specific language around costs. They talk of efficiency (the ratio of outcomes or activity to input resources) and effectiveness (the impact they have given the resources provided). Public sector financial objectives almost always include cost objectives that reflect aspects of efficiency and effectiveness, as well as working within their budgets. Sometimes it is useful to show a second level of cost implication. A fire and rescue service I worked with had financial objectives for their efficiency and effectiveness but, as they were funded by local government taxes, they had a second order financial objective, 'keep our impact on overall council tax to below 0 per cent'. This represented their desire to minimize their part of the overall council tax bill which provided much of their funding. Similarly, charities often refer to their costs as a percentage of donations received or funds distributed. So a charity might set objectives for the costs of raising donations (perhaps 1 per cent of total donations) and the costs of providing the charitable services the donations enable.

Developing Characteristics and Measures for Financial Objectives

Financial measures are the easiest to develop. They are often directly derived from the objective. Improving cash flow will require the financial measures of cash flow; improving revenue will include the financial measures of revenue, for the relevant type of client. Do not try to shorten the process and leap straight to the measures. Still start with the financial objectives, develop their characteristics and then choose what to measure. This allows you to describe the qualities of each financial objective, so you can choose the few specific financial measures that best show progress and best communicate your intention.

Remember: financial objectives are not financial process objectives or financial capability objectives, though you will undoubtedly discuss improvements to both the financial processes and the capability of the organization. Capture these discussions, but make sure you record them in either a process or learning and growth section associated with finance, where you can use them later.

Look for both lead and lag financial measures for the various financial objectives. So, for the objective, 'increased revenue from new clients', revenue received is a lag measure. In contrast, the value of orders placed (but not yet delivered) is a leading measure of future revenue. Similarly, revenue invoiced but not yet paid is also a lead measure of forthcoming revenue and can be used, alongside predicted costs and payments, as a predictor of future cash flow.

Table 11.1 shows an example of the objective framework with the characteristics of a financial objective. It uses the example of the objective, 'increased revenue from new clients'. This clearly shows how the objective can be measured in a variety of ways. It also shows how some of these measures will be lag measures of the objective, whilst others can be leading measures that show progress is being made.

Table 11.1 An example of a financial objective and its characteristics

Overall objective: 'increased revenue from new clients'	
How will we know we are making progress? (Lead)	How will we know we have got there? (Lag)
Proposal Value of proposals for new clients that suit our bid criteria Value of won projects from new clients Projects being delivered Expected margin on engagements with new clients Billed revenue from new clients that arrives on schedule	Revenue received from new clients Revenue received against actual costs Final margin on new client projects

This framework can be used for any of the financial objectives. For an objective such as, 'optimize material costs', the lag (eventual) measure could be the actual cost of the material. If the organization is operating accrual accounting, a leading measure of costs will be those services or products that are ordered, but not yet paid for. An even more leading measure will be the predicted costs for the project, production run or service for the customer.

Remember that lead and lag measures exist relative to an objective. They are the lead and lag from the perspective of the person who owns the objective. A project manager tasked with 'operating projects to cost and quality' will have the lag measure as the ultimate cost of the project. For them, the lead measure of costs will be the predicted costs. In contrast, for the manager whose division is affected by the project, and whose objective may be 'operational efficiency', both the predicted and eventual project costs are lead measures. It is the improvement in operational costs that is the operational manager's lag measure.

Financial measures are usually *direct* measures of money, be they revenue, costs, cash flow or interest. You rarely need to use an indicator of money (that is, a value that *indicates* performance rather than directly measures it). There will be some exceptions; for instance, for an objective such as 'increased revenue from new clients', the credit worthiness of the customer (measured in their credit rating), may be an indicator of the likelihood that they will pay. Similarly, you may have to use an indicator of social or environmental costs rather than being able to establish them accurately. Mostly, you will have direct measures of the financial objectives.

Finally, be careful not to mix financial inputs with financial outputs. This is to mix forecasts of budgets and the allocation of resources with the actual amount used or produced. A budget is a forecast, it is not the out-turn. The financial objectives represent the out-turn. Of course, accurate budget figures are a precursor to achieving the budget, but the process of budgeting sits within the process perspective. The capability to forecast expenditure accurately is within the learning and growth perspective. The ability to deliver your objectives with the allocated budget is the overall process of management and implementation and, if successful, will lead to the financial objectives you envisaged.

Link Questions to Lower Perspectives

Having developed the financial perspective's objectives, it is now time to find out what objectives in the lower perspectives support the achievement of the financial objectives. There are two sets of questions that reveal this. One set of questions links the revenue to the customer perspective; the other questions link the other, non-revenue, financial objectives to the process perspective, as in Figure 11.3.

Questions that lead to the *customer* perspective:

Which customer groups will these revenues come from?

What do our customers need to be satisfied with to pay money?

Questions that lead directly to the *process* perspective:

What do we have to do well to deliver this financial (cost, cash flow) objective?

What has to be different to achieve this financial (cost, cash flow) objective?

It can be worth using a slightly different question when dealing with the financial risk and compliance objectives:

What do we have to do well to mitigate these risks?

What do we have to do to satisfy these (new or changing) compliance needs?

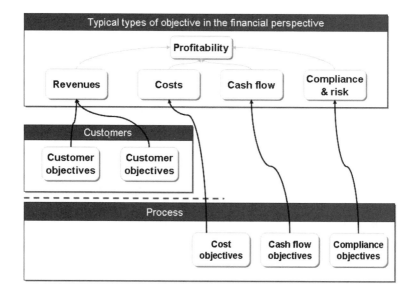

Figure 11.3 Linking financial objectives to objectives in the lower perspectives

Conclusion

You need to keep several things in mind whilst developing the financial perspective. Are the financial objectives contributing to the overall purpose of the organization? Is the ambition set out at various points in time from the tangible vision articulated in the financial objectives? What is the gap between the ambition at points in the future and today? Then, what will bring these changes about? Are they operational changes or changes to the expectations of customers?

Whilst working on the financial perspective you will be constantly moving backwards and forwards between this perspective and the customer and process perspectives, whilst ensuring that the financial model makes sense. All the time you are checking for cause and effect, avoiding strategy by hope and magic, so that it is clear what will cause the changes to happen. The financial perspective provides an important anchor point against which the logic of the strategy and the lower perspectives will be judged.

12 *The Environmental and Social Impact Perspective*

This chapter explains how to incorporate an environmental impact perspective into your strategy map and balanced scorecard, and how to capture, measure and manage environmental and social impact on your balanced scorecard.

The importance of an organization's impact on the environment and the demands for environmental management reporting have made it easy to argue for a dedicated environmental impact perspective in the balanced scorecard. The Kyoto agreement, ratified in 2005, established national greenhouse gas emission targets, with various governments passing laws to ensure reporting of the environmental impact. Environmental issues are now being incorporated into annual financial reports (Institute of Chartered Accountants and the Environment Agency 2009). Carbon trading has been introduced in the EU (EC directive 2003). ISO 14001, the standard for environmental management systems, makes it clear that it is designed, 'with the commitment of your entire organization... to address the delicate balance between maintaining profitability and reducing environmental impact'. There are taxes on the disposal of waste and landfill (HMRC 2010), and new standards for recycling are being introduced across industries. Individual industries such as paper, electrical components and forestry have introduced their own standards for sustainability. Using an environmental impact perspective also helps to dispel the misconception that the balanced scorecard model is ultimately profit driven.

For many organizations, their environmental impact is only a part of their wider corporate social responsibility (CSR) agenda. The CSR agenda includes the organization's impact on its community and the parts of society it interacts with. It can include charitable and philanthropic work. It includes the consequences of the organization's approach to ethics. It includes the supply chain, with many organizations having codes of conduct to ensure a responsible approach towards suppliers, considering their rates of pay, and their working and living conditions. Increasingly shareholders are looking at the CSR records of companies to determine whether they should invest in them or withdraw their funds. Porter and Kramer (2011) suggest that truly integrating CSR thinking into your business and your supply chain will be the next way to create sustainable economic value in organizations. Many organizations already think this way. They have moved beyond the 'greenwash' of appearing to take on environmental issues, and have taken such issues to the heart of how they work and think. Having a social and environmental impact perspective within your strategy map and balanced scorecard, that is tightly linked to your strategy, is becoming mandatory.

I first used an environmental perspective in a strategy map for balanced scorecard design in 1998, and have continued to use it ever since, with a wider scope, to capture both social and environmental impact. You will notice that I refer to these as capturing the environmental and social impact. This is because all the activities associated with environmental and social responsibility are captured in the objectives in the lower perspectives.

This chapter explains how to represent your environmental and social impact and describe your environmental and social strategy. It will help you measure and manage your environmental and social impact. It will also help you improve how you communicate the importance of environmental and corporate social responsibility in your organization.

Avoiding Common Mistakes

This perspective is frequently misused and misunderstood. It is more sophisticated than merely adding an environmental perspective and putting anything and everything associated with environmental issues into that grouping. Rather, you need to reflect different ways in which environmental and social *impact* is thought about (as a strategic issue) and capture the drivers of environmental and social impact through the existing perspectives. This makes sure that the thinking is more deeply embedded in your strategy.

Putting absolutely everything associated with environmental topics within that single perspective often happens when the environmental perspective omits the impact part of its name. As a consequence, it is seen merely as a topic. The cause and effect relationship is lost. Anything associated with environmental or social issues is placed in the category and the whole causal structure collapses. This also misses a great opportunity to embed environmental and CSR thinking into the entire organization.

Another mistake is to create a theme that covers environmental issues, alongside other themes that the organization may have. Treating all issues of an environmental nature separately, whether in their own dedicated perspective or in a theme, effectively isolates the topic and forces them to be seen as side issues. Whilst the intention might be to signal their importance, you are actually sidelining them away from the other objectives and removing them as embedded thinking.

This is solved by what I call the 'render unto Caesar' approach. Rightly, environmental aspects associated with the processes and the learning and growth of the organization should be put in the objectives within the process, and learning and growth perspectives. If you wish to bring them out as a set, then treat them all as a theme that spans many objectives and the breadth of organizational responsibility.

Overall Approach

The environmental and social impact perspective is treated as a separate perspective, alongside the other organizational outcomes of financial and customer objectives as shown previously in chapter three (see Figure 12.1). The external perspective only captures the objectives that represent the environmental and social consequences of the organization's activities. The existing lower level perspectives identify what the organization is doing to improve these outcomes or results.

If you wish to split out the social impact and environmental impact of this perspective because they are each especially significant, please do. Just be aware of the emphasis that that provides. Changing the name of the perspective to say, 'CSR perspective', again has implications for the message that you communicate, potentially downgrading environmental impact and emphasizing all activities. What matters most is that you model and capture the impact appropriately and communicate your message correctly.

Figure 12.1 shows how the perspective contains objectives that relate to the environmental and social impact and separately the lower perspectives capture the drivers and causes of environmental and social change. Here you are embedding the drivers within the rest of the strategy.

Where your customers have environmental demands, place their demands as an objective in the customer perspective. You are effectively creating an embedded strategic theme of environmental and social thinking and action.

The way Figure 12.1 is drawn, there is no direct link from the environmental impact to the financial perspective because, typically, it is not a strong *direct* driver of the organization's financial performance. If you believe it is, then you can add one, but do be explicit about how the relationship actually works. Do not include such a link just to make the diagram look right (every arrow has to have a meaning). You can include the costs, savings or benefits of your environmental activities in your financial perspective, as long as the source is clear through the cause and effect relationship.

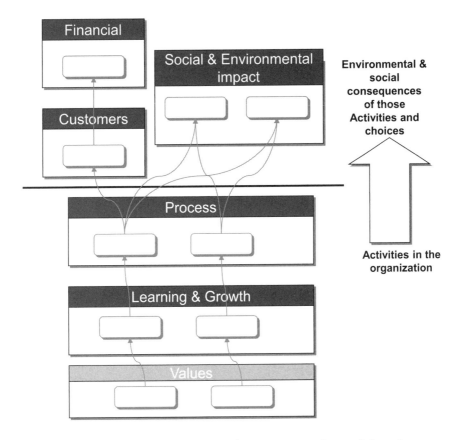

Figure 12.1 The environmental perspective captures the social and environmental consequences

Many organizations see their environmental activities as having an influence on their shareholder value through their reputation with the investor community and shareholders. Figure 12.2 shows a generic example of this. This organization believes that its environmental credentials influence investors' perceptions, and their regulator's comments, thereby positively influencing their share price. Clearly the opposite can occur, as with BP in 2010 when the oil spill in the Gulf of Mexico caused the share price to drop considerably, due to the consequences of both the clear up and the potential fines.

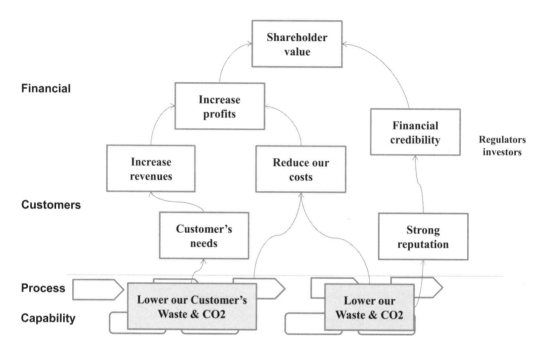

Figure 12.2 Environmental reputation can have financial implications

Figure 12.3 shows how the regulatory department of a water utility company saw their role in influencing the regulator, getting benefits from how the regulation applied to them as an organization and how this would ultimately affect their share price.

This environmental regulatory department sought to develop their capability across three themes: ensuring the quality of the water, setting the standards by ensuring water quality standards were understood, and directly influencing their regulatory environment. In each theme they identified capabilities they needed to develop as well as processes that they wished to improve.

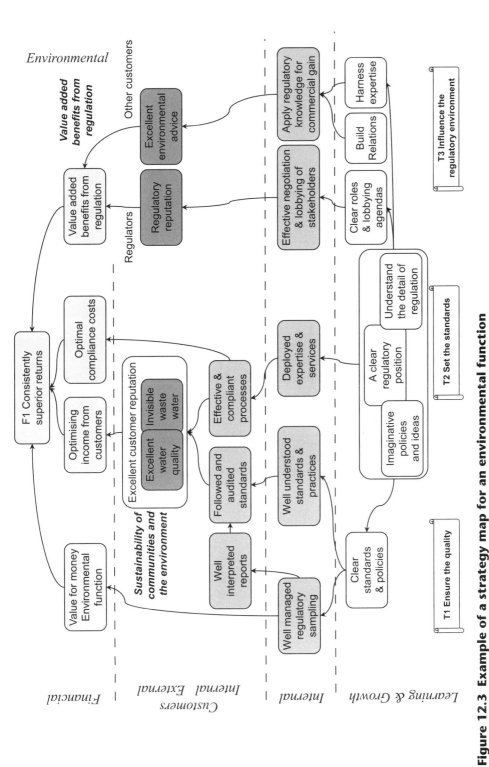

Figure 12.3 Example of a strategy map for an environmental function

Detailing the Environmental and Social Impact

So how do you represent the variety of social and environmental issues?

ENVIRONMENTAL IMPACT

When developing objectives in this perspective you are interested in capturing the impact of the widest operations of the organization on the wider environment. Your considerations should include the whole supply chain from first and second tier suppliers through to end users. You need to include the whole life cycle of products, from production through to reuse and recycling or disposal. In some industries such as the wood/paper supply chain, industry standards have emerged for quantifying and improving the impact on the environment. Some countries now have carbon trading and rules limiting the emission of greenhouse gases and other air pollutants. In other areas such standards are still emerging. Make sure you consult with industry bodies to monitor standards as they are developing.

Ensure you look at the wider impact on the environment. This might include your use of electricity, water, chemicals, and the sustainability of sources of raw material. There is a temptation to convert all impact into the CO_2 consumption or carbon footprint, but this should be avoided, as some conversion is still in discussion and other impacts are not appropriate. First identify the impact of your material so you are clear what your primary footprint involves, be that, say, chemicals disposal, water consumption or transportation miles. This way means you can address the primary source of the impact. Only when you have this should you consider the second stage of conversion, where appropriate, to a carbon footprint, or another standard if such is available.

SOCIAL IMPACT

With social impact, as with the customer perspective, it is absolutely vital you identify which particular groups in society you might be affecting before you start detailing any impact. This perspective requires you to look beyond your immediate customers, and also beyond their customers. You might look at the impact on the wider population around your organization. You might include impact on the local economy and how you, as an organization, contribute to that group in terms of charitable contributions, help with developments or supporting part of the economy. You might consider the impact beyond your immediate customers, for instance a pharmaceutical company might be thinking about the effect of the care of a patient on that patient's family, or the consequential health costs if a patient deteriorates. You might affect your suppliers, wherever they are located in the world.

Again, take a two stage approach: make sure you identify the groups that might be affected by your organization and then establish the various impacts on them. Make sure you are thinking of objectives from both their perspective and yours. For instance, you might want to foster good community relations (process perspective), with the effect that you are able to gainfully employ people with learning disabilities and so help their development and contribution to society.

With social impact it is useful to adopt the same approach as with the customer objectives: that is to identify archetypes and look at the processes they go through as a result of your social, or environmental, interventions. Then deduce your impact on their lives within that framework.

ENVIRONMENTAL IMPACT DIRECTLY ON CUSTOMERS

As you think through this perspective you will come up with some objectives that should by rights fall into the customer or financial perspectives. You may, for instance, alter the environmental impact of a customer and their supply chain. Here you would include objectives in the customer perspective that reflected that customer's demands upon you, e.g. 'lower my carbon footprint'. In the environmental perspective you might wish to include the total carbon footprint saved for your customers by your products or services.

You might also have demands on your environmental performance from legislators or regulators, and again it may be appropriate to include these in the environmental perspective or to treat the regulator as a customer. Make sure you include the environmental impact somewhere, but be sure not to double count.

FINANCIAL COSTS (OR BENEFITS) OF ENVIRONMENTAL THINKING

You can also include the direct costs or direct financial benefits of your environmental activities in the financial perspective. That is, how much do your improvements to how you handle environmental issues cost to implement and ultimately save for the organization? Where there are direct costs incurred by the organization associated with the environmental or social impact, then these costs would by rights fall into your financial perspective objectives. The same goes for the savings you have achieved. Whether these are captured in the financial perspective of the highest level strategy map or highlighted in a lower level strategy map would depend upon their importance within your strategy.

Where you have saved environmental costs for other people that are not reflected in your revenues – for instance, you have saved costs for your customers – again this would be captured in the customer perspective with an objective that might say, 'reduce my environmental costs'. In each case be clear from whose perspective the savings have occurred.

Integrating Social and Environmental Thinking into your Strategy

The most effective way to communicate your environmental intentions is to include appropriate words in the objectives of your strategy map. You can show in the lower strategy map perspectives how you bring the impact about. When I worked with the Environmental Services department of Peterborough City Council, nearly half of their objectives included the word 'sustainable' or 'environment', reflecting their intention to be a city with a reputation for its environmental credentials. Including reminders in the objectives helps to communicate the message.

Another client, a manufacturer of buildings, thought it unnecessary to show their environmental credentials in their top level strategy map. Their credentials were embedded within their objectives and in their lower level strategy maps. For them, sustainable buildings and environmental thinking were already a natural part of their culture and way of working. They designed buildings that had a low carbon footprint to build, were efficient to run and had a long lifespan, incorporating solar panels and very effective insulation into the designs.

Whichever way suits you, make explicit choices about how you bring your environmental and CSR credentials to the fore.

Managing Environmental Issues

There are various ways to think about environmental management. Each can be represented in your overall strategy map, but you may choose to have a strategy map that looks explicitly at your environmental management. For this scenario, here are five themes directly associated with your environmental thinking and activity. Each one of these themes will have aspects that reflect capability, information, culture and behaviour (learning and growth perspective), and aspects that are about what you do (process perspective).

MONITORING THE ENVIRONMENTAL CONTEXT

You may well be monitoring environmental legislation to ensure you comply and monitoring environmental trends to anticipate how the technology is moving. This is analogous to monitoring the environmental context. It represents your process for monitoring legislation. Of course, you may need additional skills, knowledge and capabilities to do this well, which will appear in your learning and growth perspective. Fail, and there will be financial costs.

COMPLYING WITH THE ENVIRONMENTAL LEGISLATION

You will need to ensure you are in compliance with existing legislation, and you will therefore need to include processes for monitoring your compliance with the legislation, as well as identifying which operational processes need compliance attention. The cultural piece may be about embedding environmental thinking into the activities of production or maintenance, and this would be represented in the learning and growth perspective. Fail here and there will be financial costs. The customers are the regulators.

REPORTING STATUTORY ENVIRONMENTAL COMPLIANCE

You may need to demonstrate and prove your compliance with the standards of legislation and therefore need an effective environmental compliance reporting process. I put this here to distinguish it from normal organizational compliance practices. Again, you may need to develop environmental auditing skills or some other environmental capabilities. There are costs with reporting compliance. There are costs with carbon trading, in both the trades and the transaction costs.

INNOVATING WITH YOUR ENVIRONMENTAL ACTIVITIES

You may wish to be innovative with your environmental activities and improve how you help lower your impact on the environment. It may even be a source of competitive advantage as environmental issues become more important. This is about doing it better. If you have an R&D process (which some call an innovation process) and that is aimed at improving sustainability, then you will also need to develop your organization's R&D skills (learning and growth). If it is about including environmental capability and thinking in your existing R&D process, then the process remains the same, but new skills, competencies and capabilities will be needed. This is likely to directly impact your customers and the revenue aspects of the financial perspective.

PROMOTING YOUR ENVIRONMENTAL CREDENTIALS

Many organizations have learnt to promote their environmental and CSR credentials, to positively influence both customers and investors. Here you are taking advantage of your credentials and promoting them. It is useful to think of this as the public relations process for your environmental or CSR activities. If you add to your environmental credibility, then you may improve your share price, attract new customers or win awards that add to your credibility and value.

Questions to Move between Perspectives

The focus of attention in this perspective is the impact of your activities environmentally and socially. So you will ask:

What environmental impact do you wish to have?

or

What impact do you wish to have on society/suppliers/your community?

To tease out the direct financial implications for your organization, you can also ask:

What are the financial consequences of achieving these objectives?

To move from this perspective to the process perspective, you would ask, for each environmental or social impact objective:

What are the few things we have to do really well to ensure we achieve this objective?

The navigation through the objectives from this perspective is identical in principle to the other perspectives. You should expect to iterate up and down the cause and effect story, as you develop the objectives and their characteristics, to ensure the story remains consistent and is told in the correct way.

Conclusion

The emphasis in this perspective is the impact of the organization's activities on the environment and on those stakeholders affected by the organization's wider CSR activities. The perspective captures the impact. The organization's actual environmental and CSR activities should be embedded within the objectives in the lower perspectives of the strategy map. Embedding your thinking into the objectives should ensure that they are not seen as an add-on.

As with any perspective, the ultimate test is whether the content of the perspective helps you communicate the overall story of your strategy and, in this case, its environmental and CSR credentials.

13 *The Process Perspective and Process Objectives*

The financial, customer and environmental perspectives contain the *effects* of the activities of your organization. In contrast, the process perspective is inside your organization and describes what you have to do. Achieving objectives in this perspective should cause objectives in the higher perspectives to change.

To develop the process perspective, you always start from the objectives in the higher perspectives and look for the process objectives that support them. Never start work in the process perspective, before you have detailed the financial and customer perspectives, otherwise you will find yourself justifying process objectives without a higher reason. The top down approach ensures that you concentrate on process objectives that are driven by your objectives in the higher perspectives.

The process perspective answers the question, 'what do we have to do well to deliver our intended results?' Those results are the objectives in the financial, customer and environmental perspectives. The higher level perspectives are also anchored in the purpose and the tangible vision, putting emphasis on delivering the longer-term strategy and vision. Taking this wider perspective can often lead to the redefinition of processes, functions or departments.

When working in this perspective you should be aware of current structures, but you should not work to, or assume, an existing structure or process. Rather you can ask, 'what is most important for the strategy?' This approach can identify process objectives that are important, but not large. For instance, in a FTSE 100 retailer, we identified having the right store portfolio as a critical objective in the process perspective. The property function contained very few people, yet they controlled most of the asset base: property location is a strong influence on the number of visitors to a store. This had not previously been on the management team's radar. In a city council with a cost base of £130m, the team responsible for developing commerce in the city had a total budget of barely £500,000, yet their objective was important enough to appear on the corporate strategy map, alongside the objective for the education department, which had a £70m budget. Looking for what is important, rather than departments or budgets, can also help you create a more joined up organization where previously there was silo thinking and working. The links between the objectives in each perspective should look similar to those in Figure 13.1.

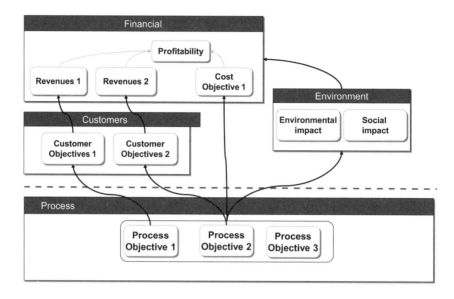

Figure 13.1 The objectives in the process perspective may support objectives in several higher perspectives

The overall approach to developing the process objectives is:

1. Understand the scope of the organization, and the particular processes you are dealing with
2. Develop the objectives for these processes, by linking
    a. from the objectives in the customer perspective
    b. from the non-revenue objectives in the financial perspective
    c. from the environmental impact perspective
3. Check the scope of the processes to ensure nothing significant has been missed.

Having a Clear Organizational Scope

When discussing and developing the process perspective, make absolutely sure you are clear about the scope of the part of the organization you are dealing with. The scope should have been clear when earlier perspectives were discussed, but any ambiguity in scope is usually exposed when the process perspective is discussed.

It is quite common for the strategy (and strategy map) to be limited by location, geography or the departments you are working with. Sometimes it will be determined by the customer segment. Whilst you are dealing with these factors, they will all ensure you check and validate the scope of the process objectives.

In an insurance company, the scope of the work was limited by the type of customer. The scope of the strategy map was to concentrate on the change in strategy for commercial customers and ignored changes to the services provided direct to consumers.

You also need to be aware of organizational boundaries and where contracting out arrangements stop and start.

> *A different insurance company required a rich picture of how well it 'treated customers fairly' (TCF), to demonstrate its compliance to its regulator, the FSA.[1] Even though the customer service function was outsourced, with a clear responsibility boundary, it was still necessary to collect information that demonstrated how the insurance company was treating customers fairly across all of its operations, even parts that were outsourced.*

Be clear where the organization makes its profit, from whom it receives revenue and where it incurs costs, as this will help you ensure you cover the entire scope of the activities and processes. You need to be absolutely clear of the ranges of products, services and offerings that the organization provides, and the limits of the strategy and strategy map.

> *Having listened for half an hour to the chief executive of a commercial service company describe the business, I was still puzzled. Eventually I had to ask, 'Where does your profit come from?' He replied, 'Oh, the profit comes from the property portfolio'. It turned out that the service company made almost no money at all. However, owning the land it was sited on meant that rent was charged to the holding company, and this was where the profit came from. There were also some other property assets that provided income. Suddenly it became clear: this was both a service company and a property company in the same ownership. The question now was whether to do two strategy maps or one that represented both (separate, but linked) businesses. It was decided to concentrate on the service company and keep the property part separate. This would focus the management's attention on the service company strategy. The separate property strategy would be discussed with the family that owned the overall business.*

Sometimes a part of the strategy is ruled out of scope. Often this is to ensure that the management team focus on delivering their part of the strategy, and to avoid distractions.

> *With a technology company, the scope of the strategy map was the international operation of the constituent organizations. However, whilst there was work underway to identify and acquire further companies into the group, the acquisition theme was considered out of scope.*

Sometimes the reason is to do with group structures and how the organization fits into the overall corporate portfolio of companies.

> *A retailer was part of a larger group that covered other high street companies and also a manufacturing and distribution business. These other pieces of the business were out of scope. The management team's objectives were set by the group, rather than the company's board. This meant that when these objectives became an issue, the company's chief executive had to raise the issue with the group management team rather than with his own board.*

---

1   TCF was an initiative introduced by the Financial Services Authority in the UK to ensure that consumers received a fair deal when dealing with financial services firms. It is based around six outcomes. Further details can be found at: http://www.fsa.gov.uk/pages/doing/regulated/tcf

Whatever type of organization you are dealing with, it is absolutely vital that you are clear about the scope of the strategy and the consequential scope of the process perspective. Have these elements of scope in mind as you work through the questions and develop the process objectives.

Generic Approach to the Process Perspective

The process perspective contains objectives that describe the strategy within the organization's processes. It will not include all of the organization's processes and their objectives. Rather, it will be the few that will make the biggest difference to the higher perspectives. Establish the process objectives with reference to the customer, financial and environmental objectives that you have already developed.

LINK FROM CUSTOMER OBJECTIVES

I prefer to start working from the customer objectives, despite the financial objectives being at the top. The customer objectives are where the revenues come from in commercial organizations, and customers' needs are also the main focus of not for profit organizations. Getting these right helps you validate the consequential financial objectives. We do this by working through the customer objectives, one by one. For each customer objective we ask:

> To deliver this customer objective (naming the objective), *what are the few things that we have to do really well, that will make the biggest difference?*

As usual the question emphasizes the few things that make the biggest difference within our processes. You can then run through the general questions, making them more specific to the customer and process objectives.

1. To achieve this customer objective, what do you have to do really well as an organization?
2. How well do you perform these processes? (Marks out of 10)
3. What do you have to do differently to ensure the (process) objectives are achieved?
4. What stops you delivering this?
5. If you deliver these process objectives, will the customer objective be delivered? Will they make it a 10?

You should repeat this for every customer objective in turn. Of course, you may find that some of the process objectives are common and will serve several of the customer objectives. So you can amalgamate them once you have finished working across the customer objectives.

Figure 13.2 shows an organization, part of which seeks to persuade politicians to fund help for people with numeracy and literacy difficulties, as well as working with adult literacy providers. This example shows only the persuasion (advocacy) part of their strategy map. You can see how each customer's (politician's) objectives are matched by objectives in the advocacy process. It shows how the politicians must first be convinced there is a need, and that they will want to see real evidence that policy will make a difference. Once convinced, they will want help with policy development and ultimately policy implementation. This process of convincing and helping the politicians is matched by the objectives of the advocacy process. Advocacy seeks to engage people with the problem, convince them it is a priority, help the civil servants and politicians to set policy, and help with both implementation and demonstrating that the policy is having an effect. Of course, this last piece is important to the politicians, who want to demonstrate that their actions have made a difference, and to the advocates, who want to see that their work has resulted in improvements in literacy and numeracy levels.

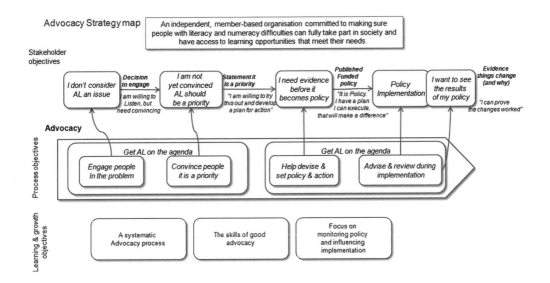

Figure 13.2 Example showing how customer objectives can dictate the structure of the process objectives

This is a good example of where the customer perspective reflects the stages you want them to go through, rather than what they might necessarily want: a subtle but useful approach to use where the customers are to be persuaded to buy or use the services.

LINKS FROM THE FINANCIAL OBJECTIVES

With the financial perspective, the revenue only comes via customers, so do not try to link the revenue objectives directly to the process perspective. They will be linked through the customer objectives. You only need a cause and effect link from the non-revenue objectives (e.g. cash flow, cost, risk). The process for working from these financial objectives is the same as for the customer perspective, only varying the name of the objective:

1. To achieve this financial objective, what do you have to do really well?
2. What do these processes have to achieve? What is the performance gap?

3. What do you have to do differently to ensure the (process) objectives are achieved?
4. What stops you delivering this?
5. If you deliver these changes, will the financial objective be delivered? Will they make it a 10?

The most significant objective is likely to be the overall cost of the organization, including the impact on the strategy of the cost of sales and the cost of operations to deliver the customer objectives. This is most easily represented by a link that surrounds the appropriate processes and links them to the cost objectives. For instance, you might want to isolate the cost of sales or the costs of manufacturing or servicing.

There will be specific process objectives that will bring about the financial changes – perhaps changes to how cash flow is managed or a major investment in manufacturing that will decrease operational costs. These are shown as specific links from the process objectives to the financial objectives.

LINKS TO THE ENVIRONMENTAL IMPACT PERSPECTIVE

The links from the environmental and social impact perspective are developed in exactly the same way as for the other two perspectives, with the questions adjusted to refer to the environmental and social impact objectives.

1. To achieve this environmental/social objective, what do you have to do really well?
2. What do these processes have to achieve? What is the performance gap?
3. What do you have to do differently to ensure the (process) objectives are achieved?
4. What stops you delivering this?
5. If you deliver these changes, will the financial objective be delivered? Will they make it a 10?

As well as developing objectives specific to the environmental and social impact perspective you will find it worthwhile asking how each objective contributes to the perspective, and identifying where any tensions might apply.

Strategy Maps with Various Process Perspective Designs

You can see how this generic approach works in the example of the manufacturer of modular buildings that are later assembled on site (see Chapter 4, Figure 4.9). We discussed the customer perspective previously. Six process objectives have been identified, which correspond to the various customer objectives as the building is conceived, designed, built and eventually handed over for occupation.

These six process objectives (numbered P1 to P6 in the diagram) were deliberately designed to bridge across the organizational departments and ensure that the organization operated in a joined up fashion. The organization was divided into sales and marketing; the design team; the supply chain that managed input and output logistics; manufacturing, which built the modules; and after sales, which ensured the modules were assembled correctly and resolved any warranty problems.

The six process objectives can be matched to these departments, with some overlap, but have been deliberately described to encourage the departments to work together. For each process objective, you can see how it relates specifically to a customer objective and, in the detail, each link has a specific meaning that is understood by the team. For example, 'P2 Effective propositions' requires input from both the sales team and the design team. The design team find ways to provide architects with solutions that allow the architect to be flexible in design whilst still allowing the building to be manufactured. Objective 'P3 Quality design and support that balance performance and price' contains elements of the design of the look and feel of the building, as well as how the building is designed to simplify its manufacture and therefore lower costs.

The example in Figure 13.3 shows a different approach. This comes from an organization that rents, sells and services commercial vehicles (trucks and vans). In this case the business was divided into two separate parts, and it made sense to continue this split in their strategy map. So there are two main, separate sets of process objectives that have been developed: one set for vehicle provision, covering the vehicle rental and sales (the theme of providing quality vehicles), and another set for the after sales operations that keep people on the road.

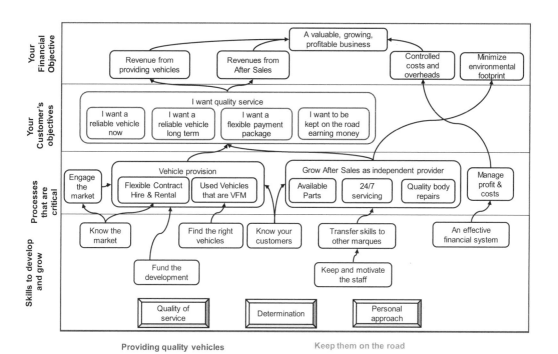

Figure 13.3 Strategy map for a commercial vehicles company

A Strategy Map for a Detailed Process

Figure 13.4 provides an example of both a detailed process and of a not for profit organization. This is actually a detailed strategy map deep within a hospital and applies to the Ear, Nose and Throat (ENT) outpatients clinic. It is a good example of how once you get several levels down in the organization and start to deal with a specific department or process, you often develop what looks like an outline process map. In this example, you can see how the issues within this particular clinic have been included on the map. The overall process in this clinic will be similar, if not identical, to the processes in all the other outpatients clinics. So, this design is generic enough that the approach could easily be mapped across to help identify where problems might lie in other clinics. This would allow you to look across clinics for consistent themes and problems.

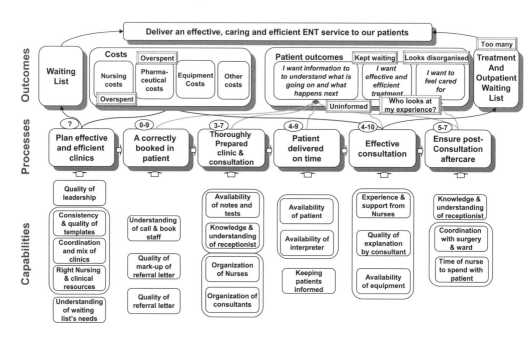

Figure 13.4 Strategy map for an outpatients department in a hospital

The first two objectives ('Plan effective clinics' and 'Book the patient in correctly') refer to activities that lie outside the direct remit of the clinic, yet they have a dramatic effect on its efficiency. They involve planning clinics to account for the demand for care and the waiting list. They must also ensure that sufficient time is allocated for different types of consultation, depending upon the referral from the GP or the presenting symptoms. The patient booking system is strictly outside the scope of the clinic, yet the clinic relies on this to ensure that patients are booked in properly and know their appointment times, and that 'call and book' staff understand the needs of the clinicians in this type of clinic. This is a good example of looking at the influences of other processes on the performance of a particular process. In this example, the process the clinic follows is represented very closely by the strategy map. With conventional process mapping, the focus is the process.

In strategy mapping, the focus in the process perspective is the objectives of those processes: what is to be achieved, not how it is done. The higher perspectives show the consequence of the process objectives. The lowest perspective shows the skills knowledge and capabilities needed to improve the processes. This is a really valuable technique for analysing a process in a wider context than traditional process mapping techniques use.

WORDING PROCESS OBJECTIVES

How you phrase process objectives makes a significant difference. It is extremely important to phrase process objectives as the end result of the process, rather than the activity of the process. The example below shows this contrast (Figure 13.5). The first set of process 'objectives' from the clinic example are expressed as activities rather than outcomes. A good clue here is the use of words that end '...ing'. These suggest an ongoing activity: planning, booking, delivering, etc. In each case they are an activity rather than an outcome.

The second set of objectives shows a set of process objectives that express a desired state in each case. It was not about the activity of 'Planning the clinic' but rather the objective 'Plan effective and efficient clinics'.

Wording an objective correctly ensures that you concentrate on the objective of the process, rather than its current activity. The retailer we looked at previously named their store portfolio objective 'put us in reach of every customer'. This is far more open and useful than the original statement, 'manage the store portfolio' because the interpretation of what is good management was too open. Using 'right store, right location' gives more scope to discuss land values and property rents. The final version, 'put us in reach of every customer', allows other channels, such as the internet, to complement the physical stores.

These examples clearly show how important it is to detail the characteristics of an objective as well as giving it a succinct and memorable name. That name should only be finalized once the more detailed characteristics have been developed and understood, to ensure that the name chosen is representative of the underlying detail.

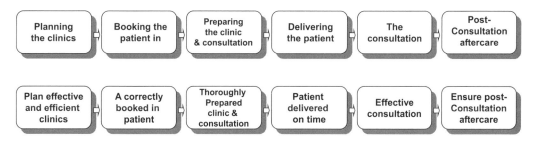

Figure 13.5 Contrasting alternative wording for the process perspective

USING PROCESS MODELS

Make sure you do not get lost in the detail of a process. If you wanted to develop a performance model of the processes, you would map them in detail and then look for the measures that gave information about the activities, quality, times, resources, etc. along the various stages of the processes. We are not doing this. It may be useful analysis, but it is not the intention. The strategy map is looking for those pieces of a process that need most change or improvement and that will make the biggest difference to the customers or the financial results. We are looking for where the management judges that the improvements will have most impact on the strategy. The more detailed model provides a basis from which you can evaluate the effectiveness of the processes and determine the source of problems.

The strategy map will show particular aspects of a process, not the whole process. Fixing just a particular part will make the difference. It might be the front end of the process where things go wrong, or somewhere along the way. Perhaps it is something about the links between this process and others. If manufacturing is only performing at a six out of 10 level, because the designs it receives are poorly configured or the supply chain is so tight that the parts are not always available, then the problem is prior to the manufacturing process. The problem will be in the links and relationships between elements of the process.

This approach has a useful application when considering the impact of the management of knowledge in an organization. The learning and growth perspective contains the knowledge, skills and capabilities that the organization needs to develop to deliver change in the process perspective. It provides a direct link to the eventual impact on the customer and the financial consequences. This is extremely useful for developing the business case for knowledge management and also ensuring that knowledge management activities concentrate on delivering their benefits.

Whatever the approach to process improvement, the outline process model allows you to look at the whole process and ensure that you are addressing the points that will make the biggest difference.

CHECK PROCESSES' SCOPE TO ENSURE NOTHING IS MISSED

This approach of looking at the whole is also useful at any level when checking the scope of the process perspective. I find the best way to do this is to map out the outline of the processes in perhaps four or, at most, six steps (just as in the primary activities of the value chain model). Any more is too detailed. Any fewer often misses key pieces and can be too general. I often use this approach to scope out a discussion and ensure we are talking about the same processes and activities. It makes establishing which steps will make the biggest difference easier. It also has the effect of acknowledging the more detailed processes, which may well be scoped out in a lower strategy map, so that any director who owns one of those areas and its processes knows that we will come back to the detail.

Do be careful to ensure that this approach is not used to develop bottom up thinking, warned about earlier. Tackling the process perspective's objectives this way can lead to bottom up justification, rather than deriving the objectives from the strategic intent.

After the directors had presented their strategy maps to the 50 middle managers, we asked the managers to demonstrate where they thought they could contribute to the strategy by placing sticky notes on the various strategy maps. Unfortunately the legal and audit teams took it a bit too literally and stuck a yellow sticky note on every single objective they could find, explaining how they might make a difference. Of course they were right, operationally they could make a difference everywhere, but not the significant difference that the management team were looking for.

Be conscious that the discussion will move to 'what is wrong today', rather than 'what is needed for the future'. The 'what is wrong today' discussion is useful, but often produces a more operationally focused set of process objectives and a more operational strategy map. You have to be sure that the improvements support the longer-term, improving the previously established financial and customer objectives, rather than just fixing operational issues for the sake of it.

It is vital that you concentrate on the objectives for the processes, rather than the steps of the processes. The objective descriptions become the axis around which the processes fit. This is important because the processes around which the organization is currently organized may not be the most appropriate for the strategy. This way of thinking helps to break down existing processes that are causing problems with the delivery of the organization's objectives.

The approach can also be useful where an organization has a more operational focus and wants to fix short-term issues, and where clarity over the processes will help the organization tease out what is most important within them. It is valuable to know and understand the processes, but still be driven by the need to deliver the objectives higher up the strategy map.

Joined up Working: Eliminating Silo-Based Thinking

The opportunity to avoid silo thinking occurs during the interviews. When you are interviewing a functional director about the strategy map at board or corporate level, it is vital that you ask them to answer as a board director rather than as a functional director. The answers will then be from the corporate perspective, rather than the narrower functional perspective. When you interview a board director and their team about the strategy map for their function, you can later ask them to answer from the perspective of their department. By this time you should have a wider context to work in, so that they can also think about how they as a function can contribute to the delivery of any or all of the objectives on the corporate strategy map.

This next example is from a public sector organization, included here specifically to demonstrate how you can break down silos and create joined up organizations (see Figure 13.6).

If you use process objectives that reflect each department, such as customer services, sales or production, it will only encourage and perpetuate silo thinking and working. However, if you choose objectives that are jointly owned by various departments you will start to break these silos down. This happens when you start with customer objectives and ask, not 'how can this department serve this customer's need?' but 'how do we *as an organization* serve this customer's need?'

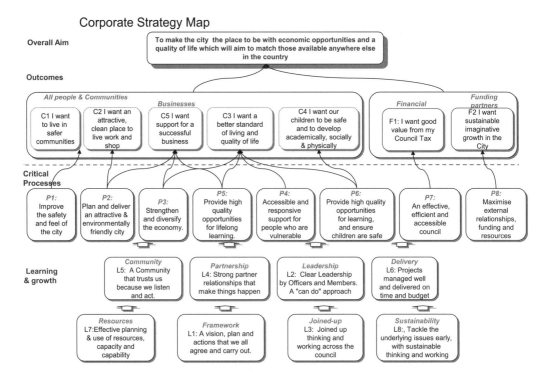

Figure 13.6 Strategy map for a city council showing process objectives deliberately chosen to break down silos

In this city council example, the chief executive was concerned that her team were operating as separate functions and worked in silos. This is not untypical of an organization that has such diverse services as street cleaning, planning, adult social services, schools, adult education and childcare. At the same time, the council was redeveloping its city centre, looking for business partners to develop the economy and trying to satisfy central government demands for targets and financial performance. The chief executive believed that one way towards a more effective overall service and lower costs was to encourage joined up thinking and working across the organization. She also recognized that this started with her management team.

Having developed the customer and financial perspectives, and the demands of central government first, two alternative designs for the process perspective were produced.

The first design reflected the current organizational divisions of the organization, creating a traditional functional split. The second design was quite different. It reflected much more closely the structure of the customer perspective.

The chief executive was offered both. She wanted to move to a more joined up organization, and considered whether she might initially go with the functional design, moving to the more joined up approach over the following two years. She decided to go straight to the joined up model.

The effect, at the management team level, was that each director jointly owned several of the process objectives, and each process objective was shared amongst the directors. Thus safety was shared between the director of environmental services, the director of community services and the director of contract services. Planning and delivering an attractive city was shared between the director of environmental services, which included the planning department, and the director of community services, who had the business development team within her remit. Prior to any management team meeting, the directors had to review progress as a team. Any one of the directors with responsibility for a particular customer objective could then talk about, report on and answer questions for that objective. In fact they would take it in turns, backing each other up as necessary.

This joined up working at the director level caused their teams to have to come together, in many cases to meet with people they had never met before, to discuss the wider aspects of delivering each of the objectives. It also meant that as the objectives cascaded, each director needed to look across the corporate strategy map for any objectives that they could support in addition to those they were directly responsible for.

The traditional approach to joined up working is to try to create a new organizational structure or design that solves the joined up thinking and working by placing people in new departments. Of course, this costs immense effort and often money, becomes political as people fight for fiefdoms and distracts the organization from external delivery for anything from nine to 18 months. In contrast, this alternative arrangement leaves people in place but encourages them to simply talk to others who can help them deliver what they need to. Picking up the phone and meeting with people in other departments is far cheaper than massive reorganizations, yet can achieve a far better result.

Conclusion

This chapter has explained how your process objectives can be linked to your objectives in the higher level perspectives. We have also looked at various ways in which the choice of process objectives affects how the strategy map is used.

At the organizational level, there is an obvious temptation to develop a set of process objectives that reflect the existing divisions or functions of the organization. Resist this easy option. Rather, think hard about the few things that will make the biggest difference *across the organization* to achieving the customer and financial objectives. Think objectives rather than activity. Ask directors to think as general managers rather than functional heads. Choose wording that encourages cross-functional thinking and opens up opportunities rather than narrows them down.

Of course, reflect the themes of the strategy and ensure that these are the dominant thread around which the story of the strategy is woven.

Finally, remember that you are concentrating on the few things that will make the biggest difference to your strategy, at the level of the organization you are currently dealing with. This means that some aspects will undoubtedly be omitted. That is fine *at this level*: they will eventually be included at an appropriate level of the cascade of the strategy map. Avoid the temptation to put everything in. The question is, 'what are the few things we need to do differently to deliver this strategy?' When you are clear on this you will be in a better position to develop the objectives in the learning and growth perspective.

14 *The Learning and Growth Perspective and Objectives*

The basic model within the balanced scorecard and strategy map is that the 'human capital' of the organization underpins its strategy, creates its value and drives performance. What makes the difference are the skills, knowledge, capabilities and culture of the organization, the ability to exploit and deliver technology, the quality of the people and the management. These can create sustainable and persistent capabilities that underpin the organization's delivery of its strategy and create value. It is the choices about which capabilities to develop and the ability to nurture, build and grow them that will continue to give the strategy an edge and underpin its delivery long-term. Representing this is the role of the learning and growth perspective.

The perspective is called 'learning and growth' because the focus of attention is, 'what do you need to learn and grow as an organization to deliver your strategy?' This perspective is about the organization's ability to recognize that to succeed it needs to develop and grow its capabilities, to evolve, to re-evaluate itself and even reinvent itself, growing new capabilities. This perspective should contain objectives that describe the skills, knowledge and capabilities that the organization needs to focus its attention on in the long-term.

The learning and growth perspective is both wide and specific. It should consider the whole range of potential aspects of learning and growth that the organization could develop, but also the few specific ones that will deliver the strategy, set it apart from its competition or position it for the future. This is the challenge when developing objectives in this perspective.

Changing the Name from Learning and Growth is a Big Mistake

The concept of learning and growth is fundamental to strategy maps and strategy focused balanced scorecards. Too many practitioners miss this point and rename this perspective 'people', 'culture', 'employees', 'staff' or something similar. They think they are being helpful and are making it clearer. In fact, they have undermined the value and intent of the perspective. As soon as they rename the perspective they remove the ideal of learning and growth. They undermine the strategic thinking and the strategy map. This perspective is not about measuring the current attributes of the people in the organization or the current culture and skills. It is about focusing on what the organization needs to develop, learn and grow for the future. The original name was given for a reason.

There are three good reasons for keeping the name 'learning and growth'. First, names such as 'employees', 'people' and 'culture' are fundamentally static. The name 'learning and growth' was deliberately chosen and designed to suggest movement. What do we have to learn? What do we need to grow? It is about change, rather than being static. When organizations rename this perspective 'employees' they place static information about their staff in the perspective. They are no longer thinking of the strategy and change. They are providing information on where the organization is now. Useful perhaps, but not strategy and change.

Secondly, changing the name also changes its scope. If the name is changed from learning and growth to 'people' or 'employees', what role is there for technology, data or physical capability? What about behaviours? What about skills and knowledge? What about intellectual capital? What potential is there to discuss, learn about and develop alliances, suppliers and partners if only your employees are considered? If the perspective is only about employees, where is the contribution of management and leadership? Any of these could help to deliver the strategy, so it is foolish to exclude them. Basing the perspective only on people or employees narrows the perspective. Learning and growth opens up the scope.

Finally, changing the name changes its relationship to the other perspectives. The name 'learning and growth' asks the question, 'what do we need to learn and grow?' The title 'people' or 'employees' at best poses the question, 'what people or employees do we have or need?' This leads to the narrow path of resource allocation and utilization. The question might be useful, but it is a very narrow view. The learning and growth agenda opens up a wider set of questions and potential answers. It puts the emphasis on the organization's wider capability, rather than just its people.

I admit I do sometimes change the name but keep the intention. In the public sector I will sometimes use the phrase 'growing capacity and capability'. Public sector organizations use the language of capacity and capability to cover similar aspects to those which learning and growth covers. This reflects both the capability of the organization to deliver and the capacity of the resources. However, use 'growing' or 'developing' in front, to emphasize its dynamic nature. The important message here is about the message you convey, in the language of the organization, without losing the rich meaning. It is the same as the point about the arrows between objectives in different perspectives having meaning and questions attached. These questions have to be explicit and clear. How you label this perspective helps to make them clear. If you change the name and lose this meaning, you will lose the effectiveness of the strategy map and a critical aspect of the organization's strategy.

Deriving Learning and Growth Objectives

There is only one way to derive the objectives in the learning and growth perspective. It has to be from the top, downwards. That means starting with the objectives in the process perspective and working down to the learning and growth objectives that support them. The story of the strategy only makes sense when you can say:

To achieve this process objective, what we do we need to learn and grow as an organization?

Of course the phrase 'learn and grow' is somewhat ambiguous, so make sure you have explained its scope before you start asking this question. You can also make the question clearer and prompt the specific thinking by asking:

To deliver this (name of process objective), what skills, knowledge, technology, culture, behaviours and capabilities *do we have to learn and grow as an organization?*

Notice how this question deliberately covers the gamut of learning and growth without specifically heading for one type of capability. You could ask, about each of these aspects individually, what culture do you need? What behaviours do you want? What technology will support this? Do not try this as you will have to second guess which is most important – knowledge, behaviours, skills, capacity, technology or culture – and ask the questions in the right sequence. These very specific questions will narrow the range of answers that you will receive. If you always ask about behaviours or culture, you will always only get responses about behaviours or culture. These are not the only answers. How you ask the question frames the response you will get.

The way around this is to be sensitive to the topics that are raised as the process objectives are characterized. As each process objective is detailed and its characteristics set out, you will naturally pick up comments about skills, knowledge, behaviours and culture, which do not fit within the process perspective but rather fit in the learning and growth perspective. As you notice these, use them to help you to be sensitive to the common themes that are developing across the process objectives.

Trying to develop the learning and growth perspective any other way will lead to problems. Too often I have seen someone try to develop the perspective from the bottom, thinking what might also help. I hear people saying, 'we need to develop this capability, skill, behaviour, *because* that will improve this *process*'. They may be right, but to what extent will it improve the process objective? The question is, 'is that one of the most critical, important and highest leverage capabilities that will make the biggest difference?' Quite often it is not. There are often many others that may also improve it. To check this, you can ask, 'to bring about the changes you want in the process, in the timescales you want, is that one of the *few* underlying pieces that will make the biggest difference?'

Structure of the Learning and Growth Perspective

Look for learning and growth objectives that transcend the organization and are fundamental to the strategy: objectives that will cascade through the organization; objectives that may manifest themselves in different parts of the organization in different ways, but have a common theme. This is how you build a sense of 'this is what the strategy means for us'.

LEARNING AND GROWTH OBJECTIVES DERIVED FROM PROCESS OBJECTIVES

Because you are developing the learning and growth perspective from the top down it is normal to have a set of learning and growth objectives that are initially linked tightly to the individual process objectives. You are likely to identify two or three learning and growth objectives attached to each process objective. The perspective will look confusing with too many learning and growth objectives. On closer inspection you will start to see common themes emerge and notice that several of the learning and growth objectives will actually be similar and can be merged. For instance, you may find that leadership is a common objective that manifests itself differently in different areas or processes within the organization. Your first run through the perspective will quickly be rationalized so that you end up with perhaps five or six learning and growth objectives, each supporting multiple process objectives, in various ways. What you will have developed are the common strategic learning and growth objectives that apply through the organization.

This rationalization process is extremely common in strategy maps at the corporate level. As you work through the organization, the application of objectives will become more specific. The leadership necessary in the supply chain might be quite different to that applied in sales or alliances.

Even at the corporate level, you are likely to find some learning and growth objectives that are specific to only one process objective. In the corporate strategy map for the manufacturing company (Figure 4.9) the learning and growth objectives are quite specific to one or two of the process objectives. This reflects the different capabilities that are required in different parts of the organization. At the same time there are three learning and growth objectives in the lower part of the learning and growth perspective that appear to float free. These are common across the organization. Trying to draw lines from each of these to all the process objectives would create a mess, visually and logically.

Having some learning and growth objectives that are quite specific and others that are more general provides a useful way to show different levels of detail in the perspective.

THEME SPECIFIC LEARNING AND GROWTH OBJECTIVES

When developing a strongly thematic strategy map, it is quite common to find separate learning and growth objectives (and therefore capabilities) being developed in each theme area. These are specific to their theme and are designed to specifically drive the performance of that theme. Consequently, as the theme cascades, so do the learning and growth objectives.

This approach was applied in a technology company, where the group strategy was cascaded to other companies within the group. In this case the assessment of the strengths, or weaknesses, of each company was used to identify where synergy might occur as one company supported the development of another's capabilities or knowledge.

COMMON AND SPECIFIC OBJECTIVES

As you develop the learning and growth perspective, look out for these potential patterns. How you group the objectives, or make them specific, will influence how the story of the strategy is told. It is also useful to look at the overall capabilities that the organization needs to develop, across themes and through its cascade. Having these capabilities transcend the themes helps to ensure that the corporate message and imperatives are clearly communicated. As the strategy maps cascade, you may find that the objectives apply in a similar way in each theme or functional area. In other cases, the themes and functional areas may need to apply different interpretations of what is needed to close the gap, for them. Either way, the lower level department must ask, 'what do we have to do to improve our capability in this area?'

Forms of Learning and Growth Objectives

There is a very broad set of learning and growth objectives from which you might choose. Be careful, as some 'balanced scorecards' will suggest that particular learning and growth objectives should always occur. I am not in favour of presuming that particular strategies or particular organizations should be adopting particular learning and growth objectives. My experience is that companies, even in the same market segment with the same customers, will adopt quite different underlying learning and growth objectives that reflect their particular positioning and direction in the market. However, there are some types of learning and growth objectives that frequently occur in management discussions, and this section is a short guide to them. As you work through these and think about their applicability to your organization, I encourage you to be specific in your language.

SKILLS AND COMPETENCIES

Skills and competencies are very common in the learning and growth perspective. Sometimes these are technical skills and other times they may be managerial skills. These often initially arise in discussions as training initiatives, but are identified as persistent capabilities the organization needs to focus on and develop long-term.

You are not looking at competencies against existing demand, but rather where you want, or need, to be in the future. You are not trying to assess whether existing activities or projects have the right competencies, though this might also be important; rather, whether the organization as a whole needs to develop. A person may have adequate project management skills for their current role, but that does not mean they should not be developed for future needs. When you later come to want to measure competencies it is relatively easy to develop competency matrices that map available skills against current and forthcoming demand.

KNOWLEDGE AND INFORMATION

A very common learning and growth objective is associated with knowledge. This might be technical knowledge, industry knowledge, market knowledge or even knowledge about specific customers. Just as with the competencies, knowledge matrices can be developed to reflect the current and desired extent of knowledge of the people in the organization, and a similar approach can be used to develop it. Where information is required, for example in market research or knowledge of specialist technologies, exactly the same approach can be applied. Sometimes this knowledge might be brought in or purchased. Other times it might be systematically collected by the staff.

TECHNOLOGY AND RESEARCH

With organizations involved in research, there are often learning and growth objectives that reflect their ability to manage research projects, develop intellectual property and communicate that research.

Quite often companies refer to innovation. When I encounter it, I will deliberately deconstruct their use of the word and also ensure that they are clear how innovation works across the various perspectives. Innovation is far more useful as a label for a theme that transcends objectives in several perspectives than as a solitary learning and growth objective. The theme provides an overarching thread which each objective can detail and make specific, leaving less to the imagination and interpretation.

Technology companies often look for uniqueness of their technology as an enabler. They will want to be at the forefront of technologies, and often create intellectual capital or intellectual property to protect their position. Such companies will frequently want to retain their best staff, so often have learning and growth objectives that are designed to make their workplace a supportive environment that acknowledges and rewards their deep technical expertise.

ORGANIZATIONAL CULTURE

Culture is the vaguest word that finds its way into the learning and growth perspective, competing heavily with the word management in the process perspective. Organizations who like to head straight to measures, rather than developing the description and characteristics of an objective beforehand, tend to quantify culture with measures such as employee satisfaction, absenteeism and staff turnover in their balanced scorecards. However, there is a more subtle approach that looks at relationships and how culture originates and evolves. It is much more about seeing what behaviours are accepted and what are not. It is about how managers behave. It is about how people learn what is acceptable behaviour and what is not. It is about peer pressure, the way people do things, the limits that exist and the permission managers give their staff. It is about how people behave on a day-to-day basis.

> *Whilst I was working with one team of senior managers, they complained that their staff were persistently late for meetings. I paused and looked at them. I then asked them, as a team, what time they had turned up to start the workshop that morning. They were silent for a while, until the penny dropped. They were habitually late for meetings and so their staff had become used to it and turned up late. No-one had challenged this before, or pointed out that they had actually trained their staff to be late. It was their behaviour that had taught their staff. If they wanted their staff to change, they needed to change first. They needed to signal that being late was no longer acceptable with their own actions.*

It is this ability to explicitly challenge the rules, create new permissions or set new boundaries that will often change cultures. The wording of your learning and growth objectives needs to make this explicit, so that both the intent and permissions are expressed clearly by managers to their staff and new behaviours can be learnt and adopted.

Sometimes culture can be about relationships within teams or between teams, sometimes internal and sometimes external – involving partners, suppliers and customers. It might even be between parts of the company operating in different countries or continents.

COMMUNICATION

Often 'communication' will arise as a learning and growth objective. Again, be specific. Who needs to improve their communication of what to whom? It might be about improving the quality of the message. It might be about improving the quality of conversation amongst people in a team. It might be about engaging the market and customers in different ways. Whichever it is, be specific.

MANAGEMENT AND LEADERSHIP

Quite often learning and growth objectives will express the need for the management to ensure they set an example by behaving in particular ways or by focusing their communication, so it is clear what is important. This might be about how they demonstrate leadership, explain the strategy or set direction. It might involve starting to do something differently or stopping doing something (and making it clear that they are doing so). Often, it will be about creating the space for people to perform or explicitly giving the permission for new behaviours. It may be about building accountability, responsibility and trust, and delegating. Quite often teams I work with recognize that they need to step back and make more time to address the strategy and even let their managers manage. Management can often be about improving the quality of the conversation within the management team.

Learning and Growth for the Management Team

So far, we have been talking about building organizational capability. Quite often there are capabilities that the management need to develop and demonstrate to make the organization change. Examples of this may include 'clear leadership' or 'making the time to do the right things'. These are capabilities for the management team, as distinct from those capabilities that apply to the whole organization (though some will certainly apply to other layers of management).

Sometimes it is useful to develop a strategy map specifically for the management team. This will be exactly the same as the one for the organization with a complementary set of management capabilities added to the learning and growth perspective. This represents the objectives that that specific team have to pay attention to. So, at the end of every meeting they can ask themselves whether they are playing their part in helping the organization to change.

Dangers with Learning and Growth Objectives

There are many dangers and traps in the learning and growth perspective.

WHATEVER I CAN FIND TO MEASURE

The first, and most common, trap is to go straight to measures without thinking through the objectives. I have met many human resource people who are cynical about the balanced scorecard approach because they were tasked with finding measures of the people for the learning and growth perspective. They weren't engaged in the strategy discussion, but merely asked to develop 'HR measures' to create 'balance'. Following this instruction they created a 'people' perspective with measures of their activity instead of a learning and growth perspective. The favourites amongst these are: staff turnover, absenteeism, diversity, and health and safety. These may all represent useful operational information, but are rarely about the underlying capability of the organization to deliver its strategy. These hygiene measures have a use, but rarely drive strategic change. One solution is to report these as a separate set. Parmenter (2007) suggests creating a separate perspective for them, but avoids explaining how that would help the learning and growth perspective. Include them if you want, but make sure you are clear which are used for regulatory and operational purposes and which should drive strategic change.

Staff turnover is a typical example of this sort of measure. It is readily available, but what does it mean? Do you want it to rise or fall? Are the people leaving those that you want to leave, or are they the better people that are leaving for a reason? Are some leaving simply because of personal circumstances? The staff survey is another common inclusion. These are often general surveys of satisfaction rather than surveys specific to the few things of culture, knowledge and capability that will make the biggest difference. The survey is often annual and so of limited use for day-to-day or month-to-month attention, action and management. It is also extremely rich and complex, yet vague, containing many pieces that aggregate into an overall view. What specific aspects of the culture do you really want to concentrate on? A general survey may be useful for an annual review, but you need something more specific to address on a month by month basis.

I am suspicious of strategy maps and balanced scorecards with too many of these types of measures in them. Their owners are missing a big opportunity. Such scorecards are useful items of information about managing staff, but they are not about the underlying capability of the organization to implement and deliver its strategy, fundamentally position itself in the future and develop new capabilities, or bring about change. I doubt whether they were derived by asking precise questions about what would improve the process objectives. This perspective needs to be about the growing capability of the organization and it learning new capabilities.

AVOIDING OTHER VAGUE WORDS AND PHRASES

As with the descriptions of objectives in any perspective, you should be careful to avoid single, well meaning words that are open to wide interpretation. Alongside 'culture', common examples of this in the learning and growth perspective include 'professionalism', 'leadership', 'quality' and 'management'. These words are nominalizations that are so wide in application that they can mean everything and nothing to anyone. They lack precision: it is not clear what aspects of them need to be applied. They lack specificity: what specifically should I do to demonstrate better management or more professionalism? They lack applicability: where do they need to be applied? They lack clear purpose and objectivity: how shall we know when we have achieved our ends and so should move our emphasis somewhere else?

As well as being vague and unhelpful, they can often insult. One managing director I worked with was frustrated with the information his staff provided and had taken to saying to them that they 'needed to be more professional'. Probably true, but hardly a statement that would encourage change. Saying we need to be professional suggests we are being amateurish at the moment. On the strategy map we took the same message but changed it to, 'demonstrate our professionalism'. This phrase presumes staff *are* already professional, while putting the emphasis on them to provide the evidence and demonstrate it. This clearer message provides a better starting point and a far more positive message about what to do differently.

To get beyond such vague words, ask, specifically, 'what aspect of culture, leadership or quality needs to be displayed?' If they can't answer this question, it suggests that the team are unsure of what they really mean and need to find out. If you fail to do this, the vagueness problem will persist and you will be unlikely to make progress.

BOTTOM UP JUSTIFICATION AND OTHER STRANGE PATTERNS

Beware when you see a pattern like the one shown in Figure 14.1 on a strategy map. In this case someone has decided that the objective supports everything. This is, of course, bottom up justification.

A variation on this is where you see a pattern like the one in Figure 14.2. Every learning and growth objective is attached to the same process objective. This suggests that there are too many aspects being considered important and that there is a failure to identify the few that really make the difference. The alternative explanation is that the process objective is a much larger objective that may need to be broken down into separate objectives, each of which would have only a few learning and growth objectives attached.

When you are working in this perspective, personal agendas will come strongly to the front. This will manifest itself as, 'we need this capability' or 'you can't forget...' Be careful where people are seeking to justify their roles and departments being included, rather than asking what the strategy needs. This behaviour is most common where people are concerned about their roles and seeking to justify their presence in the strategy or ensure

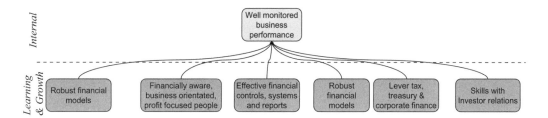

Figure 14.1 The sign of bottom up justification of an objective

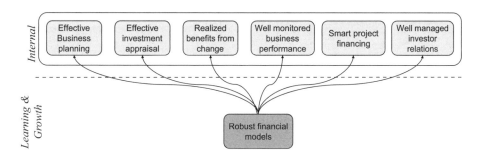

Figure 14.2 Too many learning and growth objectives support a single process objective

they are represented, in case their role is chopped, outsourced or shrunk. It is often a sign of concern or fear and suggests something about the culture of the organization or the esteem of the individual manager. In reality, if the objective is important, it will appear in a lower level of the strategy map.

I have experienced several cases where, given the opportunity, the legal department will attach a legal implication to every single activity (process objective) across the whole organization (and its strategy map). I do not single out the legal function for this, as almost any support function might play this same game. Many objectives may have legal implications, and the legal department should be thinking about this, but that is not the point. The question is, what will make the biggest difference to achieving the higher level objectives? What capabilities, skills and knowledge will make the *biggest difference* to this strategy happening? Frankly, including legal input may be necessary, but it is rarely the determining success factor.

If you do not have any aspects of a particular function amongst the learning and growth objectives in the corporate strategy map, it is not necessarily a concern. The corporate strategy map of a FTSE 100 company I worked with contained no specific information technology objectives in the learning and growth perspective. At the corporate level, it was all about the skills and knowledge they needed to develop, rather than the need for better technology. Actually their systems were pretty good, with innovative customer data collection and profiling. Their IT improvements were more local and tactical from a sound base. The information technology contribution emerged as some specific IT projects at the top level and as a contribution to some learning and growth objectives in the second level strategy maps.

TRANSIENT ACTIVITIES AND PROJECTS, INSTEAD OF PERSISTENCY

As with the process perspective, a common mistake in this perspective is to word the objectives as activities or projects rather than express them as persistent capabilities.

For instance, 'sales training' is either an activity or might even be a short project. In contrast, 'a sales team with relationship sales skills' is a persistent objective that could be achieved in a variety of ways, which would be supported by training and other management activities. Likewise, 'build customer database' is a project that should have a completion date. In contrast, 'know our customers' is an objective that has persistency: an objective for which the organization should be able to define what aspects of the customer they need to know and what capabilities they need to develop to get to know this detail and to maintain it. It then becomes a persistent objective, perhaps supported by various short-term projects. One way to move from a project to a persistent capability is to ask, 'what capability is this activity or project designed to improve?' This moves attention away from the activity to its purpose. You can then ask what other activities might also be going on that are also designed to improve this capability long-term.

This move from projects to objectives is really important. It makes the difference between a persistent strategy map and one whose lower levels become a series of short-term activities, projects, actions and initiatives. If you really want a *strategy* map, you should be asking about those capabilities that are persistent. Which capabilities will change and develop the competitiveness of the organization, in the long-term?

OVERWHELMED BY LEARNING AND GROWTH OPTIONS

Sometimes you may be faced with a bewildering amount of information about the skills, knowledge and capabilities that an organization believes it needs to develop.

> *A retailer had a tremendous range of potential learning and growth objectives. In reviewing their 'strategic literature', we identified nearly 80 different statements of skill, knowledge, culture and behaviour that were being suggested for development across the organization: far too many for any clear strategic intent and persistent capability. We created a list on a single page, categorized into groups, in the hope that the directors being interviewed would be able to say which were most important for their strategy. When we asked the question in the interviews, given the context of the few main process objectives they had identified, this list of 80 came down to only six main areas of skill, knowledge and capability: the six that were most critical to the development of the strategy.*

The lesson from this was to be open-minded about the potential answers that come out, but to look for specific themes that are really driving the strategy, as opposed to merely being useful initiatives. It was the persistent retailing skills, the development of customer insights and an expertise in their particular segment of the market that was most important for their strategy.

Testing the Logic and Checking the Strategy

Finally, when you have your learning and growth objectives developed, test the logic of the story up and down through the themes across the perspectives. Move down and up through the cause and effect model and check that the story makes sense. Check also that the learning and growth objectives are sufficient to close the performance gaps in the process objectives. If they are not, then revisit the 'few things that will make the biggest difference'. Also check the scope of the learning and growth objectives to ensure you have considered the full gamut of knowledge, skills, culture, technology, behaviours, etc. Finally, look for underlying issues. The 'what stops you?' question is particularly powerful as it will expose the barriers and help you get to the underlying causes.

The learning and growth perspective is the one that really distinguishes the strategy map approach from other ways of describing organizations and their strategies. As an executive team you should be looking for persistent capability that will underpin your ability to perform better than you have, or to take you forward. You are looking for persistent, sustainable capabilities that will distinguish your organization in the minds of its staff and ideally its customers. You are looking for the few things that your organization needs to learn, grow and develop that will drive the performance of your processes and make a significant difference to your customers and ultimately your finances.

15 *The Organizational Values Perspective*

When I started helping organizations to design their strategy maps, the lowest perspective always contained the learning and growth objectives. Most learning and growth objectives were specific to the process objectives and themes directly above them, whilst others were more general and transcended the organization's strategy and cascade. Both these types of learning and growth objectives were covered in the previous chapter.

However, after a while, a third characteristic of learning and growth objectives emerged that did not fit comfortably into either of these previous characteristics. These were the organization's values. Organizations almost always cited these as critical to their success. They transcended the organization, but they were different from the learning and growth objectives. They were often more persistent and deeper than the behaviours and actions that normally went into the learning and growth perspective. There were often around six or seven values statements displayed around the organization. Usually much time and effort had gone into choosing them, defining what they meant, communicating them and reinforcing their message around the organization.

It soon became clear to me that these types of objectives were best represented by a new and separate perspective: one that represented how the organization's deeply held values underpinned the strategy. Placing the organization's values in their own perspective underneath the learning and growth perspective positioned them to underpin the culture, behaviours and thinking of the organization.

The Benefits of Including a Values Perspective

The first time I used a values perspective explicitly on a strategy map was early in 1999 while working on the strategy map for a major retailer. The values were talked about as a part of the strategy and needed to be represented on the strategy map. The values of the organization were, as one director put it, 'the values of trust, integrity, honesty and authority [which] reflect the origins of the business'. Some of the values came from their original business nearly 100 years previously, even though they now positioned themselves as quite a different organization. These values were persistent and clearly showed through in their actual and expected behaviours and ways of working. It was clear that their values were different from the learning and growth objectives and needed to be a part of the strategy map.

Nowadays, I always put the values on a strategy map. If the strategy and business plan documents contain values statements, I will always place them on a draft strategy map. As a minimum, it checks that they are still valid. If I cannot initially find the organizational values, I place blank holding positions for the values to be inserted. Even having blank values on the strategy map is useful. It draws attention to the underpinning values of the organization and invites the management team to think what the values are and how they relate to the rest of the strategy.

I like to represent the organizational values in the shape of a keystone. This symbol has the effect of visually including and embracing the objectives in the higher perspectives. It also symbolizes a stabilizing stone that underpins the strategy map. It is purely visual, but seems to work. Having values on your strategy map confers three important benefits: emphasizing their role in the strategy, helping to stabilize the strategy map and helping to ensure consistency through your cascade.

VALUES EMPHASIZE THEIR IMPORTANCE TO THE STRATEGY

Simply including your organizational values on the strategy map makes them an explicit part of the strategy and also helps you to test their role in telling your story of the strategy. They underpin the strategy map, ensuring they are seen to support the strategy. They naturally become a part of the story, so that when the story of the strategy is told using the strategy map, from the top to the bottom and back again, the organizational values are included as a fundamental underpinning component.

ORGANIZATIONAL VALUES HELP TO STABILIZE THE STRATEGY MAP

The second benefit is to stabilize the bottom half of the strategy map, especially the learning and growth objectives.

I have had some organizations that have maintained their strategy map with basically the same structure for over five years, though the structure does evolve. As the strategy map evolves, the objectives in the upper perspectives tend to remain relatively stable, though the targets might change. The objectives in the process perspective also tend to stay relatively consistent. Of course, within this persistency and consistency of the objectives, the measures may be refined and developed, the targets will change and be updated, and the projects will get implemented and new ones will develop.

There is a greater rate of change, generally, amongst the objectives in the learning and growth perspective. As improvements are made and the strategy is implemented, the objectives in the lower perspectives, particularly learning and growth, will be achieved and new ones may be needed. This is a balance of persistency against growth and development. Without the values perspective, I found that management teams tended to choose learning and growth objectives that were more transient. In contrast, putting persistent, deeply held organizational values at the bottom of the strategy map demands a more long-term approach in the learning and growth components. The learning and growth objectives are still developed with reference to the performance gap they need to close in the process objectives. However, they are also chosen with reference to the more persistent organizational values in mind and therefore more persistent learning and growth objectives are chosen. The values inform the choice, emphasis and content of the learning and growth objectives. Overall they help to stabilize the development of the strategy map.

INCLUDING VALUES HELPS WITH THE CASCADE

The third advantage of the values perspective is that it helps communicate the organization's values as the strategy cascades through the organization. Most organizations have one set of organizational values that they apply through the whole organization.

As you cascade the strategy maps through the organization, you start by placing these organizational values at the bottom of each strategy map, just as you place the purpose or mission at the top. These values, along with the organizational purpose, become the anchor points for each and every strategy map in the cascade. Every strategy map then tells its story with reference to the same organizational values. The organization's purpose or mission statement and the organization's values serve to frame the strategy.

> In a manufacturing company the organizational values 'working together', 'taking the lead' and 'sharing' were inherited from their parent company. It became clear, relatively quickly, that the team managing the subsidiary needed to both work together better and take the lead in explaining the strategy. In this case, the managing director was able to use the corporate values to emphasize the importance of working together: first as a management team and secondly as an organization. For them, the organizational values became a natural part of explaining what needed to change and telling the whole story of their new strategy.

If there is a different culture further down in a part of the organization, placing these values explicitly on the corporate strategy map sends a clear message about the corporate values. Should an organizational unit, when it is developing its strategy map, choose to put on a different set of values, it would show up as an incongruity within the cascade of the strategy. Were a unit to omit the organizational values it would prompt the question, why did they do that? Do they perhaps not believe in the organization's values? Having the same set of organizational values on all strategy maps ensures a consistent story and helps to check organizational alignment.

VALUES AND STRATEGIC LEARNING

The strategic learning model is framed by the future thinking, the external environment and the organizational values, as shown in Figure 2.3. They form a part of the frame that creates the space for people to perform. If you as leaders give people the vision and the values, they can make their own decisions about how to perform. Including the organizational values on the strategy map helps to communicate this space where leadership happens and how leadership happens.

What are Organizational Values?

It is helpful to recognize that there are different nuances of organizational values that play different roles in organizations. Whilst we experience organizational values through our interaction with people, we most often see the organizational values as framed statements in the organization's reception that are repeated in posters throughout the building. There are usually around six such 'values' statements. One way to think about organizational values is as norms of behaviour, that is, what people are expected to do.

Generally people conform to established patterns and standards of behaviour and do not transgress them.

Why are there only six organizational values? Generally people don't steal or murder people, and are polite enough to let others through a door first. These do not usually need stating. The explicit espoused values are often ones that the organization wants to particularly emphasize or enforce. This principle of the ones that need emphasizing was backed up by a managing director with whom I was discussing organizational values. In his view, the values slowly evolved. They represented the deeper behaviours that people needed to pay most attention to at the time. He said that he only referred to the values on recruitment as a way to introduce people to the culture. The real values were being developed and refined as the organization repositioned itself and changed for the better. For him, they were a rallying cry and statement of emphasis. Perhaps this was because of the extent of change that his organization was going through. In this case organizational values had an important role to play in communicating the change and the strategy.

It is helpful to think about organizational values as a meme, a set of cultural ideas that bonds a group together (Dawkins 2006), or as an ethos, that is a culturally standardized system of organization of the instincts and emotions of the individuals in a group (Bateson 1972: 108). Organizational values exist within a cultural context which encourages particular types and patterns of behaviour. You can see, and experience, this in organizations with very strong and specific cultures. I have seen this in the partnership culture of various accounting and management consultancy firms, in a variety of investment banks and even in charities and not for profit organizations. In this sense, the values represent persistent standards and expectations of behaviour that are reinforced: things that the organization stands for, and therefore the people within it should stand for.

Some organizations have a set of values statements that acts like a brand and defines how the organization should operate, particularly in relation to their customers. Examples of these values statements include: 'customer first', 'integrity', 'honesty', 'passion for innovation', 'high ethical standards', 'technical excellence', 'teamwork' and 'quality'. These are as much a statement to customers about the brand as they are to the organization itself. Of course, such statements might also be calling attention to how the organization should operate and be managed.

There are quite often organizational values statements about social responsibility and environmental awareness that are reflected in organizational values. Again, these are both a directive to act internally and an external positioning statement.

These organizational values might provide statements and criteria against which the strategy can be assessed. They may be a rallying call for its underlying purpose. Whatever their purpose, remember that these are statements that the organization has chosen to adopt. So respect them. Ensure you have the correct set and that you represent them correctly on the strategy map. If you find that the management team start to challenge the statements themselves, then so be it. At least you have given them the chance to review the relevance and coherence of their values statements against their strategy and have invited them to think about how they will play a part in the strategy's communication and implementation.

The reason for making these distinctions amongst values statements is to help you recognize how different types support the strategy and play a role in the communication of the strategy. The more aware you are of the history of the organization's values statements, where they came from, why they exist, how long they have been there, who knows about them and what effort has gone into communicating their importance, the better you will understand how they fit into the story of the strategy.

No matter how the organization's values arose, the challenge for management is to act them out, communicate them and help people to understand them well enough to apply them as they make decisions during their working day. Just as an understanding of the future thinking and strategy helps those in the organization to understand what they are trying to achieve, the values should act as a guide to how they should achieve them.

Measuring Organizational Values

I am often told that organizational values cannot be measured. Rather, 'you just know them'. If I had believed that organizations needed to know how to measure everything before it went on the strategy map, then the values would probably not have appeared in the first place. Because I ignored this constraint, I was happy to put organizational values on the strategy map, where they are just treated as a different type of objective in a different perspective. Interestingly, most clients put the values on their strategy map and do not worry about measuring them on their scorecard. Usually any measurement involves observation and monitoring rather than using specific measures, but you can measure them, as you probably do today. To consider how to do this, think about your reactions and answers to the following questions.

EXERCISE:

1. If a person espoused the value 'teamwork', yet consistently operated alone, you would know about it wouldn't you? So how do you know?
2. Think of a time when someone has 'trodden' on your values. How did you know? How did you react?
3. Ask a peer whom you know well whether your team holds true to the organization's values. Then ask for examples. See what answer you get.

You will notice that, in each case, the answer is to do with observable behaviours or language. It is usually behaviour, or the words that people use, that indicates holding, encouraging or transgressing values. Observable behaviours and language are how values are described and detailed. Many organizations go beyond the simple statement of a value to explain the behaviours that they want to encourage. This is also how they are monitored, rather than explicitly measured..

Conclusion

Placing the organization's values in a separate perspective beneath the learning and growth perspective has several positive effects on the strategy map. It is symbolic in the communication of the strategy map. Having the values underpinning the strategy map emphasizes how the organization's values underpin the strategy and the underlying behaviours, culture and capability. This clearly shows how the organization's strategy map is now framed by its vision and values.

It also helps in the operation of the strategy map and the management of the strategy. The values perspective has the effect of stabilizing the bottom half of the strategy map. As strategy maps are used, the objectives in the learning and growth perspective are often the first to be achieved, revised and changed. Refined and new capabilities, skills and knowledge are included. The values perspective acts as an additional and stable point of reference when choosing new learning and growth objectives. Finally, and most importantly, it ensures the values are connected to the strategy and its implementation.

16 *The External Perspective*

The external perspective widens the traditional balanced scorecard and helps you to monitor and manage the implications of your environment for your strategy and performance. It also helps you widen the vision of your management team and your staff, so they also look outside their functional boundaries, and outside the organization, at the wider context in which they are working. There are typically three uses for this perspective:

1. Understanding the context of performance, especially when the context might change
2. Making an informed, fair comparison between similar units with different contexts
3. Monitoring the external environment for changes that may undermine the strategy, or at least mean it needs refinement.

This perspective sits alongside the strategy map to provide the context, as shown in Figure 16.1.

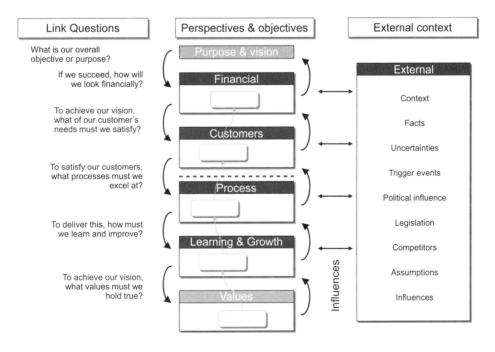

Figure 16.1 The external context sits beside the cause and effect model

This chapter also provides a checklist of the breadth of external information that you might consider monitoring for your organization. This wide scope of the external perspective is shown in a structured onion diagram in Figure 16.2.

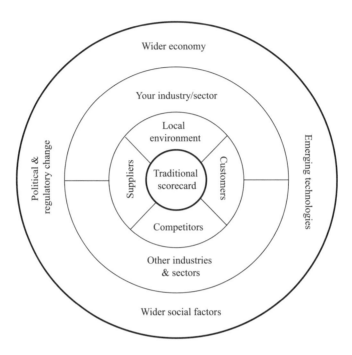

Figure 16.2 The potential range of external context information

Explaining the Changing Context

An explanation of the context and environment helps you build an overall picture of where performance is taking place and why it is taking place. The context in which performance takes place may be considered, but is rarely documented, especially when setting targets based on forecasts. What happens when the context changes but the targets are not revised? You get dissatisfaction, at the least. At worst, you create people who are motivated and incentivized to deliver targets that are no longer appropriate. The information in the external perspective explains the environment in which performance is taking place: the external drivers of performance. Knowing this context ensures that should the context change, then the assumptions behind the level of performance achievable will also change, which will have implications for any targets which have been set.

The most obvious example of a changing environment is the credit crisis that hit in 2008, restricting access to funds, changing buying patterns and causing uncertainty in markets. However, there can be more mundane external changes. A leisure business operated near where a set of major roadworks operated for most of the holiday season. Not surprisingly, visitor numbers dropped at a time when they were expected to be at their peak for the year, significantly affecting turnover for the year. In similar circumstances, large retailers with similarly affected outlets have been known to target the customers who live nearby with vouchers for significant reductions off their shopping basket in an attempt to maintain footfall and turnover. Knowing population volumes helps you plan services, especially where there are sudden unexpected changes. A city received a significant influx of immigrants, which changed demands on the council's services to exceed its expected and available funding. This happened in Leicester between 2002 and 2004, when approximately 10,000 Dutch Somalis unexpectedly moved from the Netherlands to the city, creating problems as schools and services were not funded for such high volumes of extra people.

Understanding how business volumes might change helps you make sensible predictions and decisions about costs, efficiency and acquisitions.

A life insurance company is managing the administration of its products in its service centres. However, this life insurance company's portfolio of products is no longer open to new business (known as a 'closed book' portfolio); so, as customers die, or claim on their products, the number of customers served will decline and the drivers of service centre activity will change, eventually reaching zero. This change affects the volume of activity and administration required in the call centre. Knowing this overall context, and how it is expected to change, helps them make sense of the changing activity and productivity figures within the centre. As books decline and new closed books are acquired, the information about the changing context helps them plan and manage the overall expectation of the volume and mix of work in their service centres.

Monitoring the economic situation helps you understand the wider economic drivers of business activity and performance.

A listed high street retailer set a target for creating shareholder value, consisting of share price increases together with dividend distribution. However, whilst the company might perform well, the share price would be subject to underlying movements in the stock market as a whole and their sector in particular. They needed to compare their share price performance with the share price performance of other comparable retailers. Only then could they say whether they had successfully created greater value for their shareholders, relative to the other shares those shareholders might have chosen to hold. The retailer's shareholder value target would only have meaning in the context of the overall market's performance and the performance of other players in the same market.

In both of these cases, performance is informed by the context that surrounds the organization. Understanding this context guides you towards which facts and information you need to make sensible comparisons of performance, be it the number of policies maturing this year, market share, the availability of bank lending, or the size of the population you serve. These external factors may well be the basis upon which budgets are set, for say call centre numbers or funding for schools. You need these facts and you need to notice when they change. If the context changes, the underlying targets may no longer be valid.

Comparing Parts of the Organization with Different Contexts

Context information is extremely valuable when assessing the relative performance and potential for improvement of similar parts of an organization. As was discussed in chapter seven, it allows you to make an informed, fair comparison from amongst similar activities. If targets are set across an organization for many similar units, regions or branches without considering their context, then you create inappropriate or unachievable targets. Providing the context enables you to sensibly and appropriately compare similar parts of the organization, and helps you to understand where and, most importantly, *why* ambition and performance might be different. You can then set targets appropriate to the journey that that part of the organization is on.

This was part of the scope set by an organization with many regions when they asked us to develop a balanced scorecard to help both the board and management team to compare relative regional performance.

> *Dimensions are a company that help people with learning disabilities to live the lives they want to live. The company had around 20 regions around the UK. The board and executive team wanted to compare relative performance in the regions. However, the mix of people with learning disabilities in each region can vary considerably. They may have a predominantly young population transitioning from living at home to living independently, or they may have quite elderly populations. The level of disability of the people they support can be quite variable, placing different demands on the staff in type and level of support required. One region may have been established for some time, with established management and staff. Another region may have recently taken over a contract and so some, or all, of its staff will have been recently transferred from local authority employment across to the company. For each region, the context information provided the board with a clear view of the challenges that region faced, thus allowing the board to make a more informed comparison of where each region was and the progress it could make.*

In this case the units varied as well as the context. However, even in ostensibly similar operations, the context in which they operate can vary.

> *A bank may operate many branches around the country. The mix of population that each branch serves may be quite different and therefore the mix of operations that it provides and its relative performance can vary dramatically. Three branches operating in a rural area, a poor city and an economically wealthy city will serve quite different customer groups and therefore have quite different profiles of activity. This is important to realize when branches are tasked with cross-selling products amongst their customers. The type of products cross-sold from a branch that serves an elderly or retired community will be quite different from the range sold to a predominantly younger, upwardly mobile population in a city. Both will differ from those sold in a predominantly rural economy.*

The context helps explain in each case where one business unit is at any one time. It also allows a more informed comparison of that unit with comparable units. Rather than imposing blanket targets, it informs the ambition setting process so that any targets are relative to where the units are and their potential for improvement.

It also means that comparison might be made between parts of the organization that have similar contexts. For instance, the bank may have branches that serve a variety of rural communities across the country, that do not fall into their natural regions of north, south, east, west and central. A fair comparison would be between branches serving communities with similar characteristics, no matter what their geographic location.

Monitoring and Predicting Changes in the Environment

When the environment changes, a management team might persist with their strategy for too long instead of revising it. Perhaps they made assumptions that proved to be wrong. Perhaps they were uncertain about some aspects that have become clearer. Understanding the context in which performance happens, and sensing changes to the assumptions and uncertainties that the strategy and ambition were based upon help you to improve your judgement.

Initially a management team dismissed one particular part of the market on the basis of information and experience from one of their directors. However, some six months later they realized that that sector had potential and that their director (who had now left) had been painting a somewhat black and white picture of the situation.

In this situation the information came from within the team. Later information from outside overturned their initial perceptions. In other circumstances, changes in the environment can cause the management team to have to react quickly to the quickly changing environment.

As the credit crunch started and the economic consequences started to manifest themselves, credit availability dropped and the volatility of investment vehicles increased. Those involved in the financial services industry were concerned with liquidity, solvency and capital adequacy. In more stable times, such information was normally evaluated on a monthly basis, as it was well above limits. However, as the crisis deepened, it became a daily regime of assessing the impact and monitoring the solvency levels to ensure that financial covenants were not breached and regulatory limits were maintained.

In both these cases the management team had initial views of their environment which they monitored and later changed. Had they not, they would have missed opportunities or potentially been caught exposed. Both organizations increased their monitoring activity as a result of what they had learnt: one increasing the range of potential markets they were concerned with and the other increasing the frequency with which they monitored the changing markets.

The Range of the External Perspective

These examples deliberately cover a wide range of potential situations and external information. What you choose to monitor will be based in part upon the strategic analysis and the information gathered during the strategic thinking and planning phases. It will have also come from the work developing a tangible future and the value chain, and developing the objectives in the various perspectives of the strategy map.

To help you think through all the potential sources and changes, Figure 16.2 provides a framework against which to consider potential external information. The normal information used to manage the operation of the organization is represented by the central circle. Out from this there are three layers of increasing breadth: your immediate context, your industry and other industries, and your wider economic and social changes.

CUSTOMERS, SUPPLIERS AND COMPETITORS

The first layer is monitoring the immediate context and environment. This most easily relates to your customers, suppliers and competitors, as well as local economic drivers. For instance, asking, 'what are our customers' concerns?' and 'what are our suppliers' concerns?' will help you look at the influences they have and their part of the market. Monitoring your organization's immediate competitors will help you notice changes as they occur. I know some organizations that regularly interview people who have left their competitors: as a minimum they get to see good people and, as a bonus, they get an insight into their competitors' activities.

For a smaller unit of the organization, the first layer will encompass the factors that dictate their local economy, such as the volume of customers served or, in the example of a bank branch, the state of their competition and the volume of immediate customers.

YOUR INDUSTRY AND OTHER INDUSTRIES

In the next level outwards you should be looking at the state of the industry and industry trends. What is changing in the economics of the industry? What new technologies are emerging? What new competitors are entering? Many industries organize events where peers meet to present their wares or explore the state of their market. These provide an opportunity to explore trends and changes.

Do not restrict yourself to your existing market, but look beyond to other markets. Many companies have been caught by a technology emerging from another industry and undermining the economics of their industry. Make sure that what you consider as industry best practice is not merely common practice in your industry and poor practice when other organizations are considered.

THE WIDER ECONOMY, MARKETS AND SOCIAL CHANGE

At the wider level, make sure you are plugged in to the wider economic and social trends that might bring about changes and may eventually manifest themselves as opportunities or threats. Monitoring the state of your immediate economy and the state of the economy in supplier and customer markets is a good place to start. Also monitor other economies to see how things are developing and where opportunities may lie. Obviously social change can be as important as economic change. Looking at behaviours and trends, and then asking how these might affect your business, is a basic part of being strategic in thinking and action.

Monitoring, not Measuring, Facts not Targets

With the external perspective, the emphasis is on monitoring, not measuring. This is not a place for targets. This is intelligence gathering and assimilation. You may look for movements between levels, and how trends are developing, but in the main you are doing non-judgemental collection of information which you can assimilate and review.

The information from your strategy will help you identify where assumptions, risks and uncertainties may lie. You are looking for trigger events that might tell you that something you were uncertain about is becoming certain, or that your assumptions are turning out to be false.

You are gathering facts and information. This information might only make sense at a later stage, once you have had the chance to compare it with other information from other sources. This relies on the non-judgemental collection and sharing of information. You are looking for trends, discontinuities and information that suggests things might be changing. Ideally you want a leading indicator that things are going to change. For instance, political unrest might be a leading indicator of potential disruptions to oil supplies, which in turn might lead to a rise in the price of oil. In some cases you will know what trigger events to look for. In other cases identification of an event will encourage you to pay more attention to a particular aspect and monitor it more deeply or regularly.

There are typically six stages that you go through when using an external context:

1. Identify what is needed and how it will be collected
2. Monitor and gather external information
3. Identify trends and consistent signals
4. Discuss and assess the implications: how they may affect the strategy or plans
5. Act upon the changes
6. Continuously review the signals coming and the information that is needed.

Do be careful of decision rationalization. This is where you look for information to explain or justify your decisions (Doll and Torkzadeh 1998; De Wall 2002: 137–140). Also be careful of selective attention, or sustained inattention blindness (Simons and Chabris 1999, 2010) as demonstrated by Simons and Chabris in their popular video, where as you concentrate on counting the number of times a basketball is passed you completely miss a bizarre incident that happens during the counting.[1]

Presenting the External Perspective

When presenting context information, I find it useful to create for clients a three page pack. This pack's first page contains the contextual information, followed by the strategy map and then the scorecard. This works when you are identifying changes for a single external context and when comparing a set of units with different contexts. An alternative arrangement is to have a vertical column alongside the strategy map where the contextual information is shown, as in Figure 16.1. I have used this with clients, but the

---

[1]   I do not want to ruin this for you. Suffice to say when asked afterwards approximately half the people who watched the video missed the unexpected event.

space is often limited and it causes the strategy map and the contextual information to be squeezed. As a result, I tend to support a separate sheet for the contextual information, as it is little hardship to turn a page.

When clients are dealing with the softer intelligence associated with looking for changes in their environment, then two approaches are useful. The first is where you have information against specific issues you have already identified, such as an assumption you are monitoring. Then it is helpful to keep the information in the context of that assumption and its implications. Were you assuming that a competitor was not developing a particular technology, then any reports that updated that situation would be presented in the context of competitor information and the implications of that for your development, production or sales schedules.

When you are monitoring the wider context for potential opportunities then it is helpful to provide this as raw and interpreted intelligence in regular briefings and updates. This may be away from the context of the strategy map, except where the implications of the intelligence have direct implications for the strategy that the strategy map explains.

Whichever approaches you use, the important thing to encourage is the quality of conversation around this information. Making sure you understand the facts and context before assessing performance ensures that you are looking at the information in an appropriate context and that you can do a fair comparison against others. Make sure that the context is discussed as much as the information that describes the performance and results.

With the intelligence, the important quality of conversation is about non-judgemental review and being open to what the information might be telling you. Bearing in mind that often this information is in the informal knowledge of your colleagues, it is important to create the space and time for discussion of such information and the beliefs and sources behind it. Such conversations will help you stay plugged in to the market and environment, and be better able to judge the appropriateness of your strategy and your next strategic move.

VI *Alignment*

Part VI is about organizational alignment. Aligning the organization behind the strategy is fundamental to its success.

Chapter 17 explains how to align the investments in change through projects and programmes with the strategy captured in your strategy maps. This approach as rich consequences for both savings and the realisation of the financial benefits of the strategy. Executives will appreciate the additional discipline and control this brings. Practitioners will appreciate the tools to assist in alignment as well as integrating programme and project management disciplines into the overall approach.

Chapter 18 is about the alignment of budgets and budgeting. This chapter will help you avoid mis-understanding about how strategy maps and scorecard capture the finances. It will also help you align the organizational budgets with the strategy, without potential changes to the accounting systems. This chapter will also help you move from annual budgeting to rolling budgets and forecasts, creating a more flexible responsive organization.

Chapter 19 addresses the controversial issue of balanced scorecards and risk. Risk and risk management is an important topic in governance and board rooms. Many believe, incorrectly, that the balanced scorecard does not include risk. This chapter explains how strategy maps and scorecards do indeed capture a class of risk appropriate to their role in governance: that class of risk associated with strategy implementation. So this chapter has important lessons for executives involved in overall governance, practitioners dealing with risk management and auditors and others concerned with risk compliance.

17 *Aligning Programmes, Projects and Investments in Change*

Strategic choice is about the allocation of scarce resources and where to invest in programmes and projects to bring about change and improvements.

The financial benefits of the techniques in this chapter can be considerable. If your capital investment in projects concentrates on what will make the biggest difference, then you are more likely to get the maximum 'bang for your buck'. If, on the other hand, you have many projects that are sapping energy, time and financial resources then you may not deliver all you hoped to. Meanwhile, you have spent much money for little tangible reward. This chapter is about making sure this does not happen, so you can concentrate resources on delivering the right benefits, with confidence, for your strategy.

Projects and programmes are drivers of change, which can be aligned against the objectives on a strategy map and your scorecard. This will ensure that they contribute to the achievement of the objectives and the delivery of the overall programme and strategy. This approach also helps you to track the delivery of the benefits of programmes and projects. Surprisingly, tracking the execution of projects that contribute to the strategy is not as common as you might expect. Executives in a McKinsey survey (2006) said tracking and accountability were central to strategy implementation, yet only 56 per cent said that their company tracked the execution of its strategic initiatives. Whether you are in the 56 per cent or not, this chapter will help you.

How you define the rules for investment and make investment choices is as important as how you run your individual programmes and projects. As Figure 17.1 shows, the strategic learning model can be applied to the more specific role of managing your strategic choices and learning about change. This includes how you think about your investments, managing investments, your overall approach to managing change and your choices about what sort of programme and project management approach to take. The operational management level is about the effective management of projects and programmes. You make choices at both levels.

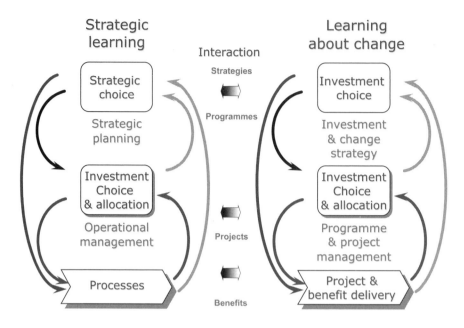

Figure 17.1 Strategic learning and learning about organizational change are related

The Basic Model

The basic model we use is to have projects as investments in change that influence objectives in either the process or learning and growth perspectives. Projects exist for only a limited timescale. They aim to bring about a step change in the performance of an objective.

PROJECTS ARE DISTINCT FROM OBJECTIVES

Projects are quite distinct from objectives, and the two should not be confused. An objective describes something that the organization wants to achieve persistently. A project is a specific activity that has a start and a finish. The example in Figure 17.2 shows how the introduction of a new bid process is a project that has a beginning and an end. It is designed to improve how bids are chosen. Likewise the learning and growth objective 'marketing knowledge, skills and resources' may be improved through a number of projects that 'train staff in marketing', 'gather market research' and 'recruit new skills'. Each has a beginning and an end. Once all the staff have been trained, the knowledge gathered and the recruits recruited, these projects will be complete. The benefits should start to show in the performance of the bid process. The continued update of the market information is now an operational management responsibility.

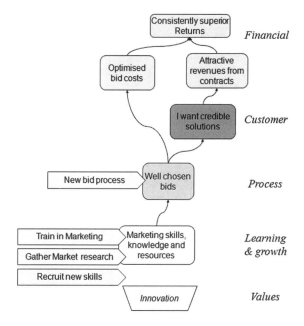

Figure 17.2 Projects help process and learning and growth objectives to improve

THE BENEFITS OF PROJECTS SHOW UP IN THE OBJECTIVES' MEASURES

A project should bring about an improvement in its specific objective. You should be able to trace the effect of the projects, using the cause and effect model, through to their eventual impact on your customers and your finances. You should be able to measure the effectiveness of your delivered projects through improvements in the measures of the objectives that the project is designed to affect.

A training project designed to change a skill or behaviour would be aligned with a learning and growth objective, and once completed we would expect a measurable improvement in the skills of the trained staff. The benefits of a delivered project are measured through changes in the measures associated with the objectives that the project is designed to influence.

STRATEGIC THEMES PROVIDE NATURAL PROGRAMMES OF CHANGE

The themes of the strategy map provide the natural basis for identifying and structuring programmes of change, and bringing together related aspects of projects that affect different levels of the strategy map, with a common overall aim. The four projects in the example are all associated with the bid process and could be described as a 'programme' of change for that theme.

How you choose to group projects and programmes will depend upon the size of the projects and where those projects are targeted. It is useful to group projects as a programme, where the whole programme addresses a particular aspect of the organization (say, sales as distinct from operations), addresses particular parts of the strategy (perhaps existing product sales vs new product developments) or particular customer groups (say commercial and consumer). We are of course talking about strategic themes, as introduced previously. Knowing that strategic themes naturally create programmes of change helps you to design a programme of change and its projects, or can help you to realign an existing set of projects with a new strategic theme.

Typically a programme of projects is owned by a theme owner, who would be responsible for ensuring that the projects delivered changes to certain aspects of the operations of the business. This alignment of projects, theme and owner makes a natural grouping.

PHASES OF PROJECTS AND PROGRAMMES

Programmes of change will often have phases of implementation, which should provide clear deliverables along the way. For instance, a three year programme of change could be divided into six to nine month phases to ensure that the projects from the first phase start to deliver benefits whilst the second phase is being developed. You should start to see improvements in the measures of the objectives once each phase of the project is complete.

In the bid process example, once the first phase of implementation was complete you might consolidate the improvements before you moved on to another phase of potential improvements with a second phase of projects.

CHANGE ALSO COMES FROM OTHER SOURCES

Not all change comes from formal projects. Changes in management style, better communication of the strategy, a revision of the goals in the appraisal system, a clearer understanding of the customer's needs and many other activities can also bring about change. These 'initiatives' and 'management actions' may not be formal projects in the sense of having project managers and budgets. They still influence change, still require concerted action and still need to be the responsibility of someone to manage, track and follow through. For this reason, the definition of 'project' in this chapter is necessarily loose, as it includes both formal projects and less formal management initiatives and actions. Do not lose sight of these less formal management actions, alongside the formal projects, as together they will make up the overall programme of change. It is sometimes useful to associate two columns with an objective: formal projects and shorter-term actions that need addressing.

Top down and Bottom up Alignment

If you have the luxury of a clean sheet of paper and are designing the programme of projects for a new strategy, then you can use a top down approach. This is used when developing a strategy afresh and when you wish to create the portfolio of projects that will deliver the strategy. The top down approach starts with each objective in the process and learning and growth perspectives. For each it asks, 'what projects do we need to deliver the amount of change and the benefits in this objective?' The top down approach should ensure a close alignment between the objectives and the benefits the projects should deliver.

In reality, most organizations have a large number of existing projects that are in various stages of implementation. It is always worth collecting all these projects and doing a bottom up approach. Here you test the existing projects against the new strategy, asking whether and how they are contributing to the strategy. This bottom up approach offers an audit of projects as well as helping an organization to get overall control of its project portfolio.

The combination of top down and bottom up will help you to design a new programme of projects that will deliver the new strategy and cull non-productive projects. Where projects don't align, it will provide the opportunity to cull some projects and free up resources. These resources could be saved or re-aligned to support the strategy more effectively.

The Tests of Project Alignment

The purpose of project alignment is to identify which projects contribute to the strategy. The projects are aligned against the strategy map's objectives. In the same way that measures are only developed after the objectives, project alignment should always start once you have the objectives developed. To test the alignment of projects with the strategy, there are five questions to ask about the alignments of a set of projects against an objective:

1. Which objectives does this project support?
2. Are these projects necessary for the delivery of that objective?
3. Are they sufficient to deliver that objective?
4. Are they cost-effective?
5. Can they be delivered?

These questions will reveal whether you can save money or whether you need to invest more, whether you need to change emphasis or find other ways to achieve the changes. It is assumed you have gathered the existing projects from around the organization.

The questions also require that you understand the scope and proposed benefits of each project, because the alignment requires more than just the project name and a short summary. It will require an understanding of the project scope, costs, timescales, benefits and current progress. Is the project on course and will it deliver the benefits to the level originally promised? Questions about resources may require a more detailed assessment of the project demands, timing and the availability of scarce resources.

WHICH OBJECTIVE DOES THIS PROJECT SUPPORT?

Before you can apply any of these tests you need to understand which projects support which objectives on your strategy map. Figure 17.3 shows the initial alignment of around a hundred projects against a corporate strategy map carried out by the executive team of a FTSE 100 retailer. The projects, represented by the various numbers, were placed next to each objective on the strategy map. These projects amounted to around £100m of investment. The alignment revealed that over £40m's worth of projects that the organization had underway were not aligned with the strategy. This gave a potential pot of recoverable projects that more than paid for the consultancy services.

Be careful when you do this sort of alignment. When you ask people to align projects against objectives, they will often place projects against objectives in the customer and financial perspectives. However, projects should only be aligned against objectives in the process and learning and growth perspectives. Projects change the capabilities or the processes of an organization. If you align a project directly against a customer objective, then you are suggesting that the project directly affects the customer without affecting the processes or capability of the organization. This would not make any sense. The project must in some way change the processes or capabilities of the organization, so that customers experience something different. The same is true for the financial perspective. You can't simply change the financial outcomes without first affecting the financial or operational processes or capability. When this misalignment happens, establish what the project directly affects and move it to a more appropriate objective in the lower perspectives.

For simplicity, in the example of Figure 17.3 the projects are only shown as numbers, with the detail held elsewhere. This is useful when you have very many projects to align, but it does require you to look up the meaning of each number. Normally I attach the project name to the objective, so that the logic of the alignment can be checked on a single view.

Even with the simplification, the picture shows up some typical issues that appear when this alignment exercise is done. Some objectives have very many projects associated with them, whilst others have none. This might suggest a cluster of activity. However, it transpired that many of the projects associated with 'develop innovative solutions' actually represented a pipeline of innovation projects (over 20) that the executive team were extremely keen to monitor and follow.

Some areas were devoid of projects. Looking at more detail revealed that some projects had aspects which supported these specific objectives but, as is often the case, the projects had such a wide remit that impact was spread thinly across several objectives. This is a common problem that often suggests a vague project scope.

It is curious that there are many projects clustered around L5, 'leadership agenda', and L4, 'innovative culture and people'. Yet there are none around retailing skills. There is only one attached to 'developing customer insights', which was a fundamental piece of their strategy. These discrepancies can only be answered by understanding the characteristics of these objectives, the various projects and the management team's intentions.

Sometimes you will find projects with a wide scope that are designed to deliver both capability and changes to a process. It is useful to identify these aspects, so you are clear which parts of the project deliver at which level. This makes understanding the scope and accountability for the project much easier. You may find it useful to have the next level strategy maps available, so that the projects can be aligned with more specific objectives. This makes it easier to tightly align the projects to the most appropriate and specific objectives.

Having completed this overall alignment, you can then take each objective and its projects in turn and apply the four detailed tests, which assess how each project supports the objective to which it is attached.

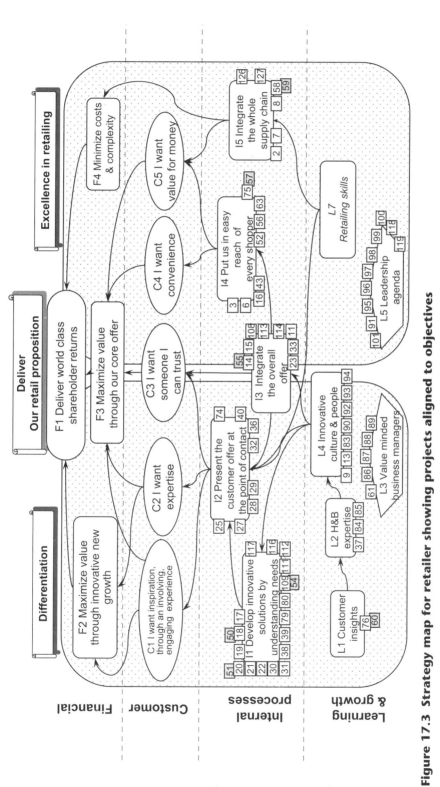

Figure 17.3 Strategy map for retailer showing projects aligned to objectives

TESTING THE ALIGNMENT OF PROJECTS AGAINST THEIR OBJECTIVES

There are four tests we can now apply, know as 'necessary', 'sufficient', 'cost-effective' and 'deliverable'.

1. Necessary?

    For this objective, are all these projects necessary for the achievement of the objective? Are any projects redundant? Are there any overlaps that could be removed?

2. Sufficient?

    For this objective, do we have sufficient projects to deliver the level of change demanded by the objective? Are there any gaps that need filling to ensure the objective is fully delivered and the level of ambition is achieved? If we deliver all these projects will we have the desired change, or are other pieces necessary?

3. Cost-effective?

    Is the level of investment demanded by this group of projects worth the level of improvements? Will we get the return on these projects, in the timescale envisaged? What risks should we factor in to these projects? Is there a better, more cost-effective way to achieve the same thing?
    The final test needs to be considered for each objective and for the programme of projects as a whole.

4. Can they be delivered?

    Do we have the capacity and resources to allocate to all these projects? Do we have the capability to deliver them? Can they be delivered in the timescale required? Are the risks sufficiently managed?

These four tests work together in helping you find the most appropriate combination of projects to deliver the desired improvements for each objective.

Investment Profile, Timing and Cost of Change

As you build up the project portfolio, you should develop an overall view across the programme that shows all the projects, which projects are running at the same time and when benefits are promised. Assessing this overall programme of projects for a complete strategic theme, or the organization as a whole, allows you to check its overall feasibility and impact. You should cover the timescale of your strategy so the programme of projects can be seen as a whole. You can assess whether the timings of project benefits are aligned. You can also identify dependencies between the projects. You can assess the overall demand for investment in capital and resources, and its impact on the operations of the organization, which will show up any overambitious or under-resourced programme of change. You can see how and when the projects will influence the measures and targets in different perspectives.

I recommend you use a Gantt chart to lay out all the projects, using a timescale that often extends two to three years out. I recommend that you divide the projects into phases, so that deliverables are no more than nine months apart. This ensures that some benefits are always on the horizon. It is useful to arrange the projects by the strategic themes to see the overall impact of a programme. I also recommend looking at the projects from the perspective of the organization's functions, departments or divisions to ensure that no one department is overloaded with too much to deliver at one point in time.

A second approach is to look at the overall impact of the programme on the measures, objectives and investment. Figure 17.4 shows how the strategy map, scorecard, phases of projects and their investment profile all fit together in a programme of work from which you can check the impact.

The example shows the objectives from a single theme of the strategy on the left hand side (1), with the measures of those objectives (2) as the left hand side of the table. In the centre is a table that shows how the values for each measure are expected to improve over time, in this case showing four quarters of year one and then years two and three. Beneath the table are, in this case, the five phases of the programme. As these phases are delivered, they should bring about improvements in the measures above them. This way you can check the overall coherence of the improvements of the measures against the promised timescales for the project benefits.

You can also analyse the investments in projects against the operational benefits and costs of change. To the right of the measures is the total investment in the projects for each objective, together with the date of the anticipated benefits (3). This gives you the investment in these projects across the life of the programme and the strategy (4). Here, there is a total project investment of £470,000.

The final, right hand column shows how the operational costs of this part of the organization are expected to change as the strategy rolls out, the projects are delivered and their benefits ripple through (5). In this case they are expected to increase, due to increased activities and improved revenues. However, were the projects designed to reduce costs, you would see improved operational costs against the project investment. You can compare these improvements against the investment costs (6) and check that the phasing of the projects (7) and the promised benefits (8) align with the planned improvements in performance.

This systematic analysis allows you to develop a coherent and complete view of a programme of change, its timing, effects, costs and how the benefits should trickle through. It allows you to assess whether the benefits are tangible and financial, or whether you are initially changing capability that should start to show a measurable improvement in the revenues or costs once it starts to be applied in a process or department. Having this mechanism to define programmes and phases of work helps you to ensure their benefits are delivered. We will look at this example in more detail in the next chapter, which explains how to link strategy maps with budgets and finance.

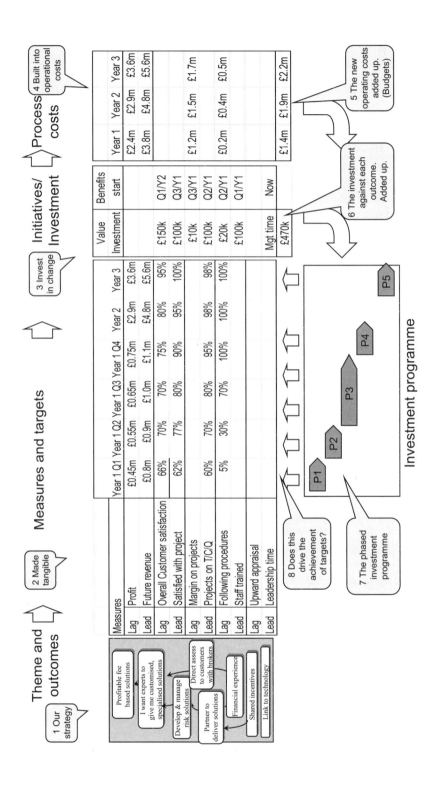

Figure 17.4 The strategy map drives an investment in change which ripples through to improve the operational costs

Gathering and Assessing Projects

This section explores some of the issues that come up when gathering the portfolio of projects. It also looks at the different types of projects that organizations undertake and their implications for alignment with the strategy.

GATHERING THE PORTFOLIO

Some organizations may already have a full register of their projects. They may have project and programme offices in place and have a clear view of how their projects support their strategy. This makes collecting the project portfolio for alignment very easy. However, it may be necessary to collect and collate information about which projects are in the organization and to gather basic control information about each of them. For each project this would typically include:

Project name

> Sponsor and project manager

Has a business case been developed and approved?

> Beneficiary

> Nature of benefits

When delivering

> Status information (on target, behind schedule)

> Is it going to deliver what was intended?

Outline of costs

> Budget holder

> Anticipated costs

> Sunk costs

> Remaining costs

> Other resources consumed (e.g. people)

What else is needed to help it deliver? (projects that it depends upon)

This is a minimum amount of information. In a rich project environment with a project office and well managed projects, more information should be available. Many organizations will have projects 'under the radar' for which this minimal information will have to be teased out or may not be available at all.

Which projects need to be counted? When do you stop collecting projects? When doing this I use the 'coal seam' analogy. I take coal out of the seam until I hit the rock that surrounds the coal, and I expect to take some of the rock as well. That way I know I have probably got to the edge of the seam. There will be parts of the seam where further gathering of projects becomes uneconomical. This is not where there is excessive resistance to projects being declared, but where there are very small tactical efficiency improvements, or projects which sit on strategy maps two or three levels down from the one being analysed.

In my experience, this exercise usually digs out around 120 to 150 projects before the coal seam becomes uneconomical. The exercise can be repeated at other levels in the organization once strategy maps have been cascaded, so that local project alignment and optimization can take place in the context of the larger change programme that may sit above.

You may think you determine the limits, but others will be trying to decide whether to include or declare their projects. The question of which projects need to be counted has a different meaning for them: 'which projects should I legitimately declare to the group and which can I keep to myself?' Projects may not be declared for a number of reasons. Quite often projects are hidden in 'business as usual'. Sometimes, they are small improvement projects under local autonomy. At other times, you may encounter projects that have come off the rails and are being hidden. You may come across objections to projects being collected or declared. Take a note of the objections and behaviours that you encounter. They will be revealing about the culture of the organization and the way in which projects are managed and controlled in the organization. This will provide useful clues about which parts of the culture need to be addressed.

Not all projects are 'strategic'. When you are doing a project collection exercise there are a number of things to look out for and a number of pitfalls to avoid.

INTERNAL AND EXTERNAL PROJECTS

Confusion often occurs where *the business of the organization* is delivering projects for its customers. Many organizations run projects for their customers. They might be building a software product, managing a construction contract or delivering a consultancy engagement. For this type of organization, delivering customer projects is business as usual. In these cases you need a clear distinction between *projects for customers* and *projects designed to change the organization's capability to deliver* projects for customers.

Organizational change projects are designed to change the way the organization works. They have an internal focus. The objective of the project is an internal change that will eventually filter through to the customer and the finances. A customer may see the ultimate effect of these changes, but they are not involved in the project. Projects for customers are not designed to improve the organization, except to bring in revenues. They have an external focus. The question for these sorts of projects is, 'are they appropriate for our market and product portfolio?'

A simple way of telling these two types of project apart is whether they are a source of revenue (that is directly from customer payments) or are seen as an investment in the business funded by cash or capital (such as the company's short- or long-term funds).

Some projects will be designed to improve the organization's capability to deliver external projects. A project may be designed to improve the quality of project delivery, making the bid process more effective or finding smarter ways to maintain the software. These improvements enhance the organization's capability to deliver external projects for their customers.

If you fail to distinguish between these two types of project when collecting the project portfolio, it will cause confusion and misunderstandings. Collect both, but ensure you are clear which are which.

CONTROL AND LEGISLATION PROJECTS

Some projects will be a necessity because of legislation. Examples include projects to ensure compliance with financial and accounting governance, to improve health and safety, to ensure accounting controls are in place, to manage financial risk, and to improve the controls in the organization. They are important in the sense that they need to be done, but they are not strategic in the sense that they will differentiate the organization in the market. Everyone else in the same industry has to implement the same compliance requirements. These projects support the governance section of the learning board model. They will appear on the strategy map where there is an objective such as, 'ensure compliance with current legislation'.

Such projects will necessarily probably not appear on the higher level strategy maps, unless the organization is recovering from a compliance breach, is concerned about potential breaches or it is a particularly high profile change. Such projects are often important, and often need to be delivered by a particular time. They are not strategic in the sense that they will not distinguish the organization from any other organization in the industry that will also have to comply, but they are important. Of course, how to implement them and the cost of implementation can be a differentiator and is your choice.

PROJECTS FOR OPERATIONAL PERFORMANCE IMPROVEMENT

Not every project is strategic in the sense that it is designed to implement the strategy and bring about change to support the strategy. The strategic learning framework is also useful in filtering the projects and teasing out what is a strategic project and what is not strategic but may still be a project that is useful to the organization.

Some local projects might simply be incremental operational improvements at a local level: cost-effective, short-term and sensible investments to improve operational efficiency, rather than intended to bring about substantial change. They may have a sensible business case based upon their financial return. These projects should not necessarily be discarded as non-strategic without thinking through the consequences and their advantages, for example their simplicity to implement or their mandatory nature. When aligning such projects the main criterion is often the availability of scarce resources. Whilst they all might seem to make sense, the question becomes, 'do we have the resources and management capacity to do them all sufficiently well?'

Such projects often hide inside 'business as usual' budgets. In part, they may simply be the initiatives going on in a department: work that simply has to be done. These improvements might be part of the way of working of the organization and ones that should be encouraged.

Be careful of budgets hidden within departments that hide the extent of change and so may not be exposed to appropriate scrutiny. Minor change can be hidden. Responsibility for major change can be held in a separate budget outside the main budget. In one case, the budget of an IT department seemed to be £21m. However, all the change activity was found embedded within the user community as business as usual and amounted to an overall budget of around £42m. Of that only £19m was IT operational support and the other £23m was all investment in IT-based change projects spread across IT and their user departments. This was a situation that was not clear to the management, either inside or outside IT.

Take care as what is tactical at one level may be strategic at a lower level in the organization. The project may position a part of the organization to deliver its part of the overall strategy better. When dealing with these projects you will find that they may align with objectives on lower level strategy maps, support objectives in support functions, or that they bring about an improvement in capability and support objectives in the learning and growth perspective. As you cascade the strategy maps through the organization, you can review these lower level projects against the more local strategy.

JUSTIFYING PET PROJECTS

Sometimes an organization or manager will justify a project, 'just because it feels the right thing to do'. Whilst such a phrase falls far short of a clear justification, discussion may reveal that the project supports the core values or purpose of the organization. An example of this sort of project might be a scheme to help the local community, investing in environmentally friendly technology or making a donation to the community. The justification is not a pure cost benefit case, but a case of 'we ought to be doing this, because it is right to do it'. It may be driven by values, or sense of purpose. The key, of course, is to recognize the difference between these projects and projects which have a poor cost benefit case where the owner resorts to emotional arguments because their case is weak.

It is more likely that someone is not driven by core values, but is simply trying to justify a pet project that has a poor investment case and does not contribute to the strategy. An example of this was the building of a millennium garden outside a newly developed head office. The chief executive was convinced that it was the right thing to do to enhance the look of the offices and provide staff with somewhere to sit outside at lunchtime. However, there was no cost benefit case. The case was based entirely upon it being the right thing to do. When we did the project alignment exercise with the management team the chief executive would walk past and put the project on the strategy map, but in a corner, not attached to any objectives. A few minutes later another director would walk past and move it down again into the 'non-strategic' projects. It was quite amusing watching the project move up and down every few minutes as the various management team members aligned the projects.

INFRASTRUCTURE PROJECTS

Some projects fall into the category of infrastructure. They do not directly provide top line benefits, but facilitate other parts of the business so they can provide the benefits, or operate more efficiently. Implementing them should enable other areas to operate more effectively or facilitate other projects. Failing to complete infrastructure projects may undermine the capability in other areas and stop things working or being delivered.

Examples often come from support functions such as IT, finance or HR. One major change programme totalling £100m was designed to dramatically change the sales force of an insurance company. Embedded within this was a £3m upgrade of the PC technology that was necessary to support the working practices and systems: not strategic in itself, but an enabler of the strategy. Other examples might include upgrading the network infrastructure, ensuring that data security and back-up is in place, or introducing technology to enable home-working.

These projects may be local to a part of the organization only directly affecting IT, finance, HR or production. As a consequence, they may be hidden inside business as usual. In other cases they may be laying infrastructure for the organization as a whole, the benefits of which will not be apparent until other projects have been delivered. Well organized staff training and appraisal records, for example, provide HR with the information they need to make decisions, as well as helping line managers do their jobs more effectively.

These projects are a part of the strategy of the support function and would be fundamental to the delivery of their part of the overall strategy. However, because they do not appear in the front line strategy maps, the concern is that they will be dropped. So often there is the (misguided) imperative to put such infrastructure projects on the top level strategy maps. Such projects often have wide effects, supporting infrastructure improvements across many departments. They are also depended on rather than being a direct driver. Showing such projects at the overall strategy map level only clutters the overall picture. Resist the temptation to put infrastructure projects on the corporate strategy map, and put them in their rightful place as a central project within the strategy map of a support function. As a part of a larger programme, they will show how they contribute to the eventual improvement. Just because they are not on the top level strategy map (and therefore not seen as strategic) at the corporate level does not mean they are not important or that they could be dropped. They are simply below the radar of the corporate team, but perhaps the local responsibility of a functional director to deliver (or inform his or her colleagues if the project is hitting problems).

Some projects involve the continued maintenance and refreshing of technology or capability. Examples of this are upgrades to server technology or renewing the PCs and operating systems in use in the organization. Likewise, production machinery wears out and needs replacing. Failing to do this type of project will impair the operation of the organization and may result in creeping cost increases as incremental inefficiencies occur, or prevent more important projects being implemented.

Conclusions

This chapter's techniques will ensure that your investment in projects will make the biggest difference. Have we got the right programme of change to make sure the strategy happens? Are we investing as efficiently as possible in that change? Have we eliminated unnecessary investments? Investment alignment may involve the design and creation of a new set of programmes of change with completely new projects. It may cause existing projects to be realigned, incorporated or even culled. This can save you a considerable amount of money, time and energy.

We have also seen how to align the programmes with the profile of investment and return. This makes a clear cost benefit case that links the projects, strategy, budgets, change programmes, investment and the financial implications for operations. We shall develop this further in the next chapter.

18 *Aligning Budgets and the Budgeting Process in a Learning Organization*

We have handled the financial outputs of the organization in the financial perspective of the strategy map. We have also examined the financial implications of projects and initiatives designed to bring about change. This chapter links the strategy map to the case for the investment in change and its impact on the operational costs of the organization. It also explains how strategy maps can help the budget and the budgetary process to be more flexible.

The financial perspective of the strategy map and scorecard should already be linked to a financial model of the organization, one that demonstrates how changing costs, revenues, funding, risk and cash flow will affect overall profitability (or surplus) and financial outcomes. You might also have made connections to external social or environmental costs. You should also have a clear link to the activities and changes in the organization that bring about these financial improvements.

We have not yet made explicit connections from the objectives and measures in the various perspectives to the internal costs of the organization. This chapter explains how you do that. This chapter explains how your strategy map and scorecard can be linked to the budget and the budgeting process. Different ways of linking will achieve different ends, and depend on the extent of change you are planning. You might be changing the organization and changing the planning and budgeting processes. This chapter provides you with ways to progressively integrate the strategy maps with the budgets and the budgeting process.

Whenever you work with the budgeting process, work closely with the finance director, with management accountants and with product or project accountants. They hold the knowledge of how the finances fit together. It was important when we addressed the financial perspective. It continues to be important as we link strategy development and budgeting.

Finance, Governing Variables and Learning

To understand how the strategy map and balanced scorecard link to the finances, it is only necessary to have a basic understanding of budgeting and investment appraisal. However, when dealing with the organization's strategy it is useful to appreciate the wider financial management and financial context in which these more basic financial processes occur and strategic and operational decisions are being made.

When you are dealing with the financial management of the organization, it is useful to recognize that there are governing financial choices and variables. The organization's financial choices and financial strategy are a part of its overall choices and strategy. The financial strategy includes its choice of investment returns and hurdle rates for investments; the type and sources of capital; the cost of capital; financial governance; financial risk management policies; the hedging or mitigation of financial risk such as currency, trade or commodities; and the choice of use of capital and surplus funds for either distribution or reinvestment to bring about improvements.

At the operational level these higher level financial policies influence the budgeting policies, investment criteria, financial control and risk management processes, and the choice of allocation of funds and scarce resources. The financial management and financial control processes operate within these wider rules and influence how individual managers are allocated or acquire funds, use cash and report on their financial performance. Just as we have double loop learning with governing variables for the strategy, the financial policies act as governing variables over the financial processes (see Figure 18.1).

These higher financial choices can have unforeseen consequences on the way the organization operates and how decisions are made.

A company's business model was to acquire land for development and then recapitalize the costs against the building that was subsequently rented out. The development stage was funded by external investors with covenants on the loans allowing only traditional building contractor arrangements. The company wanted to use alternative contracting arrangements that would have more reliable build times, but this was prevented by the covenants. Once they recognized the constraint, they were able to discuss and agree alternative funding terms with their investors, which allowed alternative contracting options, and so the buildings could be built more reliably and at a lower cost.

Figure 18.1 Strategic learning applied to the organization's financial management

At each level there are choices to be made that affect the context in which you are working. Trying to establish a project's benefits will be difficult if poor project financial controls or reporting are in place. Trying to move to a joined up organization when the management culture is divisive will be almost impossible. Trying to introduce rolling budgets into an organization which is funded on an annual basis will cause the method of funding to conflict with the budgeting process, unless the wider funding context is also addressed. In each case, the higher level policies constrain the lower level processes and decisions. Be aware of these constraints when you are dealing with the organization's finances and its financial strategy.

I have highlighted these issues to raise your awareness of these wider constraints and financial implications that you may encounter during strategy discussions. If you are developing a strategy map for the finance department, think first about the financial strategy of the organization and do that first. The finance department's strategy should support the financial strategy. However, to apply the techniques in this chapter, only a basic understanding of budgeting and investment appraisal is required.

Integration with Annual Budgeting, and Planning and Investment in Change

How do strategy maps and balanced scorecards relate to budgets and investments in change? The previous chapter explained how investments in change programmes and individual projects are aligned with the changes and improvements that they should bring about in operational costs and potential revenues.

To understand how strategy maps and balanced scorecards are integrated with budgets, it is best to start with the simple case where functional areas align with the scope of a strategy map and its objectives. Then we can look at more complex cases where the process objectives are used to create joined up thinking and working.

First, it is helpful to understand how the accounting coding structure organizes the individual cost codes, against which individual budget items are identified and costs are posted. Examples of this would be salary costs in a department broken down perhaps by wages, national insurance, other insurances, pension costs and bonuses. In another area it may be material and labour codes for a product. Another set of codes might cover software licences, maintenance costs, contractors and consultancy fees. These are then aggregated in the chart of accounts to build up the overall cost of a department. In this way the organization's overall costs are divided into cost centres and cost codes, starting at the corporate level and continuing through to the divisions, departments and eventually teams or even individuals.

The key to identifying where budget responsibility lies is to align the objectives in the process perspective with the departments and teams that own the cost centres in the accounting system. As with all strategy mapping work, first ensure that the scope of your strategy map lines up with the scope of the part of the organization you are dealing with.

A SIMPLE ALIGNMENT OF PROCESSES TO COST CENTRES

The simplest case is a strategy map whose scope is a single organization or a single part of that organization (say a functional department). In this case the organizational scope will be the same as the scope of the budget for that organization or department. The scope of the budget is the same as the scope of the process objectives.

It becomes even easier where the individual objectives in the process perspective correspond with the organizational sub-units which, in turn, have their own cost centres or departmental cost codes. Thus each process objective will have a simple mapping to a unique set of cost centres within the accounting system. The expected budget out-turn at the end of the year for the department (its target for cost) will be reflected in the cost objective in the financial perspective.

The reason you only need to map the process perspective to the cost centres is that this is the only perspective where operational costs truly occur. The learning and growth perspective describes the capabilities that the process has. The learning and growth objectives do not represent cost centres. They do represent an improved capability of the cost centres, but this will not be reflected in the costs unless the capability has changed the operational costs. Finding clients might necessitate a database subscription, which would increase the sales team's operational costs. Implementing a customer relationship management (CRM) system might save time, lower operational costs and increase effectiveness, but at the same time it may incur additional support costs. Both of these change the operating costs of the operation and therefore the costs of the process objectives. Of course, the investments in these projects are not usually funded from the operational budget but will come from a capital or investment budget.

This is a simple alignment between each process objective in the strategy map and the various cost centres that make up the budget of the same department, as shown in Figure 18.2. Changes to the capability, costs or performance of the function should be reflected in the forecasts of how these cost centres' budgets will change.

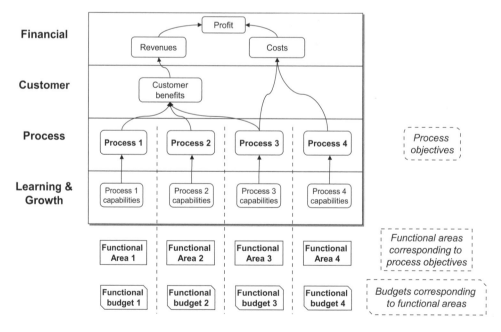

Figure 18.2 A simple alignment of functions and cost centres with objectives in the process perspective

When you are dealing with a simple cascade of strategy maps and scorecards based upon the existing organizational structure (and by implication you would expect this to align with the current chart of accounts which would also be based upon the same organizational structure), then the scope of each strategy map will probably correspond with a functional area that has a corresponding set of entries in the account coding structure.

A MORE COMPLEX ALIGNMENT WITH JOINED UP WORKING

This approach works easily when the themes and strategy maps follow the existing functional and costs structures. However, in most cases, for good reason, your strategy map will not have process objectives that map in a simple way to the functional departments and cost centres. They will overlap. This will be especially true when you are breaking down silos using joined up objectives, or even when simply using a themed strategy map structure. An understanding of how budgets and coding structures work is therefore useful.

The budget system and budget coding structure is designed to break down the organization into parts. These are parts that are owned and budgeted for individually. If you are trying to create a more joined up organization where the parts think and work together in a more joined up and collective manner, then the existing chart of accounts and coding structure that defines this breakdown may also need to change to reflect the new structure. Changing coding structures is not simple and yours may be difficult to change. There is a simple, but powerful, technique that enables you to step aside from the constraint the chart of accounts may impose and develop budgets for the joined up working without having to alter the established budget structure and chart of accounts.

When you have process objectives that cross functional boundaries, it is quite likely that an existing function (and its cost centres) may have to be allocated to and shared between several objectives or themes. At this point you will be faced with a question: what is the total cost of the activities and support for the scope of this strategy map or joined up objective? Getting directly to this answer could be quite difficult. To make it easier, before we can answer this question we need an answer to an intermediate question: just how much of our organization, and which parts, actually supports this strategy map or objective?

To answer this question, we create an allocation matrix that maps the main cost centres to the objectives in the process perspective. Figure 18.3 provides a template for this. You start this allocation matrix by placing the process objectives along one dimension and the major cost centre budgets along the other. You complete the matrix by filling in, at the square they intercept, the amount of a particular cost centre that should be allocated to a particular process objective.

If you do this for a single strategy map from a cascade, you may find that not all of a cost centre is allocated to the objectives on this strategy map. Part may lie within another map's objectives at the same level. When this happens, simply ensure you cover the whole scope of process objectives and budgets by creating a matrix whose sides include all the process objectives (at a given level on the strategy map) and all the corresponding cost centres. Obviously the totals along each row and column should add up to 100 per cent of the budget unless some part of the wider budget falls outside the scope of the strategy maps.

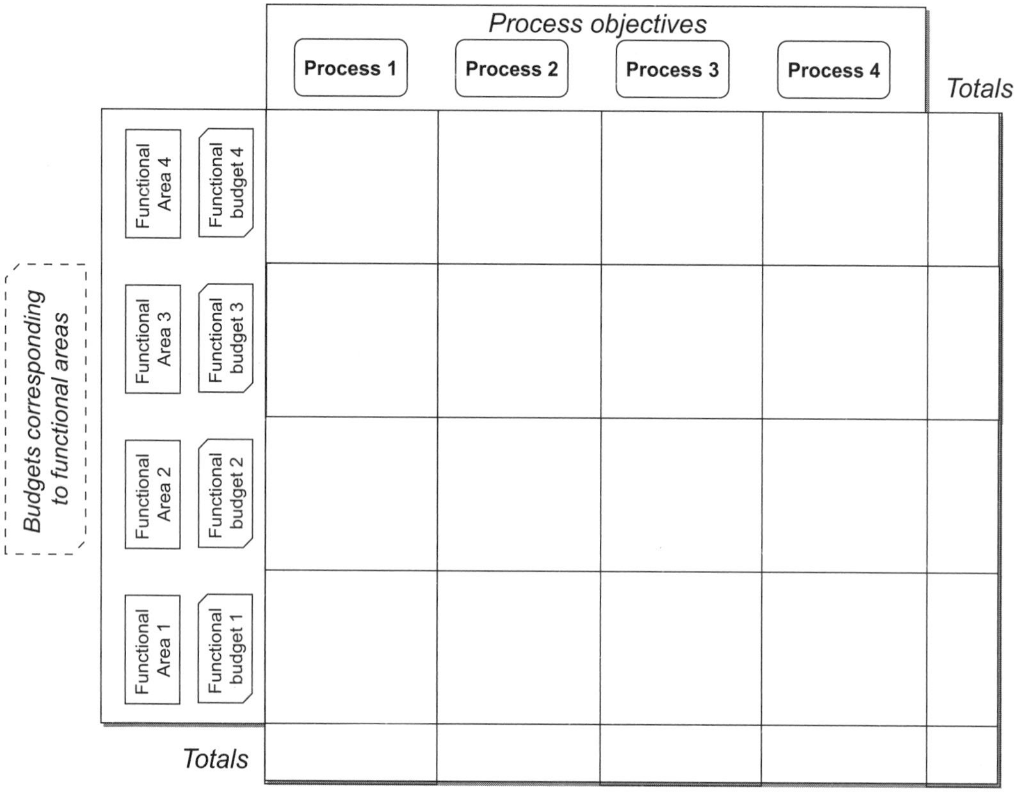

Figure 18.3 Matrix for allocating budgets amongst process objectives

Work with the people who understand the scope of the business units and the new strategy map, as well as the costs structures. You can use this approach to make an initial costs estimate about the allocation of the cost centre budgets to the objectives on the strategy map at, primarily, the process level. Then you can repeat the exercise in more detail to verify the allocation with those who developed the strategy maps.

This allocation matrix has one big advantage. It is far easier to simply follow the allocations from the old accounting system's cost structure to the new strategy map structure than it is to try to change the, probably long established, coding structure of the finance system. Designing a coding structure for an organization can take several months for a reasonable sized organization. Trying to design *and implement* a substantial change to coding structure can take far longer. The allocation matrix provides a valuable bridge from the new strategy maps to the existing cost structure. It is a bridge that can provide a useful base of information for understanding the drivers of costs, as well as winning time whilst a new design of structure settles down and becomes firm.

Using Strategy Maps to Document the Thinking Behind a Budget

For a moment, think what happens when a budget is constructed. To construct a budget, you have to have the strategy in your head. Someone is saying, 'this part of the strategy means this expenditure on these items, and this investment, over this period, to achieve this change, with these operational costs and these expected revenues. It will yield this cash position which means this level of funding'. Then, it becomes subject to negotiation, horse-trading and some centralized (sometimes seemingly arbitrary) decision making.

The budget is only one dimension of the completed strategy, expressed as financial numbers. Hopefully, the assumptions are documented. Sometimes, however, the assumptions are implicit. When someone receives the budget, they either understand the strategy well enough to know what assumptions were made and how they link to the strategy, or they have to deduce them. Imagine for a moment you were arriving to take over a department, without a handover, and were looking at the budget. How would you know how it was deduced? Hopefully the budget assumptions would be documented somewhere.

This sort of information tends to be documented in a whole variety of spreadsheets prior to reaching the accounting system. The catch is that Microsoft Excel is the most undocumented programming language ever used. Assumptions in one spreadsheet might be carried across to another, but they might not. There is no change or version control with a spreadsheet, so a user can release a version as final and then update it later. A version can be changed by someone else without the originator knowing. Maintaining consistency of data relies on trust and conversations and a tight central discipline, usually by a single person. Amongst all of this the assumptions and thinking may go undocumented or can get out of step with the changes to the figures.

In larger organizations collaborative planning software is often used, where spreadsheet-like functionality is placed inside workflow tools with proper version control embedded in them. Multiple worksheets on many different people's computers are replaced with a single central database with controlled access. This provides much tighter control on versions, consistency of data used in the various sheets and an audit trail of changes. Such software makes the distributed budget planning process across multi-site and multinational organizations far easier to control and manage. The other feature of these collaborative planning tools is the ability to run scenarios for different situations without disrupting the main model. From the main model of the business, the planners can experiment with different costs, the effects of various change programmes, and differing revenue streams from sales and deduce the consequences for cash flow and profitability.

However, there is still a need to document the changes. These might range from small tactical changes to a major shift in strategy. Strategy maps with linked objectives in perspectives make this much easier. Not only should the versions of the collaboratively produced plans be controlled, but these should be related to the relevant strategy maps and balanced scorecards, which should be version controlled in synchronization to capture the changed thinking and assumptions. Whilst this seems an obvious step, the links in the software tend to be implicit rather than explicit at the moment. Perhaps this will be an area of future development.

The need to link the budget changes and thinking to the strategy will become stronger, and more challenging, as rolling budgets are introduced. The light strategy documentation approach provided by strategy maps will definitely help.

Integrating Rolling Budgets and Strategic Learning

So far we have concentrated on creating a strong link between the strategy maps, balanced scorecards and the budgets for both the operation of the business and investments in change. However, this link has been a single, one off link, as the budget is constructed. We have not yet discussed how the budgets would be revised as the strategy evolves and the projects develop.

We are moving towards a strategy that evolves as you learn from it and where you can update the strategy maps and scorecards as it evolves, so how can we also maintain its relationship with the budgets? If the strategy is being refined and the budgets stay the same then the management is asking the organization to do something different without the appropriate resources, i.e. those that were allocated on the basis of previous assumptions. This is a constraint you do not want.

For this reason, rolling or continuous budgets have been popular and introduced in a number of organizations. For a detailed rationale for the introduction of rolling budgets and how they operate, see Hope and Fraser (2003). Rolling budgets provide a six to nine month forecast of the budget in detail, followed by a less detailed budget that extends perhaps to 18 months or two years. This rolling budget is revised every month, bimonthly or every quarter as information comes in, based upon the latest information about sales, operations, prices, performance and the strategy. The advantage is that the budget process does not try to predict in detail everything for a long way forward. Nor does it only operate a budgeting process once a year – a process that is often lengthy and time consuming. Rather it predicts the detail short-term, less detail longer-term, and refines these predictions as the information evolves. Effort involved in budgeting is more evenly spread through the year and requires less crystal ball gazing. It means that the budgets are more realistic in the period that would normally be characterized by 11 month old predictions.

Most importantly, if the environment or the strategy changes, strategy maps and their scorecards are far easier to update than a thick, written strategic plan. They can be refined and their associated budgets updated with the consequential changes. This allows strategic thinking, learning, testing and refinement to become a continuous process that is unhindered by budgetary process constraints. The strategy maps and balanced scorecards are updated consistently with the budgets. Any changes can be communicated easily, together.

Working with Finance

In developing this integrated view and testing its logic, you will have created a financial model that represents how the strategy will drive changes within the financial model of the organization, how that strategy will be funded and where the financial implications reside. The finance function may have used a combination of financial models to develop this. There may be a revenue model to examine the impact of increased sales or alterations to the sales mix. There may be operating cost models that assess the changes in fixed and variable costs associated with the strategy. There will be a cash flow element that assesses the changes in cash requirements or the funding of investments. There will be a profit analysis (either marginal or overall). There may be an investment analysis model that uses discounted cash flow and hurdle rates, or some more sophisticated value added analysis such as Economic Value Added (Young and O'Byrne 2000). They may also run a number of scenarios to understand the effects of different timing and options. Some may use sensitivity analysis to determine how variables affect changes in profitability.

These financial models contain detail, summarized in the corporate strategy map, that can be used through the cascade of strategy maps and their balanced scorecards. The same financial models will be used to set the financial measures and targets within the lower level scorecards. These financial models are vital to a successful scorecard, underpin the financial model perspective and ensure that the strategy is based upon a sound financial footing. However, as with all financial models, they tell only part of the story. They are great at documenting the financial assumptions and consequences, but poor at documenting the thinking behind the model. This is where a close integration with the strategy map and scorecard plays an important role, particularly due to the cause and effect model.

Conclusions

The accounting and budgeting systems are powerful mechanisms of control in organizations and are a powerful way to communicate change and intention. Making strong and effective links between the budget, the strategy maps and the corresponding balanced scorecards sends a clear signal about alignment and intention. It also acts to align important mechanisms of control and influence, and to communicate the strategy.

If you do move to a more responsive organizational style, but leave the accounting practices, structures or budgets in place, they will do a marvellous job of contradicting and undermining your strategy. It is not just the capital investments and change programmes that need appropriate funding: the operational budgets need to be tackled as well. Updating the budgeting process can demonstrate that even the accounting systems, budgets and practices are changing. This can be a useful message to the organization alongside your other actions.

It is a two way path. Strategy maps provide a powerful way to tease out changes to operational costs and to investments. Strategy maps also help the budgets come to life and provide a flexible and effective way to communicate the strategic decisions implicit in budgetary decisions. Strategy maps and budgets work naturally together, once the links between them are understood.

19 Representing and Managing Risks in Strategy Maps and Balanced Scorecards

The way that strategy maps and balanced scorecards represent risk is one of the most misunderstood areas of their design and use. Many suggest they ignore risk, but this is far from the case. This chapter explains how they do capture risk, but only a specific part of the overall organizational risk specific to the strategy and its implementation. It explains how you can capture risks to the implementation of the strategy, and how to manage those risks using strategy maps and the strategic learning model.

The management of risk has become very topical in business and in the public sector, especially since the banking crisis and credit crunch. Risk management within corporate governance has been coming increasingly to the fore since the Cadbury Report of the early 1990s and the Turnbull Report of 1999. The credit crisis has added to this pressure for the explicit identification and management of risks within organizations, demanding that organizations are clearer about a range of risks arising from external events, the organization's strategy and its day-to-day operations. In the UK, the UK Corporate Governance Code (Financial Reporting Council 2010) introduced a new requirement, applying to all companies listed in the UK, stating, 'The board is responsible for determining the nature and extent of the significant risks it is willing to take in achieving its strategic objectives'.

First we will explore and dispel the myth that the balanced scorecard does not include risk. Then we will outline what is meant by risk management and make clear the different categories of risk that an organization faces. This understanding of types of risk and how risks are managed will make it easier to explain where a strategy map and balanced scorecard do actually manage risk already and where they do not. It will explain why the balanced scorecard neither has, nor needs, a risk perspective. It will apply a 'render unto Caesar that which is Caesar's' approach, making it clear which risks are appropriate to handle within the strategy map, which can be handled with some extensions and which should be handled elsewhere. It will explain how the strategy map and learning board model also manage part of the risk landscape. We will also look at the risks' implications for strategy implementation and in decision making.

The Misconception is that Risk is not Included

Given the popularity of the balanced scorecard and the need for improved risk management, various practitioners, commentators and academics have commented on how they include and manage risk. Here is Prof Bob Kaplan (2008) being interviewed about his latest book, Execution Premium (Kaplan and Norton 2008):

> *I have recently become sensitive to a gap in our strategy map/BSC framework by not paying sufficient attention to enterprise risk management (ERM). Obviously, many large financial institutions, despite having risk management departments, have suffered massive losses from failure to understand the risks they took on. All companies, not just financial ones, need to have better methods to assess and monitor their risks.*

Other practitioners and academics suggest that there is no explicit mention of risk within the balanced scorecard or even strategy maps, and therefore that they do not manage risk at all. This is incorrect, but has led many to suggest extensions or changes, so that risk is more explicit. Ernst and Young (2009), for instance, decided that the standard scorecard needed to be extended to include Key Risk Indicators (KRIs) in each perspective. On the surface this seems sensible, except that their approach uses the inappropriate cruciform balanced scorecard model (see chapter three) and simply adds Key Risk Indicators as an extra measure in each perspective.

The strategy map's approach to the management of risk is actually more subtle and systematic than this. The problem with discussions about risk management is that the management of risk covers a very wide variety of risk types, that affect different parties, and a wide variety of ways in which those risks are managed. I like to say that risk is a lonely word: it needs company that helps to clarify what type of risk is being talked about, who is at risk and in what particular way it is being managed.

The questions we need to address are:

1. Which types of risk are covered by the strategy map and balanced scorecard?
2. How do balanced scorecards represent risks?
3. How do you include risk and how do you manage these risks?
4. Which risks should I manage elsewhere?

To answer these questions it is helpful to establish a common understanding of risks and management, especially the various types and causes of risk that an organization needs to manage.

What do we Mean by Risk Management?

To sensibly discuss the management of risks, we need to be clear actually what is meant by risks and risk management. The management of risk consists of a coordinated set of systems and activities designed to understand and control an organization's exposure to risk. More specifically, the management of risk includes: identifying and clarifying risks, knowing what risks we are running and our potential exposure; evaluating vulnerabilities, impact and consequences; mitigating the risks to minimize the possibility that the risks occur; ensuring you know when risks have manifested themselves; limiting the consequences of the impact of the risks; and ensuring you can recover. It also includes the collation, reporting and assessment of risks and the overall risk position.

Risk management also operates at, at least, two levels: risks associated with an individual activity, trade or process; and the overall portfolio of risk that makes up the overall exposure of the organization to its collective risks.

There is also the risk appetite: the level of exposure or potential impact from an event that an organization is willing to accept. Risk appetite suggests there is a threshold that, if exceeded, would cause additional risk management approaches or business controls to be put in place to bring the exposure level back within the accepted level. Risk appetite will vary depending upon the type of risk involved and the knowledge that the organization has available. For instance, you might accept no health and safety breaches, but be willing to launch a product into a competitive market.

Types of Risk

It is also useful to be clear what sorts of risk we are discussing, so we can decide which risks are appropriate for a strategy map and scorecard to capture and help manage. Also, which risks are inappropriate and are better managed elsewhere. A useful guide to the wide variety of risks an organization faces is provided by the Institute of Risk Management. In their paper, 'A structured approach to Enterprise Risk Management (ERM) and the requirements of ISO 31000' (Institute of Risk Management 2010), they suggest four general classes of risk: strategic risk, financial risk, operational risk and hazard risk. They recognize that some risks arise internally from decisions the board and management teams make, whilst other risks come from events outside the organization and from decisions made by people outside the organization, such as competitors, the market and regulators, amongst others. Their framework is shown in Figure 19.1.

This model is very similar to the learning board model introduced in chapter two (Garratt 2010), even though the dimensions are drawn in a different order and some pieces are placed in different parts of the model. There are clear similarities in the classes of risk, with a direct link between the strategic and operational views of both models. The regulatory aspect of the learning board model corresponds to the financial group (though this model has regulation in the operational box). The policy area of the learning board model broadly corresponds to the hazard risks.

What is clear from this model is that there are many areas of risk that you would not expect a management team's strategy to address. There are other risks that other aspects of the management team's agenda would be expected to identify and mitigate. It would not be normal for an organization's strategy to worry about such basic issues as, say, business continuity risk, key person risk or day-to-day health and safety. These are important, but not strategic. They are more operational risks and hazard risks than specific risks to the strategy or caused by the strategy. They are in the category of risks that you would expect to be managed by existing business controls within operational processes.

In contrast, there are risks that affect the implementation of the strategy, be they internal or due to external events. The ACCA (2008) defines strategic risks as 'those that arise from the fundamental decisions that directors take concerning an organization's objectives... strategic risks are the risks of failing to achieve these business objectives'.

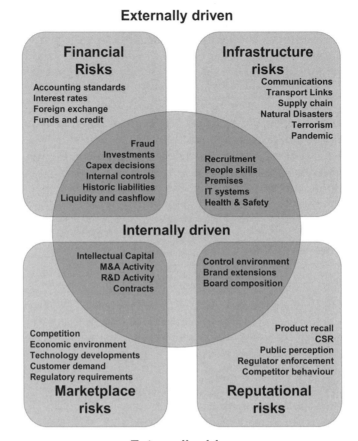

Figure 19.1 Institute of Risk Management: classes of risk

Similarly the STRATrisk project (STRATrisk 2010) defines strategic risks as 'the system of future opportunities and threats that are so significant that they could materially impact the enterprise's achievement of its main purpose or eventual survival'. These definitions helpfully extend the definition to include risks associated with internal decisions about the strategy as well as external events that might derail the strategy. They correspond with the types of risk you would have expected to identify whilst developing the context, value chain and tangible future for the organization.

What emerges from this categorization of risks is a clear view of where the strategy map and scorecard might appropriately support the management of risks and where they should not. Clearly some aspects of risk and risk management should be left to other mechanisms and controls within the organization. The strategy map and scorecard would include the risks to the strategy and the risks from the strategy's implementation. At the corporate strategy level they should not try to cover risks that would naturally fall into compliance, finance and operations.

How does this model, and its definitions of the categories of risk, help us understand how the strategy map covers risk? I believe this is a case of 'render unto Caesar that which is Caesar's'. When a strategic balanced scorecard is used for strategy implementation you would not expect it to also serve a detailed operational reporting role. It is easy to see why those using a basic scorecard in an operational role might easily be diverted into including many operational risks at the same time. They need to realize they are not creating a strategy map and scorecard for the purpose of strategy management and implementation. When you are creating a strategy map for the implementation of a strategy, it is appropriate to consider those risks, internal and external, that might derail the implementation of that strategy. You still use existing and complementary business controls and risk analysis on the non-strategic pieces that managers need to manage.

How do Strategy Maps and Scorecards Handle Risk?

Just because the strategy map and balanced scorecard do not explicitly mention risks, many assume incorrectly that the approach ignores risks. Consequently, any discussion of how to include risks quickly, and prematurely, concludes that the scorecard should be changed, or added to, to incorporate risks. This conclusion is a leap too far, too early. First it is necessary to see how the strategy map does capture a certain class of risk.

THE RISKS FROM STRATEGY IMPLEMENTATION

The strategy map and balanced scorecard have actually captured a certain class of risk. The difficulty is that they have captured the risks implicitly.

They have already captured many of the management's decisions about the mitigation of risks in the implementation of the strategy. This identification and mitigation is already included thanks to the questions that were asked during the design of the strategy map and balanced scorecard. This may come as a surprise, but think how the design came about. During the discussion and design of the scorecard, the management team were describing what their strategy was; it is therefore a strategy they have already thought through. This thinking will already have included their thoughts about how they wish to mitigate and manage the risks of the strategy not being implemented successfully. They have been articulating a strategy that already has risks considered and mitigated in their intention to implement changes, and develop capabilities and their choices of objectives, measures, targets, actions and initiatives. For instance, the risk of a process not delivering to the standard expected might be mitigated by a project and changes to the underlying skills in the departments involved. The risks to the implementation of the strategy are already embedded and expressed in the strategy map and balanced scorecard.

The problem is that these thoughts and risks are implicit in the strategy map and balanced scorecard, and the mechanisms of change that they provide.

ENSURING STRATEGY IMPLEMENTATION RISKS ARE EXPLICIT AND MANAGED

Leaving these strategy implementation risks implicit does create a problem. Should they start to manifest themselves they might get missed, not be addressed or not be mitigated. We need to make these risks, and the actions to mitigate these risks, explicit. To make the risks explicit during the articulation and design stages you can ask, for each objective, 'what risks are in here and how have you mitigated them?' Noting the risks associated with each objective allows you to create a risk register alongside the strategy's implementation plan. You can extend this to the projects in the same way if that level of detail is required.

The management of the risks associated with the implementation of the strategy is now concerned with what gets monitored, discussed and addressed during implementation. The ongoing and emerging risks have been identified, monitored and are being mitigated as the strategy is being implemented. This places the following question firmly on the agenda of the strategic review meetings: 'are we considering the risks and are we managing them appropriately?' Keeping risk on the agenda and continuously asking about new and known risks as the strategy is being implemented is the best way to ensure that strategy implementation risks are identified, mitigated and managed.

This is where the earlier approach of using KRIs made sense, but only at the objective level. It does not make sense at the perspective level that was being suggested. It does make sense to ask, for this objective, in this perspective, what risks do we need to monitor, mitigate and manage?

THE EXTERNAL STRATEGY IMPLEMENTATION RISKS

The same approach can be used for the class of risks that are external, but yet might affect the strategy. You will have identified and documented these assumptions, uncertainties and risks during the development of the tangible future and the value chain. By now you will have incorporated them into your external perspective. It is a simple step to create a risk register alongside the external perspective to note where risks arise and how you are monitoring them. The process of monitoring the external environment and ensuring these aspects are reviewed monthly is a significant part of the external risk management process.

As Figure 19.2 shows, there are already three levels of risk management corresponding to the three main techniques that have been used. The tangible future provides the mechanism to identify and then monitor external risks that affect the strategy. The strategy map and its objectives provide an overview of the risks affecting the logic and implementation of your strategy. At the balanced scorecard level you are looking at more operational and specific risks associated with each objective, the projects, measures and targets.

Figure 19.2 Risk levels and the strategic learning model

DO NOT ADD A RISK PERSPECTIVE

This argument clearly removes any question of adding a risk perspective to the strategy map or scorecard. As we have explained when discussing themes, you would not expect a strategy map or scorecard to have a perspective entitled 'risk'. There are several reasons for this. What would you put in this perspective? Would it be the value of risk, the risk to the market, the risk management activities or the organizational risk capabilities and skills? Again, we have a theme rather than a perspective: a theme of risk that might potentially apply to every objective on the strategy map. Furthermore, good risk management practice says that risk management should be embedded within the operations and management process of an organization; therefore, to separate it out as a separate perspective would be a mistake. Consideration of risk should pervade the existing objectives in all perspectives, and no new perspective needs to be added. It is sufficient to embed risks and risk management into the existing perspectives and objectives.

AVOID RISKS THAT ARE NOT IN THE STRATEGY MAP'S REMIT

As we have seen, many organizational risks are not in the remit of the strategy management and strategy implementation. These risks should be identified in objectives by managers at the level at which they would be managed (as a part of the management of the objectives). They should be managed by the appropriate risk management processes that sit in different parts of the business. Given that 'a strategy map and balanced scorecard are for a management team, and a set of balanced scorecards is for an organization', the mechanism of exception reporting between layers should escalate those issues about risks that need to be raised upwards to manage the operational detail in addition to the strategic intent. Many risks would never be expected to be in a strategy map or balanced scorecard, unless they were being used as an operational tool, or the risks were exceptions being reported up from lower down the organization.

Making Risk Management Explicit

It can be useful to make explicit the processes of managing risk. You can do this by explicitly describing risks in objectives or explicitly including how you manage risks. This approach is most useful when risks not part of the implementation of the strategy have risen to prominence.

Take, for example, the case of oil exploration companies after the events in the Gulf of Mexico. The safety of rigs and their operating procedures has become a critical issue: one that potentially might jeopardize oil companies' ability to operate as a business and their long-term future. In these circumstances one would expect to see explicit statements about safety, either in the way objectives are worded or as objectives in their own right. For example, 'safe exploration and drilling operations' would emphasize safety in the process objective. If the underlying problem is perceived as a capability then you would expect to see references to safety skills, procedures and even attitudes in the learning and growth objectives and in the values statements associated with the values perspective.

When I was helping to develop the strategy map for a fire and rescue service, the choice of objectives included both how they managed risks to the public and the risks to themselves. The process perspective was structured around their risk management process: how they identified risks, assessed risks, allocated resources against risks and delivered services safely, and the evaluation of their services so that they learnt from their experiences. The customer perspective was where the public risks were placed, with the various parts of the population they served having objectives for their safety. They also included an objective for firefighter safety (no deaths or injuries) and included the aspects of how firefighter safety was ensured in the process and learning and growth objectives. This way both the various types of risk, and their management of risk, were made explicit.

Decision Making and Risk

One final aspect of risk we need to consider is how risk is embodied within decision making. The choices made within the strategy represent a series of decisions that have been made. Some of these are about direction. Some are about resources and how to apply them. Others concern the roles and responsibilities people have and how they should change. These decisions will need to be communicated through the organization, and with these decisions comes a consideration of the risks and consequences.

At each level in the organization there should be a clear understanding of which decisions can be taken and what limits exist on decision making. This level of authority may be defined through the roles and responsibilities. It may be expressed in the way managers manage and the degree of freedom they give their staff. It is also limited by the formal scheme of delegation that prescribes limits of spending and the authority that various roles have.

Managers often wish to empower their staff, improve responsibility and increase the extent of delegation. This wish appears in the strategy map as development objectives within the learning and growth objectives, and usually involves changes to established decision making authority. In these circumstances you need to consider two things: how are we, as managers, going to support and communicate such a decision to empower our staff? And what does it mean for the people to whom we are delegating decisions?[1]

When we communicate a decision, the danger is that we put too much emphasis on measures and targets, and not enough on the objective and the wider picture and the context. This usually makes the target clear, but means that staff may ignore, or dismiss, the other aspects of the whole story. The target becomes sacrosanct, no matter what. The whole design of the strategy map and balanced scorecard is to ensure that, as managers, we tell the whole story, including the limits of action, the consequences and what we do not want.

What do staff need to make an informed decision? It is all well and good giving people the freedom to decide and the authority to act, but if they do not have the information to know what to do then they are likely to get into trouble. One consequence of delegation for those who have more authority and responsibility is the need to ensure that they think through and understand the consequences of their new decisions. What is the potential impact? What is the potential unintended consequence? What opportunity does it open and what risks does it create? What information is available to make decisions, and what are the limits of knowledge? Sometimes this understanding will come through support,

---

1   For a fuller description of such decision making from an internal controls perspective, see M. Leitch (2010).

training and experience, but we as managers need to help our staff by ensuring guidance is in place and people know how to manage with limited or unfamiliar knowledge.

Conclusions

The choices to mitigate the strategy should already have been included in the thinking behind the balanced scorecard (included, but implicit). It is better if these are explicit. You make decisions, and the risks to be managed are a consequence of your choices. Risk mitigation is embedded in the objectives, actions, projects and other aspects of the strategy map and scorecard. Reviewing your strategy map and balanced scorecard for the risks of failure is also worthwhile, to ensure that all risks have been identified and mitigated.

The consequences of risk can be represented in the external perspective (as a potential financial penalty) or as regulatory requirements represented in a regulator's perspective (where the regulator is a special form of customer). Risk can be embedded in characteristics of process objectives and also mitigated in the choice of learning and growth objectives.

How you manage risk might appear also as a capability or a process, as a reminder to continuously improve and embed how you manage risks, both operationally and during the review of the scorecard, as you implement and learn from your strategy.

VII *Communication and Use*

Part VII provides guidance for executives and managers who will be communicating their strategy and managing and refining it using the techniques in this book. It is also for facilitators who will support executives through this process.

Chapter 20 is about communicating your strategy so that you tell the story of your strategy effectively. Strategy maps have built in a number of mechanisms designed to make that communication easier. This chapter explains those mechanisms and how to exploit them during communication of your strategy.

Chapter 21 returns to the most important aspect of strategy – making sure it happens. This chapter provides an agenda for management meetings that use strategy maps and scorecards. It explains how strategy maps and scorecards support the review of the strategy. It enables the team to question, review and revise their strategy using the strategic learning model. It provides facilitators with an understanding of how managers will be thinking and working through these strategy review meetings. It also provides the management team with a tool to consider how their behaviour and actions is influencing the the implementation of the strategy.

20 *Telling the Story of your Strategy*

Central to the value of strategy maps is their ability to communicate your strategy in a clear, simple, yet rich manner. Strategy maps, together with their scorecards, help you to tell the whole story of your strategy. They help you to ensure your people understand what you intend. They help them to understand how they fit in and can contribute.

This chapter explains the deeper thinking behind how strategy maps tell that story, how to tell that story using strategy maps, and how to use strategy maps to create the level and types of engagement you are looking for. I often come across strategy maps and scorecards that have taken shortcuts or missed out a piece of the jigsaw. These shortcuts often undermine a piece that is vital to the story or that helps the communication to work effectively: subtleties that are not obvious at first glance. This chapter will ensure you do not make the same mistakes.

All Plans should be Burnt

There is a fundamental belief in this book, embodied in the idea that all plans should be burnt. This comes from the questions, 'where does strategy exist?' and 'where does strategy happen?' In any organization, strategy is being executed all the time. It is being executed in the actions and behaviours of every single person in the organization, every single day. They are making decisions, on a day-to-day basis, at some level or other that affects the strategy and helps to implement it, or not.

Yet these people are not constantly referring to the strategy or the plans. What they are referring to is what they know, believe and have learnt in their heads. The actual strategy exists in their heads. Their understanding of the strategy and how to implement it is in their heads. It is only the hoped for strategy that is in plans and documents. If an organization has successfully managed to get its 'hoped for strategy' and people's roles, contributions and judgements about the strategy into their heads, then the written plans and documents have become redundant. The hoped for strategy is in their heads as the actual strategy, and the plans can be burnt. Of course, if the hoped for strategy is not in their heads, it is a waste of time. It is not being implemented and therefore you might as well burn the plans. Consequently, all plans should be burnt.[1]

A critical part of the implementation of your strategy is how you communicate your strategy and get it, its principles and actions, and values and beliefs, into the heads of your people. If you can get the principles and values into their heads, it is easier than trying to get the detailed tasks in. You then have people who are thinking about and

---

1   Of course, auditors don't like this, but I like telling them anyway.

acting on the strategy, instead of simply following orders. This idea is developed much further in *Communicating Strategy* (Jones 2008).

The Importance of Creating Management Consensus

The stage before this happens requires the management team to leave the boardroom with a common understanding of the strategy and a common understanding of how they will communicate it. This is not necessarily the case. It can happen, but more likely there will be differences of opinion and emphasis. A vital role of the facilitator is to help the management team understand where agreements and disagreements lie. They then help the team resolve the disagreements, so that the whole management team leaves the boardroom with a common understanding of the strategy. This is about the quality of conversation that has been emphasized throughout this book. This is where the information and assumptions that were collected during the discussions, interviews and workshops are valuable. Your team should know explicitly where you agree and also be able to discuss those areas where your opinions or understanding differ. The role of many of the tools and techniques in this book is to bring about this common understanding.

Your objective is to walk from the room, as a team, knowing how the strategy will be described and delivered. On the few points where you may disagree or differ, you also need to know how you will resolve those differences. The techniques within strategy mapping help to develop this collective understanding of the strategy – a collective understanding which can then be told consistently, coherently and with integrity by each member of the management team, a story you can tell through the strategy map.

How to Tell the Story

The strategy map describes a cause and effect relationship between the perspectives, and it is this which we use to tell the main story of the strategy. As you will have noticed in all the descriptions of strategy maps throughout this book, the descriptions start at the top, with the overall purpose, and work their way through the strategy map themes to the underpinning values. Having worked down through the strategy map perspectives, you can then retell the story back up through the cause and effect relationships.

TOP DOWN

In telling the story, the best place to start is with the overriding objective, purpose or mission statement. Emphasize its importance as a persistent, overriding ambition for your organization. You then have choices about how best to work through the themes and perspectives. In a strongly themed map it is often clearer to introduce the themes first. This clearly positions the themes in the overall strategy. In another case you might cover the upper perspectives to frame the overall outcomes of the organization and then cover the themes from the lower perspectives. There is usually a natural way to cover the strategy map, given the structure you have chosen. It is often useful to explain the overall structure of themes and perspectives before you continue with the detail.

Assuming you are covering themes, you can then talk through the cause and effect description for each theme from top to bottom, moving down through the objectives in each perspective. As you do this, introduce each perspective. For instance, the customer perspective represents how your customers think. Talk about the customer objectives 'as if you are that customer'. This allows your audience to realize how you are emphasizing the perspective from a particular customer group's perspective. When you enter the process perspective, emphasize the 'we' component: 'to satisfy this customer objective, *we* have to do this really well'. Emphasize the 'we' again through the learning and growth perspective and the values.

Remember that the strategy map is not the whole picture: you can add detail from the objective descriptions, the research, the financials, the analysis, the gaps and other parts of the strategy work. The more you do this with anecdotes about the customers, facts, financial information, performance criteria, and both qualitative and quantitative information, the more you will bring the story to life.

As you work downwards, emphasize the questions that were asked to tease out the few things that make the biggest difference. Phrases like, 'we must focus on' and 'the biggest difference will come from...' serve to emphasize that the strategy map describes where the focus of the strategy is and how we are looking at the few things that will make the biggest difference.

Ending the top down story without values tends to leave a collection of different capabilities at the end of the story, depending upon the chosen themes. Ending the top down story with an emphasis on the organization's values neatly wraps up the story by emphasizing how the values, across the organization, serve to support the whole strategy and purpose.

BOTTOM UP

Having told the story top down you can then retell it bottom up. When retelling the story upwards, the linking between objectives in perspectives is slightly different. The story is that *if* we can uphold our values, and *if* we can develop our capabilities, then this means that we will be able to improve the performance of our processes and this *should* or *will* mean that we will improve the satisfaction of our customers, so that we can achieve our financial objectives and, ultimately, the overall objective. Whilst the emphasis downwards was on what will make the biggest difference, the emphasis upwards is on how important a contribution the lower objectives make to the success of the objectives in the higher perspectives.

Telling the story this way engages the audience with their experiences. Refer to their knowledge and anecdotes that they will be familiar with. Knowing where problems have lain in the past helps you to emphasize how the strategy will overcome and address these problems. Explain what will be different and why, so that no one thinks you are describing a strategy by hope and magic. Telling the story from the audience's perspective, so that you talk about how building on their skills, knowledge and experience will make a difference to them and their working lives, sends a completely different message from one that suggests they are inadequate or do not have the appropriate skills.

Remember that the whole story starts and ends with the overall purpose. Bring richness to the picture with numbers, facts and stories that back up the strategic thinking.

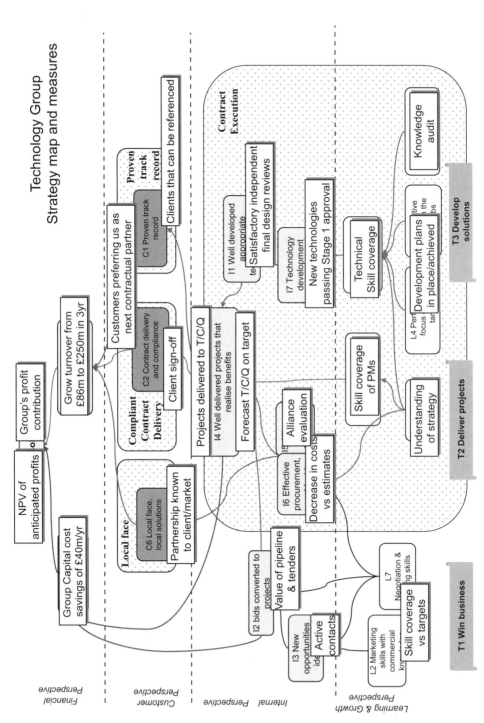

Figure 20.1 Strategy map showing objectives and their measures

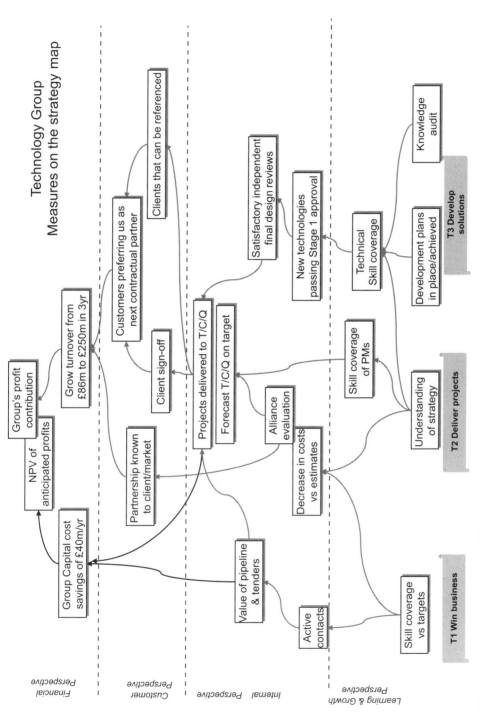

Figure 20.2 Strategy map with objectives removed but measures still telling the story

Make sure you rehearse the story so you are comfortable with it and can explain it fluently. This is not to do it parrot style. It is to tell the story with passion, commitment and belief. If you have doubts about the strategy, or how the story fits together, they will leak out as you tell it. Your staff will easily detect this and they will be unconvinced as well. Communicating Strategy (Jones 2008) provides specific techniques for developing your story and getting the message across in a powerful and convincing manner.

Using the Tangible Future

It is often helpful to use the tangible future to frame the strategy map story. However, you will find that the very detailed tangible future that you used to develop the strategy map is not necessarily the best tool for a large communication. It is often too detailed and contains information about uncertainties, which you may not wish to communicate. It is better thought of as a working document than a communication tool.

If you want to use your tangible future, create a simplified version that shows the pressures on your organization, acknowledges where you have come from, shows the challenges ahead and sets out the overall ambition. Alternatively, talk about these aspects as you explain the strategy map.

Telling the Story through the Measures

We have seen how the strategy map is used to tell the story of the strategy. In this case the relationship between the objectives on the strategy map tells the story of how the strategy will be delivered. The same should be true for the measures. You should be able to tell the story of the strategy through the measures. If not, then you have a set of measures that are either obscuring the strategy or telling a different story. In either case they might hijack your implementation and send it off on the wrong path.

Figure 20.1 shows a variant of a strategy map with the measures for each objective overlaying the map. For this client these measures told their story as well as the objectives. Showing the objectives and the measures together on the same strategy map makes it easy to check whether the measures tell the story behind the objectives and the strategy. If you want to go to the extreme test you should be able to take the objectives away and see a cause and effect model simply between the measures you have chosen.

Figure 20.2 shows the same picture with the objectives removed, so only the measures and linkages are shown. Although the objectives are missing, you should still be able to tell the story of the strategy. Your measures, if chosen well, should be as effective in telling the story of the strategy as the objectives were. Of course, there are many other measures in operation within this organization (for project management alone they listed over sixty measures); however, at the top level, as shown here, they used a select few that were driven by the design of their strategy map.

Communicating a Culture of Performance

You will want to avoid a culture of measure mania, the tyranny of targets and feeding the beast. However, it is easier to say what you don't want than what you want.

I find it helpful to define the opposite of these as the culture of performance. By a culture of performance, I mean:

A visible and explicit pattern of behaviour, actions and values...

Working to achieve the organization's overall objectives...

That encourages honest evaluation, feedback and appraisal...

And informs decision making.

It is built upon collective and individual responsibility...

Is responsive to changing circumstances...

And encourages self regulation, trust and learning.

So how do you move from the measurement and target setting culture to one of performance? Much is in the messages you communicate alongside your story. When the underlying causes of the problems are understood, it is easier to adjust your messages so that you communicate not only what you want to achieve, but the behaviours you expect as well. That way people understand how to do the right thing in the right way.

Whilst the measures should communicate the story of your strategy in the same way as your objectives, there is a good reason why you should communicate both together. Figures 20.3 to 20.6 explain the problem that occurs and how to overcome it. In this diagram there are two players: the policy setter and the policy implementer. These two players might be the management and their staff. They might be a manager and his or her team. They might be head office and the organization's divisions. They might be central and local government. The policy setter decides what needs to be done and chooses what they want to achieve. The policy implementer's role is to deliver the chosen objectives.

Unfortunately, this policy makers suffer from measure mania and compulsive target setting. They believe they must convert their ideas into measures to ensure that they can track what they want to achieve, and that they must set targets to establish the level of achievement expected. It is important to recognize this compulsion to set targets for every measure. As soon as you insist that all measures need a target, you are trying to control and influence rather than diagnose, observe and learn. Diagnosis requires facts, without an expectation of a target. Nevertheless, targets are also set.

The measures and targets are then communicated to the policy implementers. At this point the policy makers have not explained the policy, strategy or the objectives they are trying to achieve. They believe they only need to explain the measures and targets. The policy implementers are faced with a collection of measures and targets that represent, but don't describe, the strategy or policy.

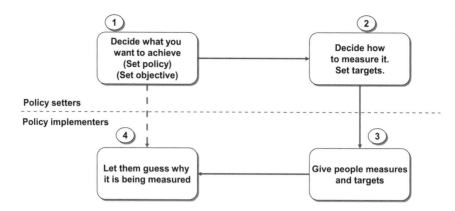

Figure 20.3 Measures culture 1: giving people only measures encourages mind-reading

The effect of this is to put policy implementers in a state of what I call 'mind-reading'. The measures and targets are an abstraction of the policy, they are not the policy. The measures and targets are the policy setters' best estimate of how to translate the policy into targets. The policy implementers were neither privy to the policy decisions nor to how the policy setters translated the policy into measures and targets. They were not consulted on the suitability of the measures and targets, even though they might be in a far better position to choose them. They have to deduce (mind-read) what the policy was from the measures and targets, as they were not privy to the thinking. Is it any surprise in this situation that the policy implementers seem disconnected from the policy and policy makers? This failure to communicate what is really intended is probably the most important reason why it is vital to start with objectives before measures and to communicate both.

If the measures are a poor representation of the policy, the situation is worsened. The policy implementers will be measuring and aiming for the wrong things. If the policy setters compensate for this by adding more measures, the policy implementers will start to wonder which measures are the most important and become even more confused. Measure mania will set in. You can avoid this by concentrating on the objective and choosing the most appropriate measures to go with the objective, dropping inappropriate ones.

COMMUNICATING OBJECTIVES

An obvious improvement to this is to communicate the policy, strategy and objective, rather than just the measure and the target (see Figure 20.4). Now you are explaining what you are trying to achieve and why you believe the measures and targets you have chosen are the appropriate ones. Whilst this could improve the situation, in a draconian punishment regime you are merely adding to the information.

An even better alternative is to communicate the objective or strategy and ask the policy implementers to choose the measures and targets that will achieve the objective. By doing this, you allow negotiation and discussion over how they are to be achieved. You are asking people how they will demonstrate they are making improvements.

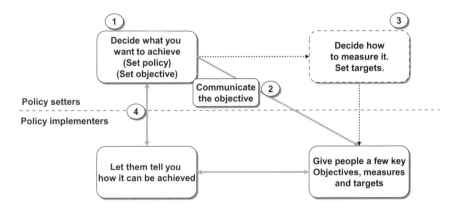

Figure 20.4 Measures culture 2: communicating objectives and asking how they can be achieved

A CULTURE OF PUNISHMENT

Whilst communicating the objective helps, it is not sufficient to change the culture. The effect of the regime will depend upon the message that is communicated with the measures and targets – the message about incentives and punishments that is also communicated to create the culture that surrounds the measures and targets.

If no message is passed down with the measures and targets, the policy implementers may believe that there is no seriousness or commitment behind the targets and may begin to think that it does not matter if the targets are hit or missed, as there will be no consequence. The performance management approach is seen as unnecessary bureaucracy. If the policy implementers are chased to report their performance against the targets, they will not worry about them being late or inaccurate. Any information will do to keep the policy makers happy. Again the performance measurement approach will fail.

Problems start to occur when the additional message of, 'you will be blamed for failure', is added into the measures and targets (see Figure 20.5). Intense management by measures and targets together with 'it is your fault if you fail' has been created. In other words, responsibility for achieving all the measures and targets is placed firmly upon the policy implementer, despite it being someone else's policy. This can easily lead to dysfunctional behaviour. When the message of 'punishment for failure' is added to the blame message, the policy implementers may resort to suboptimal and dysfunctional behaviour to avoid punishment. Their actions will be based on the fear of the consequences of failure, rather than on striving for success. They no longer have a culture of performance, but one of punishment and fear.

The complication here is that reward is not necessarily the answer. Psychologists have found that making a reward available can stop someone continuing to do a task when previously no reward was available and they were happy to do the task. Rewards may have a detrimental effect on performance in the long run (Persaud 2005: 153–55). Rather, Persaud states that 'job enrichment is the most effective way psychology knows to improve motivation' (Persaud 2005: 169).

CULTURE OF LEARNING AND PERFORMANCE

If the message that is passed down is not one of punishment for failing to hit targets, but a far more subtle message, then you start to move towards performance management culture. The message this time is, 'we want you to learn, but a failure to learn will be punished' (see Figure 20.6).

This is a very different message from 'failure will be punished'. The measures provide the policy implementers with information. They are given the opportunity to think about the situation, to make choices and act on the information they have. A similar message is passed on with 'a failure to demonstrate a willingness to change or collaborate'. If people are given an opportunity to change, and fail to take it, then they may be punished. If they take the chance, but get it wrong, then it is learning (as long as it was not disastrously wrong or they repeatedly got the same thing wrong).

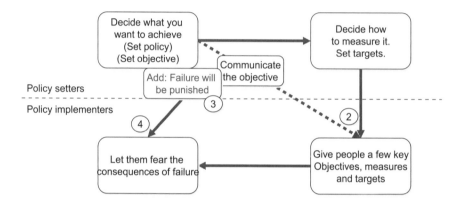

Figure 20.5 Measure culture 3: you will be blamed for failure and your failure will be punished

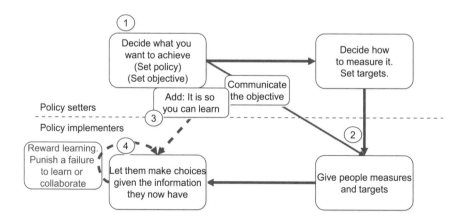

Figure 20.6 Measure culture 4: rewarding learning. Punishing a failure to learn or collaborate

A message that gives people the chance to try and improve for themselves, where only a failure to learn is punished, is far more subtle, effective and empowering than the earlier ones.

The message from these examples is clear: the cultural context that you provide around the message makes as much difference as the message itself.

The Richness of Communication in Strategy Maps

The first chapter described a situation where the strategy map exposed a team's underlying thinking and helped to resolve their disagreements. Why are strategy maps so effective at doing this? It used to puzzle me why a strategy map improved the quality of communication, discussion and understanding. The answer lies in the many ways in which strategy maps represent the strategy: a deep richness that makes them so effective.

TELLING THE STORY IN DIFFERENT WAYS

The strategy map, and the other components that sit around it, deliberately represents and tells the story of the strategy in a variety of ways. Unlike most plans, strategy maps are not only written. They do have written characteristics for the objectives. The strategy map provides a simple yet rich picture. The scorecard also satisfies the analytical need by providing the numbers that sit behind the strategy map, which can be drilled into and provide evidence and facts. The telling of the story of the strategy allows you to show your emotional connection to the strategy. It allows others to hear the story first-hand. The story is available in a variety of ways that support the variety of preferences that people have for thinking and communicating. These various ways are known as representational systems (Dilts and Delozier 2000). Broadcasting across these representational systems ensures that your message is most likely to engage the maximum number of people.

THE SUBTLE LEVELS OF STRATEGY MAPS

The representational systems are not the only way this communication works. The effectiveness is also explained by the variety of ways in which the organization is described. Dilts (1998: 34–37) also provides insights into the richness of the picture the strategy map creates and the various levels at which the model works. His model, summarized in Table 20.1, describes how people think about themselves and describe their connections to reality, in various ways. The suggestion in this neurological levels model is that the higher level components, such as mission and identity, drive the activities at the lower level. Thus, if you think of yourself as a parent, it will dictate how you see yourself in respect to a child. In the same way, if an organization thinks of itself as a growth company, it will seek to generate revenues for reinvestment rather than distributing dividends. At the lower levels, if you believe that your competitor has stolen a march on you, then you may decide to develop similar capabilities to them or to choose part of the market they have not occupied.

Table 20.1 The neurological levels model (Dilts 1998)

System and mission: What am I a part of? What is the bigger purpose? This is sometimes referred to as the spiritual level.

Identity: Who am I? What is my sense of who I am and what I am? What do I think of myself as?

Beliefs: What values, beliefs and expectations do I have? What permissions and motivations do I have or give myself?

Capabilities: How do I do things? What particular skills, experiences and ways of thinking do I have? What guides and gives me direction?

Behaviours and actions: What do I do? What specific behaviours do I exhibit? What do my skills get applied to? What specific actions are taken?

Environment: The most basic level is the environment in which you operate. This is the external influences. Where are you operating?

The neurological levels model of how an individual operates is carried over to the organization where the same levels of thinking can apply. In the strategy map we see identity and purpose statements, and capabilities underpinning the behaviours and actions that will be most successful. We also see the values of the organization. The strategy map provides only a limited view of the whole system (which is why we also develop a systems diagram and rich picture of the future). Some beliefs about the strategy and what drives change are embedded within the strategy map. Others are more implicit or embedded within the details as the story is told.

CAUSALITY

The cause and effect model is fundamental to the strategy map and to the scorecard. That there is cause and effect sits deep within the human psyche, and the work of philosophers to understand causality and to characterize it extends over millennia. In the Western philosophical tradition, explicit discussion stretches back at least as far as Aristotle (350 BC). He said, 'All causes of things are beginnings; that we have scientific knowledge when we know the cause; that to know a thing's existence is to know the reason why it is'. To suggest there is causality within the strategy suggests that it is within our control to deliver it. If we are successful, we can deliver this strategy. It is about implementation. To suggest otherwise would be to suggest we are at the whim of our markets and competitors, and that the strategy's success is more in their control than ours. These are messages that would make the management sound very unconvincing, or the strategy not sound robust. In contrast, a convincing cause and effect relationship will add coherence and credibility to the story, and avoid strategy by hope and magic. When we add to this the orientation towards the future, we can start to see why strategy maps help people connect with the strategy.

Through strategy maps' rich use of representational systems, neurological levels, cause and effect, and future orientation, both managers and staff connect with the basic ways we implicitly think about the world and represent it. This realization has important implications for how strategy maps and strategy are captured and described. In the same way that financial measures are a one dimensional representation of an organization, if you were to miss elements of the strategy map out either during the design stage or as the story is told, then you would present a limited perspective on the strategy.

Conclusions

A strategy map is not only a tool to capture the strategy, it is a tool for communicating strategy. It describes the richness of your strategy in a way that engages the maximum number of people in your audience.

The quality of thinking, conversation and analysis that has gone on behind the strategy will come through in how you describe it. The cause and effect model provides the framework to explain the strategy from the top downwards and from the bottom upwards – from the mission or purpose to the underpinning values. When you tell the story, your passion, sincerity and commitment will also show through.

The strategy map provides a framework to tell the story of the strategy through the measures you ask people to focus on. This is a valuable test of the communication quality of the measures. Look through your chosen measures; if you cannot deduce your strategy from them, then there is a good chance that your staff will not be able to either. A poor set of measures will undermine your strategy rather than support it.

A poorly structured, unclear strategy map indicates that the quality of thinking, or the quality of the strategy mapping facilitation and design is at fault. In contrast, a clear strategy map shows how clearly the management team are thinking and how well they will act. Be sure that the message you wrap around your strategy map also supports the culture that you wish to create.

21 *Managing with your Strategy Map and Revising your Strategy Map*

All through the discussion of strategy mapping design and implementation the emphasis has been on the quality of thinking and conversation. The last chapter built on this, explaining how to add in a culture of performance. This chapter is about management meetings and how you review and revise your strategy maps. It is about the quality of your analysis and action during implementation. All the work designing your strategy map and strategic balanced scorecard will be wasted if you do not use it to improve the way you manage your meetings, implement your strategy and bring about improvements.

The strategic learning model introduced two levels of performance management: operational and strategic. Around these basic processes were a wider set of questions: how are we doing operationally? Is our strategy bringing about the operational changes and improvements we expected? Is our strategy working as intended, or does it need refinement and change? Has anything in the outside world changed that would cause us to refine or change the strategy? In this chapter we also ask, 'how are we doing as a management team?'

This chapter explains how to review your strategy as it is implemented. It splits into three main parts: the review of operations, the review of the strategy and the review by the management team of their own performance.

Principles

Throughout this book, strategy maps have been positioned and designed to help you manage the implementation of your strategy better and to learn from it as it is implemented. The strategic learning model, with separate loops for strategic review and operational review, is central to how your meetings are planned, held and managed. If you are not used to looking at both strategic and operational views, the first step is to make sure that you make time to look at the business from the operational and strategic perspectives. If necessary, hold two separate meetings, at least initially, so you get used to the different focuses of attention and thinking. This also has the effect of partitioning the strategy discussion from the operational and makes more specific time for the discussion and review of the strategy. Once you are more confident as a team, you might delegate responsibility for the more operational aspects. Until then, ensure that you are giving both the strategic and operational levels appropriate attention.

MAKING TIME FOR STRATEGY

Management teams behave quite differently when their approach is focused on learning as a team, rather than management reporting and control. As Figure 21.1 shows, there is a dramatic contrast between a team that concentrates on reporting and control, and a management team that wants to learn from its strategy. Think of a team operating as general managers, rather than functional managers. This is in sharp contrast to a team whose focus is control.

To complement the strategic learning model and this approach, hidden away in Kaplan and Norton's first book (Kaplan and Norton 1996: 268) is a figure that contrasts an event-driven strategic review process with one of continuous learning. In essence, it suggests two improvements to how management teams meet. More time is to be spent discussing performance and analysing the data between and prior to the meetings, so that issues are identified for discussion. In the meetings, less time is to be spent reviewing performance and much more time is to be spent discussing the implications and reviewing strategic issues. This is designed to help your management team move away from reactive control towards learning about your strategy as it develops. The quality of conversation emphasized through the design of your strategy map should be continued as the strategy map is used and progress is reviewed.

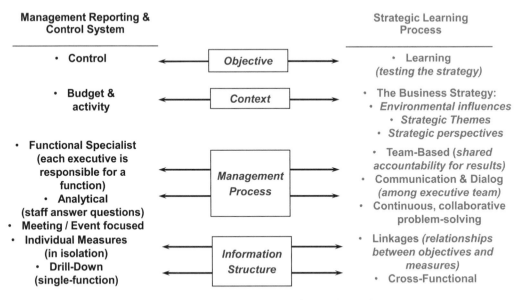

Figure 21.1 Contrasting management control with strategic learning

Your team must first have confidence that you have adequate control, as on the left hand side, before you can move to the learning culture shown on the right hand side. Once you are sure of the budgets, top level measures and targets, and have confidence in the further detail that may be available by drilling down further, you can move towards a team that learns together. The leader of the management team has responsibility for establishing the right climate for this wider, more collaborative approach. Then the rest of the team have to follow. The following two sections provide you, as leader, with agendas for both strategic and operational reviews.

It is assumed that the information on which you base your decisions is reliable and available, that the management team can arrive at a meeting having reviewed the information, that they are confident in the data and that they are prepared for discussion, analysis and decision making. If not, any problems need to be resolved, as inaccurate data will undermine the quality of conversation. Too much time will be spent discussing the quality of the data, rather than the implications of that data.

Reviewing Operational Progress (the Scorecard)

You can review the strategy before the operational detail, but there is a tendency for the conversation to drop into the as yet un-reviewed detail, and to lose sight of the strategy. It is often helpful to review the operational performance and then move up to the strategic performance review, but be judicial following this advice.

At the operational level you are reviewing individual objectives and their detail, though it is often helpful to review the objectives in each theme together. You assume that the objective and its characteristics are correct, and you are looking for progress towards that objective, using the measures and indicators of progress and the achievement of projects and actions that are targeted at the objective. It is important to review progress with the individual measures and projects. They should be working together to deliver improvement to the objective as a whole.

The main document for operational reviews is the scorecard. You should have the strategy map and tangible future to hand as points of reference. An example strategy map theme is shown in Figure 21.2 with its corresponding scorecard.

Start by reminding people of the objective you are to discuss and its characteristics. This ensures everyone is familiar with the characteristics. Then for that objective you can ask:

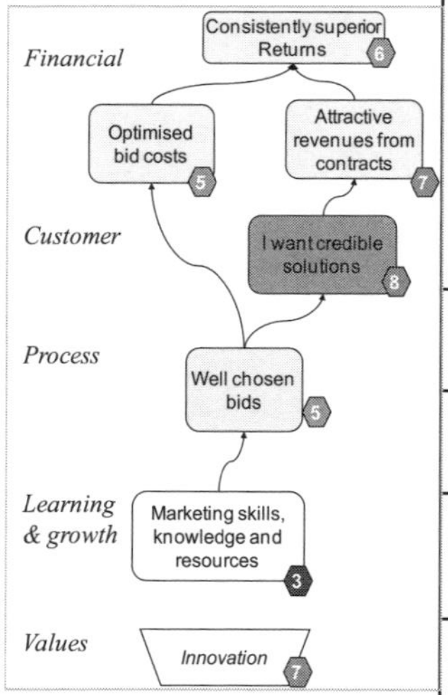

Objective and characteristics			Assessment against ambition				Projects and actions			Responsibility
	What the strategy must achieve	More specific description of the objective and how you get there	Overall assessment of progress against objective	Judgement score	Evidence of progress & achievement	Level of ambition and timing	Projects that support the objective	Actions to progress the objective	Target dates for actions	Ownership
Perspective	**Objective**	**Characteristics**	**Assessment**	**Score/10**	**Measures**	**Targets**	**Projects**	**Actions**	**Dates**	**Responsibility**
Financial	Consistently superior returns	Improve return on contracts		6		+20% be year 2				
	Attractive revenue from clients	Overall increase revenues from new clients		7		+8% per annum +25% over 3 years				
	Optimised bid costs	Lower overall bid costs relative to revenue from bidding for the right business		5		-15% per annum				
Customer	I want credible solutions	I want a supplier with a credible trackrecord		8						
Process	Well chosen bids	Improved bid process ensures we bid for the right opportunities		5						
Learning & Growth	Marketing skills, knowledge and resources	Improve marketing skills through training and application of systematic process		3			*Training ptro*			
Values	Innovation	Ensure we innovate in both marketing and bids		7						

Figure 21.2 A strategy map theme reported alongside its scorecard

1. Overall assessment and judgements:
    a. What is the assessment of the objective telling us?
    b. Does it appear reasonable?
2. What are the latest measures telling us about our objectives?
    a. How are we doing against our expectations, targets and ambition?
    b. What are the trends?
    c. What is the combination of measures for this objective telling us about achievement of the objective?
3. What state are the projects in?
    a. Are they going to be completed on time and to budget?
    b. Are they going to deliver the outcomes and bring about the changes we expected?
    c. Now delivered, are they bringing about the changes?
4. Have the actions been carried out?
    a. On time?
    b. Have they had the expected effect?
    c. What other actions are necessary to achieve the objective or address any problems?
5. Timing and change
    a. Is the change consistent with the extent and timing we expected?
    b. Has anything else changed that will influence progress?
6. Given everything, was the initial assessment accurate?

A written assessment is useful to describe the current state of progress with an objective. For instance, if a skill was not being developed, despite the training programme, the assessment would describe the situation and diagnose the underlying problem. From here, actions would be identified to address the issues.

The improvement in the performance of an objective may rely on the improvement in an objective from a lower perspective, so examine how the supporting objectives are performing. You need to be clear whether any delay in improvement is due to the failure of projects, actions, measures or communication of the objective itself; whether it is due to the failure to deliver a supporting objective from a lower perspective; or whether it is due to some combination of the two.

Review how well each objective is understood by those who are influencing it. Do they understand what they are being asked to achieve? Do they have the resources? Do they have the skills and capabilities? Do they understand the time, cost and quality demands? Where you have teams in several similar units, departments, projects or regions, it is also useful to compare the teams. How does this team's context and situation affect the situation? What might this team learn from others? What could others learn from this team?

Ask whether you are playing your part as a team. What do we have to do as a consequence to help get the message across? Are we explaining and reinforcing the strategy and objectives? Are we making the measures clear, meaningful and understood? Do we need to refine the measures to make them clearer as a set?

This operational review of the objectives is the precursor to the review of whether the strategy is working.

Reviewing Strategic Progress (The Strategy Map)

When taking a more strategic perspective it is important to remember that you are in the outer loops of the strategic learning model and the strategic performance management loop. To help you, this agenda provides a checklist that will help you think through the wider issues and focus on themes of the strategy map. The following sections add detail to these agenda items.

1. Overall context: have any external drivers, overall objectives or policies changed?
2. For each theme: review the cause and effect chain and its objectives
3. For each objective in the theme: review the objective
   a. Status of the objective – any new information
   b. Updates on measures, targets, trends
   c. Projects and actions underway to deliver change
   d. Any other issues
4. Overall issues and risks
5. Do we need to refine the strategy? At which level?
   a. Actions and projects
   b. Targets or measures
   c. Characteristics of objectives, or the objectives themselves
6. Proposed actions and next steps.

HAS THE CONTEXT OR EXTERNAL ENVIRONMENT CHANGED?

Start with a review of the overall context in case anything has changed in the external environment, outside the immediate control of the team. This refreshes the thinking about the underlying assumptions that were made. It allows for discussion of policy issues that could affect the assumptions and the strategy. Spending even a short amount of time sharing the intelligence will help the team to broaden their horizons. This question is led by the chair, with themes owners contributing. Use the tangible future together with the external perspective to ask whether any external events or new information suggest that an underlying assumption has changed, or that a particular scenario is starting to develop.

THEME REVIEW: CAUSE AND EFFECT

Next review the strategy and the themes of the strategy map. The theme review normally covers both the strategy map and the associated scorecard, but focuses on cause and effect. The strategy map's objectives create a broader basis for discussion, with the measures and targets smoothly integrated into the conversation using the scorecard to support detailed points. Presenting the strategy map with red/amber/green scores on the objectives, obtained from the scorecard, allows the strategy map to show quickly and clearly how the strategy is progressing.

You can see how the causality works with Figure 21.3. It shows a typical strategy map with the objectives marked as red (R), amber (A) or green (G). The objective for process one is green, yet the supporting learning and growth objective is red. This suggests that the objective for process one may not stay green for long unless its learning and growth objective is improved. In contrast, the objective for process four is amber and its supporting learning and growth objective is green. Therefore, one of three things may be true: it may only be a matter of time before objective four will start to turn green due to the learning and growth objective; objective four needs an additional learning and growth objective to help it to improve; or perhaps it is waiting for projects at the process level to be completed to turn it green. Only a more detailed look at the other aspects that might bring about the change and examining the detailed scorecard over time will tell this.

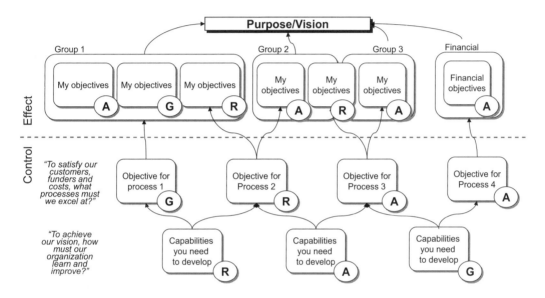

Figure 21.3 Interpreting red/amber/green status on a strategy map

Your cause and effect model describes the main long-term driver of the strategy and change. When reviewing a theme as a whole, ask whether the learning and growth objectives are improving the processes, and therefore improving the customers' objectives and the outcomes you expected. Be clear about the timescales you set and how various components are designed to bring about improvements. Has the training been completed? Is the communication understood? Are the learning and growth components in place? Have the projects been delivered yet? Remember, you want to avoid strategy by hope and magic by making explicit the pieces that you believe will bring about a change in the performance of your organization.

Where a theme is shared to create collective ownership, any of the theme's owners should be able to lead the discussion. Prior to the meeting the theme's owners should review their theme together so they bring their collective expertise to the table. They can then substitute for one another or take it in turns to present the theme at different meetings.

REVIEWING RISKS

The strategic review of a theme and its objectives is a good time to review the overall risks. These include risks already identified, those which might be occurring and any new ones that might emerge. Look at both the overall risks and the narrower operational risks. As well as the standard risk register, use the strategic risk framework from Chapter 19 as a reminder of the scope of risks that might need assessing, mitigating or reviewing.

UNDERSTANDING AND COMMUNICATION

The strategic learning model emphasizes strategic communication and looks for evidence that it is having an effect. This asks the question, 'are we seeing evidence that the strategy is understood and being executed?' Its purpose is to put emphasis on the role of the management to ensure that the strategy is communicated, checking the understanding of the strategy and looking for signs where there may be a need to re-emphasize or reinforce the strategy. Asking, 'how effective is our communication?' puts the emphasis on the management to communicate both the strategy and the operational details, and ensure that others are passing the message accurately through the organization.

Refining and Updating the Tangible Future

The normal situation for the strategic review is to check on the progress of the strategy, without necessarily changing the strategy. During the design of the strategy map its persistent nature was emphasized (strategy being a persistent pattern of behaviour). However, the review process is deliberately designed to allow you to refine, update and re-communicate the strategy as you learn from its implementation. These updates can be at different levels.

The first level of change is around those items designed to influence an individual objective. This is the choice of measures, the value of targets and the set of projects designed to improve an objective. You might decide to change the measures to ones that better represent the strategy, or add an extra initiative to ensure that the objective is achieved.

The second level of change is to the content of the objectives on the strategy map. Sometimes it is helpful to revise the characteristics of an objective or even refine their names to communicate their message better. The structure of the strategy map and the relationships between objectives is not changed. Their meaning is refined.

The third level of change is to the cause and effect model itself. This might include changing the objectives in the lower level perspectives, as, perhaps, one learning and growth objective is achieved and another replaces it. More likely, an additional learning and growth objective will be added. This is more likely on lower level strategy maps. If the design has been effective, one would expect the higher level strategy maps to be more stable and persistent.

This might not be the case where, in the normal course of monitoring the environment, you identify significant events that have changed. Such changes might cause a change at any of the three levels mentioned. They might be trigger events or warning signs that you identified when the tangible future was first developed. Changes here might be added to the external environment and the tangible future, though you will probably not need to update your tangible future more often than once a quarter. It is sensible to review the tangible future alongside the external perspective each month to see if significant information has come to light. Once these significant events have occurred, you can update the figures, timing or monitoring methods.

It is normal for some refinement at each level to occur as the new strategy map and scorecard bed in, and also as the strategy is implemented. However, be careful not to tinker constantly with the model. It was developed in a way designed to build consensus, and so you need consensus when it is refined. Apply version control and do not let one individual member of the team change it on their individual whim.

How often to Review

I am frequently asked, 'how often should we review the strategy?' My guideline is that you should (generally) be reviewing the progress with the strategy every month. Any more frequently and you will tend to have too much detail and too little movement. Leave it as infrequent as every quarter and a lot can have happened in that time. A recent McKinsey survey showed that most organizations reviewed their strategy at least monthly or quarterly.

The frequency is determined by:

1. The speed and amount of change you are trying to create in the organization
2. The external information that tells you whether your strategy is working externally (customer feedback)
3. The amount of change external to the organization that also might influence the strategy or policies
4. The time needed to get the team to think more strategically.

Initial views on the frequency of strategic review meetings are influenced by:

1. The time it has taken to get used to the new approach and develop it
2. The behavioural change of making time to move from operational detail to strategic detail.

A team with an operational focus often still need that operational detail and need to make time to also look at the wider strategy and changes they are bringing about in the organization. Bear in mind that if the management team are paying frequent attention to the changes, the message about importance will also filter through to the organization. One way to stagger the review cycle is to review the strategy map theme by theme, each week. So, in one meeting do a theme, and in the next week's meeting do another theme. Do not put the theme reviews too far apart.

One management team I worked with met every week, so we took their five themes and suggested that they review a theme a week, with a sixth week for other topics that came up. This approach meant that they reviewed each theme every six weeks. With another team with three themes, different members of the team were responsible for bringing the theme information to the table, so each month each theme was reviewed.

Whatever timing you choose, make time to do both operational detail and the strategic review. Ensure you review your progress with internal and external changes, at least monthly. Make sure your people are looking at the detail at least weekly.

How are we Performing as a Management Team?

As a management team concerned with learning, there is one other question you should ask yourselves each month. How are we doing as a team? There are two ways to check how you are performing as a team. If you have developed a management team strategy map, as discussed in Chapter 14, it is useful to review your values and learning and growth objectives, as these should be influencing your behaviour as a team. You can also assess the feelings around the room by simply asking, against each of your team's objectives, 'how are we doing out of 10?' When followed up with discussion, this provides a detailed view of how the team feel about their own collective performance. It is also important to give time and opportunity for discussion to any scores that are at variance with others. If one team member thinks that the collective leadership is only three out of 10, whereas everyone else believes it is a seven or an eight, then there is a good chance that there is an issue there that needs listening to.

How this is handled is important. Killing dissent, allocating blame or simply disagreeing with such an assessment will quickly lead to 'group think' or stifle honest discussion. On the other hand, there is a simple way to do the same as any good chairperson does. They look around the table for dissatisfaction or discomfort and bring it to the surface for open discussion. The difference is that using the previously agreed capabilities on a management team's strategy map provides a systematic assessment against several pre-agreed criteria. As usual it is not the scores that matter, but the quality of conversation and discussion that they create.

The Effect on Management Teams over Time

When you raise the level of the agenda to review strategy more regularly and systematically it often means that more operational matters can be delegated to the teams below you. What are the implications of doing this?

IMPLICATIONS FOR THE MANAGERS

As a management team take a more strategic view and spend more time looking at the bigger picture for their organization and for their role as well, they will have consequential effects on the organization. These effects need to be anticipated and managed, like any change. Initially you may continue to have operational discussions, but make space for more strategic discussions. More likely and longer-term, you may choose to move your agenda to a wider and more strategic view, and let your staff take over some of the operational detail and responsibility. You will start to delegate more and begin to learn to trust your teams.

At first this may feel uncomfortable. It means that your team will be letting go of their operational detail to spend more time on the bigger picture. For those that feel comfort in dealing with an operational performance quadrant, this can be a stretch. For others, it may bring welcome relief, even for short periods. For many, it is part of their development as a leader, manager and executive.

IMPLICATIONS FOR THE MANAGED

As your management team start to think and act more strategically, looking at the bigger picture and taking the wider perspective, the time taken for operational review and decision making will be squeezed. More will be expected of the middle managers as they are expected to handle more decisions. They may not be expecting this change of behaviour, even though they may welcome it.

These middle managers may suddenly find that the rules of their game have changed. As a management team you need to be very conscious of this, and you will have to help and manage them through the process.

A manufacturing company's management team meetings had become very operational and took up to a day to complete. They were so busy that it was the only time they spent together. They realized they needed to change, as well as helping their staff to develop. So, at the same time as they introduced their strategy map and balanced scorecard, they introduced a manufacturing management development approach, based on collaboration amongst the sales, design and production teams. Over 12 months their staff were trained in the new approach. They set up three collaboration meetings beneath the management team to focus on sales, design to manufacture integration, and delivery to customers.

Within three months, as a management team, their meetings were better focused. Within five to six months the training was paying off and their staff were starting to take more responsibility for decisions and to understand the implications of how they worked. At around nine to 12 months the new approach had bedded in and they were starting to see the benefits in the way they worked as a whole.

When a management team have been taking operational decisions over a long period of time they will have trained their staff, over that period, to bring decisions to them and push information, responsibility and decision taking upwards. The effect of this is that the managers below that management team will have developed a habit and learnt to pass decisions up.

This is a habit that needs to be broken. Doing so will pay dividends for those under the management team. As staff develop they can take on more responsibility and build a sense that they influence the outcomes of their work. Some call this empowerment. They will have to learn when to escalate issues and which ones do not need escalating. They may need training, such as in running meetings and problem solving. Through experience, they will learn and develop. For the managers it will free up time to work on the strategy, think through management development or even spend more time developing business with customers.

How a team react, and the way their staff react, will depend upon the existing practices and the way that the new approach is introduced. As with any project involving change and improvements, the changes need to be introduced, explained and managed.

USING AN OFFICE OF STRATEGY MANAGEMENT

One development popularized by Kaplan and Norton is the office of strategy management (Kaplan and Norton 2005, 2008: 281–303). In medium to large sized organizations, this is an extremely useful team to have supporting your executive team and the whole process of strategy development. However, in much smaller organizations, having a few experts who support the executive on a part-time basis is often sufficient, as long as they have sufficient time and skills.

If you decide to operate an office of strategy management, it is vital that it is clear that its role should be supporting and facilitating the process of managing the strategy. It is not where strategy is developed and designed, nor is it the team who come up with strategy maps for the organization. It is a team that help others create their own content that they own, supervised by good practice. It is a team that help others to manage their strategy better.

More importantly, having an office of strategy management should not involve abdicating any responsibility for scanning the environment, communicating the strategy, monitoring its implementation or any other aspect. The office should help with scorecard development, helping managers understand how they should align their part of the organization and bringing information together for review. As with all support teams, having people the executive respect and trust in the team is as important as the skills they bring, and you should expect their role to evolve and develop as the organization's maturity in using strategy maps and scorecards develops.

CULTURE OF PERFORMANCE: JUDGEMENT AND EVIDENCE

The previous chapter defined a culture of performance that contrasted with the dysfunctional cultures that sometimes exist. Fourth generation balanced scorecard principles involve combining judgement and evidence. Alone, neither judgement nor evidence tells the whole story. Judgement allows us to articulate how the information available may not tell the whole story. Evidence helps you to develop and support your judgement.

As judgement and evidence work together, they should encourage conversation and learning about the underlying performance, its characteristics and drivers. The richness of the conversation comes from the ability to discuss the evidence and the qualities of the objective. It is vital that time is made for these discussions, whether they be within a team, between teams performing similar tasks, amongst peers in related areas that go to make up the whole process, or amongst senior management. As you become more familiar with this approach you should expect the quality of evidence, information and conversation to improve.

Conclusion

This book began with the story of a management team who were going through the experience of having their thinking challenged and exposed during the strategy map design process.

Throughout the book, during design, communication and now implementation, the emphasis has been on helping people in an organization understand what is required of them and giving them the chance to help deliver their objectives. This requires an explicit, visible and persistent set of actions behaviours and values exhibited by the management.

It requires all to understand the overall goals, within the management team and the organization as a whole – not only during strategy development, but during the implementation of the strategy as you learn from it and refine it. My clients find that strategy maps help them tremendously with this. I hope this book helps you to do the same.

Bibliography

ACCA 2008. 'Strategic and Operational Risks: Relevant to ACCA Qualification Paper P1'. *Student Accountant* [online], September 2008. http://www.accaglobal.com/documents/risk.pdf [accessed July 2011].

Argyris, C. 1993. *Knowledge for Action: A Guide to Overcoming Barriers to Organizational Change*. San Francisco: Jossey-Bass Inc.

Argyris, C. and Schön, D. 1978. *Organizational Learning: A Theory of Action Perspective*. Reading (MA): Addison Wesley.

Argyris, C. and Schön, D. 1996. *Organizational Learning II: Theory, Method and Practice*. Reading (MA): Addison Wesley.

Aristotle. 350 BC. *Posterior Analytics*.

Bateson, G. 1972 and 2000. *Steps to an Ecology of Mind*. Chicago and London: University of Chicago Press.

Collins, J. C. and Porras, J. I. 1998. *Built to Last: Successful Habits of Visionary Companies*. London: Random House.

Coyne, K. P., Buaron, R., Foster, R. N. and Bhide, A. 2000. 'Gaining Advantage over Competitors'. *McKinsey Quarterly* [online], June 2000. https://www.mckinseyquarterly.com/Gaining_advantage_over_competitors_1057 [accessed July 2011].

Cunningham, L. A. 2002. *The Essays of Warren Buffet: Lessons for Investors and Managers*. Singapore: John Wiley and Sons.

Davenport, T. H. and Harris, J. G. 2007. *Competing on Analytics: The New Science of Winning*. Boston: Harvard Business School Press.

Dawkins, R. 2006. *The Selfish Gene*. New York City: Oxford University Press.

De Geus, A. 1997. *The Living Company: Growth, Learning and Longevity in Business*. London: Nicholas Brealey.

De Wall, A. A. 2002. *The Quest for Balance: The Human Element in Performance Management Systems*. New York: John Wiley and Sons.

Dilts, R. B. 1998. *Modelling with NLP*. Capitola (CA): Meta Publications.

Dilts, R. and Delozier, J. 2000. *The NLP Encyclopaedia*. Scotts Valley (CA): NLP University Press. Also at: http://nlpuniversitypress.com/html3/R47.html [accessed July 2011].

Doll, W. J. and Torkzadeh, G. 1998. 'Developing a Multidimensional Measure of System Use in an Organizational Context'. *Information and Management* 33 (4): 171–185.

Drucker, P. F. 1954. *The Practice of Management*. New York: Harper and Row.

EC Directive 2003. Directive 2003/87/EC of the European Parliament and of the Council of 13 October 2003 establishing a scheme for greenhouse gas emission allowance trading within the Community and amending Council Directive 96/61/EC. http://eur-lex.europa.eu/LexUriServ/LexUriServ.do?uri=CELEX:32003L0087:EN:HTML [accessed July 2011].

Ernst and Young 2009. 'A New Balanced Scorecard Measuring Performance and Risk' [online]. http://www.ey.com/Publication/vwLUAssets/A_new_balanced_scorecard-measuring_performance_and_risk/$FILE/Anewbalancedscorecard.pdf [accessed January 2011].

Financial Reporting Council 2010. The UK Corporate Governance Code, June 2010. http://www.frc.org.uk/documents/pagemanager/Corporate_Governance/UK%20Corp%20Gov%20Code%20June%202010.pdf [accessed July 2011].

Garratt, B. 2010. *The Fish Rots from the Head: The Crisis in our Boardrooms: Developing the Crucial Skills of the Competent Director*. London: Profile Books.

Godin, S. 2008. 'Tribe Management' from Seth Godin's Blog [online]. http://sethgodin.typepad.com/seths_blog/2008/01/tribal-manageme.html [accessed July 2011].

Hambrick, D. C. and Fredrickson, J. W. 2005. 'Are you Sure you Have a Strategy?' *Academy of Management Executive* 19 (4): 51–62.

Hamel, G. and Prahalad, C. K. 1993. 'Strategy as Stretch and Leverage'. *Harvard Business Review*, March/April 1993.

HMRC 2010. A General Guide to Landfill Tax. HMRC Reference: Notice LFT1 (July 2010).

Hope, J. and Fraser, R. 2003. *Beyond Budgeting: How Managers Can Break Free from the Annual Performance Trap*. Boston: Harvard Business School Press.

Institute of Chartered Accountants and the Environment Agency 2009. 'Sustainable Business, Environmental Issues and Financial Reporting: Turning Questions into Answers' [online]. http://www.environment-agency.gov.uk/static/documents/Business/TECPLN8045_env_report_aw.pdf [accessed July 2011].

Institute of Risk Management 2010. 'A Structured Approach to Enterprise Risk Management and the Requirements of ISO 31000'. Published by IRM, ALARM and AIRMIC. http://www.theirm.org/documents/SARM_FINAL.pdf [accessed July 2011].

ISO 14001 [online]. http://www.iso.org/iso/iso_14000_essentials [accessed July 2011].

Jones, P. 2008. *Communicating Strategy*. Aldershot: Gower Publishing Ltd.

Kaplan, R. S. 2008. 'Strategy Execution and the Balanced Scorecard: Interview for Working Knowledge Magazine' [online], August 2008. http://hbswk.hbs.edu/item/5916.html [accessed July 2011].

Kaplan, R. S. and Norton, D. P. 1996. *The Balanced Scorecard: Translating Strategy into Action*. Boston: Harvard Business School Press.

Kaplan, R. S. and Norton, D. P. 2001. *The Strategy-Focused Organization: How Balanced Scorecard Companies Thrive in the New Business Environment*. Boston: Harvard Business School Press.

Kaplan, R. S. and Norton, D. P. 2004. *Strategy Maps: Converting Intangible Assets into Tangible Outcomes*. Boston: Harvard Business School Press.

Kaplan, R. S. and Norton, D. P. 2005. *Creating the Office of Strategy Management*. Boston: Harvard Business School Press. Also at: http://www.hbs.edu/research/pdf/05-071.pdf [accessed January 2011].

Kaplan, R. S. and Norton, D. P. 2006. *Alignment: Using the Balanced Scorecard to Create Corporate Synergies*. Boston: Harvard Business School Press.

Kaplan, R. S. and Norton, D. P. 2008. *Execution Premium: Linking Strategy to Operations for Competitive Advantage*. Boston: Harvard Business School Press.

Kim, W. C. and Mauborgne R. 2005. *Blue Ocean Strategy: How to Create Uncontested Market Space and Make the Competition Irrelevant*. Boston: Harvard Business School Press.

Lasker, H. M. 2006. Interview Conducted by Russ Volckmann [online]. http://www.leadcoach.com/archives/e-journal/2006/2006_08_lasker.html [accessed July 2011].

Leboff, G. 2011. *Sticky Marketing: Why Everything in Marketing has Changed and What to Do about it*. London: Kogan Page.

Leitch, M. 2010. 'Making Sense of Risk Appetite, Tolerance and Acceptance (2nd edition): The Scope for Improvements in Decision Making with Limited Knowledge' [online]. http://www.internalcontrolsdesign.co.uk/appetite/full.shtml [accessed July 2011].

Levine, R., Locke, C., Searls, D. and Weinberger, D. 2000. *The Cluetrain Manifesto: The End of Business as Usual*. New York: Perseus Books. Also at: http://www.cluetrain.com [accessed January 2011].

Lindbolm, C. 1959. 'The Science of "Muddling through" '. *Public Administration Review* 19 (2): 79–88.

McKinsey 2006. 'Improving Strategic Planning: A McKinsey Survey'. *McKinsey Quarterly* [online]. http://www.mckinseyquarterly.com/article_page.aspx?ar=1819&L2=18&L3=30&pagenum=11 [accessed July 2011].

Mintzberg, H. 2007. *Tracking Strategies: Towards a General Theory*. Oxford: Oxford University Press.

Mintzberg, H., Ahlstrand, B. and Lampel, J. 1998. *Strategy Safari: The Complete Guide through the Wilds of Strategic Management*. Harlow: Pearson Education Ltd.

Neely, A., Adams, C. and Kennerley, M. 2002. *Performance Prism: The Scorecard for Measuring and Managing Business Success*. Edinburgh: FT Prentice Hall.

Parmenter, D. 2007. *Key Performance Indicators: Developing, Implementing and Using Winning KPIs*. London. John Wiley and Sons.

Persaud, R. 2005. *The Motivated Mind: How to Get what you Want from Life*. London: Bantam Press.

Pfedder, J. and Sutton R. I. 2006. *Hard Facts, Dangerous Half-Truths and Total Nonsense: Profiting from Evidence-Based Management*. Boston: Harvard Business School Press.

Porter, M. E. 1985. *Competitive Advantage: Creating and Sustaining Superior Performance*. New York: Free Press.

Porter, M. E. 1996. 'What is Strategy?' *Harvard Business Review*, November/December 1996.

Porter, M. E. and Kramer, M. R. 2011. 'Redefining Productivity in the Value Chain'. *Harvard Business Review*, January/February 2011. Also at: http://hbr.org/2011/01/the-big-idea-creating-shared-value/ar/1 [accessed July 2011].

Quinn, J. B. 1982. 'Managing Strategies Incrementally'. *Omega* 10 (6): 613–627.

Rosenzweig, P. 2007. *The Halo Effect and Eight other Business Delusions that Deceive Managers*. New York: Free Press.

Simons, D. J. and Chabris, C. F. 1999. 'Gorillas in our Midst: Sustained Inattentional Blindness for Dynamic Events'. *Perception* 28 (9): 1059–1074.

Simons, D. J. and Chabris, C. F. 2010. *The Invisible Gorilla: And other Ways our Intuition Deceives Us*. London: HarperCollins

STRATrisk 2010. Executive Summary [online]. http://www.stratrisk.co.uk/index.aspx [accessed January 2011].

Treacy, M. and Wiersema, F. 1995. *The Discipline of Market Leaders: Choose your Customers, Narrow your Focus, Dominate your Market*. Reading (MA): Addison Wesley. [Cited in Norton Kaplan 2001: 105.]

Young, D. S. and O'Byrne, S. F. 2000. *EVA and Value-Based Management: A Practical Guide to Implementation*. London: McGraw-Hill Professional.

Index

If you have found this book useful you may be interested in other titles from Gower

Benchmarking in Food and Farming:
Creating Sustainable Change
Lisa Jack and Contributors
Hardback: 978-0-566-08835-3
e-book: 978-0-566-09184-1

Communicating Strategy
Phil Jones
Paperback: 978-0-566-08810-0
e-book: 978-0-7546-8288-2

Enterprise Growth Strategy:
Vision, Planning and Execution
Dhirendra Kumar
Hardback: 978-0-566-09198-8
e-book: 978-0-566-09199-5

Making the Business Case:
Proposals that Succeed for Projects that Work
Ian Gambles
Paperback: 978-0-566-08745-5
e-book: 978-0-7546-9427-4

GOWER

Program Management
Michel Thiry
Hardback: 978-0-566-08882-7
e-book: 978-1-4094-0716-4

The Contract Scorecard:
Successful Outsourcing by Design
Sara Cullen
Hardback: 978-0-566-08793-6
e-book: 978-0-7546-8171-7

Project Success:
Critical Factors and Behaviours
Emanuel Camilleri
Hardback: 978-0-566-09228-2
e-book: 978-0-566-09229-9

Strategic Project Risk Appraisal and Management
Elaine Harris
Hardback: 978-0-566-08848-3
e-book: 978-0-7546-9211-9

Visit **www.gowerpublishing.com** and

- search the entire catalogue of Gower books in print
- order titles online at 10% discount
- take advantage of special offers
- sign up for our monthly e-mail update service
- download free sample chapters from all recent titles
- download or order our catalogue